I0091836

Traumatic Loss and Recovery in Jungian Studies and Cinema

This book explores traumatic loss, grief, and recovery through the thoughtful combination of Abraham and Torok's 'crypt' theory, Jungian thought, and film theory to guide readers through the darkest places of the human psyche.

Focusing on both the destructive and reconstructive choices people can make, the book explores prolonged grief disorder, complicated mourning, post-traumatic stress disorder, embitterment, disenfranchised grief, trauma-related rumination as well as mental, emotional, and physical pain. Presented with real life examples and fictional ones, the book connects the psychoanalytic concepts of intrapsychic tomb and theoretra with Jungian concepts such as teleological model of the psyche, dreams, alchemical operations, shadow, archetypes, enantiodromia, symbols, and compensation on the canvas of modern grief theory.

Traumatic Loss and Recovery in Jungian Studies and Cinema is important reading for psychoanalysts, Jungian analysts, and psychotherapists with an interest in popular culture, as well as cinema students, scholars, and general readers interested in psychology, counselling, mental health, and media studies.

Mark Holmwood, PhD, is a researcher, author, and photographer. Following his MA and training in TA Counselling and Psychotherapy, he creatively combined his grief experience, clinical theory, cinema, and Jungian thought for this book.

Traumatic Loss and Recovery in Jungian Studies and Cinema

Transdisciplinary Approaches in Grief Theory

Mark Holmwood

Routledge
Taylor & Francis Group

LONDON AND NEW YORK

Cover image: © Getty Images

First published 2023
by Routledge
4 Park Square, Milton Park, Abingdon, Oxon OX14 4RN

and by Routledge
605 Third Avenue, New York, NY.10158

Routledge is an imprint of the Taylor & Francis Group, an informa business

British Library Cataloguing-in-Publication Data
A catalogue record for this book is available from the British Library

Library of Congress Cataloging-in-Publication Data
Names: Holmwood, Mark, author.
Title: Traumatic loss and recovery in Jungian studies and cinema :
transdisciplinary approaches in grief theory / Mark Holmwood.
Description: Abingdon, Oxon ; New York, NY : Routledge, 2023. |
Includes bibliographical references and index. |
Identifiers: LCCN 2022023007 (print) | LCCN 2022023008 (ebook) |
ISBN 9781032274171 (hardback) | ISBN 9781032274157 (paperback) |
ISBN 9781003292630 (ebook)
Subjects: LCSH: Loss (Psychology) | Grief. |
Jungian psychology. | Psychoanalysis and motion pictures.
Classification: LCC BF575.D35 H65 2023 (print) |
LCC BF575.D35 (ebook) | DDC 155.9/3–dc23/eng/20220716
LC record available at https://lccn.loc.gov/2022023007
LC ebook record available at https://lccn.loc.gov/2022023008

ISBN: 9781032274171 (hbk)
ISBN: 9781032274157 (pbk)
ISBN: 9781003292630 (ebk)

DOI: 10.4324/9781003292630

Typeset in Bembo
by Newgen Publishing UK

To all of the brave men, women, and children who learned how to survive with a deep wound in their hearts

Contents

Acknowledgements

The contents of this book have been hidden for many years. Call it fate, call it luck, call it Karma. It really does not matter how you label it. Personal situations and global events have converged in surprising ways and brought this publication forward. As wise people say, time has a quality, and some things need their right moment to happen. This book is the product of that moment.

I first acknowledge the people who have been benevolent, given their blessings, and expressed their delight during the making of this book. Their generosity and kindness have crossed borders, travelled worldwide, and contributed to the manuscript defying all odds. In chronological order: David Thompson, Tara Bilston, Robert Connolly, Scarlet Barnett, Peter Tapp, Scott Milligen, and Erin Salvi. Many thanks to each of you.

Thanks also to Susannah Frearson, Alexis O'Brien, Katie Randall, and Priya Sharma at Taylor and Francis, Sandrine Pricilla at Newgen, and Adam Bell at Ambb Editorial for their vision, understanding, and assistance.

My greatest debt is to my husband Chris who supported me every step of the way and without whom I could not have written this book.

Permission acknowledgements

Excerpts from Hunter Cordaiy's article *Big Guys versus the people: An interview with Robert Connolly*, courtesy of Australian Teachers of Media Inc. (ATOM) – https://metromagazine.com.au/

Excerpts from the film script of *The Bank*, by Robert Connolly. Copyright © 2001 by Robert Connolly. Used by permission of the author.

Excerpts from *Rabbit Hole* by David Lindsay-Abaire. Copyright © 2006 by David Lindsay-Abaire. Published by Theatre Communications Group. Used by permission of Theatre Communications Group.

Introduction

'Hi, my name is Mark and my partner killed himself in 2005'. This was what I said when I introduced myself for the first time to other survivors in the room. It was a private meeting organised by a national charity called SOBS – Survivors of Bereavement by Suicide. It was a dry and cold evening at the end of November 2018. I did not cry when I said that because I was tired of grieving. For 13 years, I have kept this loss hidden from daylight. In return, this loss has kept me hidden from daylight, too. It was dark; it was taboo; it was too difficult and complex for people to hear, to bear, to respond to. So, not talking about it became a choice, then a habit, until I was completely sealed and silenced in an impenetrable cocoon of grief.

This silent suffering, this invisible mourning is interpreted and named differently by two scholars. Between 1968 and 1982, Nicolas Abraham and Maria Torok presented their perspectives on loss and its aftermath. They called it the crypt, or the intrapsychic tomb where the love, the loss, and the bereaved person are frozen and hidden from others.

The idea of the crypt is fairly well-defined, and it goes back to Torok's (Abraham and Torok, 1994) definition of mourning: she calls it an illness. She first shares her clinical notes based on the people who admitted that they had experienced an increase of libido after they lost an object of love. She then provides a list of her observations: these people are depressed, fatigued, full of anxiety, self-criticism, and embarrassment; their desires are repressed, and their minds are exhausted with persistent ruminations about their loss; their physical ailments complicate their suffering further. Following these observations, she clearly defines what turns mourning into an illness: the feeling of shame due to an unstoppable (and sometimes aggressive) sexual impulse (Ibid., p.110).

So, what happens when this shame is not acknowledged? The denial of these desires blocks the mourning process briefly or perpetually (Ibid., p.120). When this process is blocked, those desires, the shame, and the loved object are buried deep in the psyche, which Torok calls *the intrapsychic tomb* or, simply, *the crypt*.

Abraham and Torok (1994) return to this concept in their 1975 paper called *The Lost Object – Me*. They expand it using several case studies: first, the erotic and aggressive attraction between two brothers, Victor and Gilles; second, an alternative reading of Freud's study of the Wolf Man, the patient who was

DOI: 10.4324/9781003292630-1

haunted by the seduction of his sister; and third, an unnamed patient who was troubled by the sexual attraction between his father and his sister. In each case, the shame related to libido contributes to the unspeakable suffering of the patient and complicates the loss.

There is, however, another type of crypt which Abraham and Torok clearly acknowledge. This one is caused by separation with a compelling reason. This internal crypt, they argue, is free from any aggression. They call it melancholic and also describe how a loss might deprive people the hope of being acknowledged: not being able to put their loss into words, communicate to others, or resign themselves to grief, they choose to deny everything – the loss as well as the love. There seems to be no alternative left for these people, so they bury everything deep, the pleasure and the suffering. They lock themselves up in their intrapsychic tombs.

This second type of crypt is important for this book and for me. In this book, I examine traumatic losses that do not include shame. In other words, there is no repressed sexual or aggressive desire towards the object of affection. There is only love. Due to a traumatic separation, this love then gets trapped and unexpressed, which ultimately harms the psyche. Echoing the words of Erica Bain in Chapter 5, people change from within – they become somebody else. I know I have.

What would you do in this situation? You would – ideally – ask for help and talk to a professional. I did the same, especially after the funerals of my parents, which closely followed my partner's suicide. However, I did not find comfort in the various types of therapy I tried: art therapy; psychodynamic, humanistic, or integrative therapies; body psychotherapy. I am not saying this to imply that they are not helpful. I am only saying that they did not work for me. But something did. It was simply the act of watching films.

Birgit Wolz (2019) calls it 'cinema therapy'. I am not sure if this is the right way of acknowledging the power of storytelling and its effect on the viewer. I am not sure simply because the viewer does not actively (and individually) participate in the drama unfolding on the big screen. However, the core idea is significant: through the simultaneous process of associating and disassociating with the characters and the story on the screen, watching films can become a new tool in exploring and illuminating darker areas of the human psyche. At least, this is what happened to me. I watched and re-watched, and observed and ruminated on these characters' losses, their pain, and their choices. My emotional and psychological chaos became more accessible to my mind through the metaphors I saw in their storylines. Their terrible and terrific choices worked as a guide for me to make the right choice for my own situation. In order to heal, I had to write. In other words, this book has become the tangible creation of my personal healing, my way out of my crypt.

This is partly influenced by Maria Torok's *theoretra* concept. In her 1982 paper, 'Theoretra: An Alternative to Theory' (Abraham and Torok, 1994), Torok first describes the matrimonial Greek word 'theoretra' which is a ceremonial tradition of exchanging gifts between a bride and a groom. The gift of the bride is lifting her veil to reveal her face, femininity, and (symbolically) virginity. The gift of the groom looks more materialistic. Even though Torok does not elaborate on them, it is implied in the sentence 'he hands her gifts' (Ibid., p.253), possibly referring to jewellery, land, or other symbols of social status.

Torok refers to this marital ritual to make an important point: the exchange of gifts between two people symbolises a union where there are no secrets. The elimination of secrets is also what makes a productive therapeutic relationship between an analyst and a patient. Therefore, Torok's analogy is this: the patient hands over their secrets as gifts, no matter how unspeakable, how unimaginable, how deep, how *cryptic*. The analyst's gift to the patient is to listen, without condoning or condemning, without restricting or reducing the patient's agony with theory. Their union is what Torok calls a trance, a magical moment during psychoanalysis where the ghost locked in the crypt becomes visible to both parties. Theoretra is this moment where the distinction between theory and practice is abolished as the patient and the analyst truly and transparently meet as two fellow humans:

> In the theoretric moment there is trance. Right there, the two partners will on occasion fall asleep together, dream the same word, the same image, for an instant, and for once have a real session, a séance, to summon the specter, the spirit of the spirit of Spirit itself, assassinated by some ghost.
>
> (Ibid., p.254)

This book benefits from the concept of theoretra, because it provides a new space to discuss trauma, bereavement, crypts, and Jungian psychology without the necessity of adhering to a specific theory in any given moment. It offers a new freedom to be able to give voice to suffering without strict labelling or compartmentalising. In other words, it enables one to think outside the box when facing a person in distress.

In the same paper, Torok describes the thorny correspondence between Freud and his close associate, Sandor Ferenczi. She also points out how 'the *theoretical* Freud could not understand the *practical* Ferenczi, who, as Freud put it, merely wanted to cure people' (Ibid., p.255). She not only rejects the death drive openly in the last sentence of this paper (Ibid., p.256), but she also acknowledges the need to put theories aside, especially when they do not relate to or explain the experiences of patients fully. From calling mourning an illness to leaving theories aside, that is quite a big transformation. By publishing her paper on *theoretra*, Torok becomes forward-looking and revolutionary as she clearly offers the idea that rigid theories can stifle people further. In order to achieve a *theoretric* moment, to help a grieving person open up and release old ghosts in their crypt, clinical empathy with an open mind becomes a must. This perspective is also shared by Nicholas T. Rand who wrote the editor's note to Torok's paper:

> Theory can become a form of rigidly cold observation, even the instrument of manipulative terror, as opposed to being the reflective by-product

of a free-flowing and continuously open-ended process of sympathetic understanding. [...] For Torok, listening means to summon and welcome the voices patients cannot hear in themselves.

(Ibid., p.250)

I see the *theoretric* moment of a person opening up their crypt as a way forward, a flow of pent-up energy, an equilibrating process between pain and healing. However, in order to use this perspective productively in this book, I am doing something unconventional. I am blending theories in a way which some people may find unorthodox: I start with psychoanalytic thinking, walk through current grief theories, and finally turn to Jung in order to bypass the possible rigidity of theories on grief and loss.

The rejection of inflexible observations also played a part in Carl Gustav Jung's theories about the human mind. While he was writing *Symbols of Transformation*, which later became the fifth volume of his Collected Works, he candidly praised and criticised Freudian psychology in the foreword (CW 5, p.xxiii). According to him, Freud's research and observations about the human psyche were remarkable. However, his theoretical framework, Jung argued, was limiting the scope and the magnitude of contents harboured in the psyche.

Jung himself did not specify a conceptual framework around loss or mourning as Freud (1917) did in *Mourning and Melancholia*. However, he wrote about death and regeneration in connection with religious and mythological stories and iconography that span centuries of human history all around the globe. For example, he talks about death as a threshold for rebirth (CW 5, para.354), meaning people symbolically go back to their mother's womb. He refers to different rites of initiations as ways of rebirthing education (CW 4, para.783). He even describes how the human brain is more in tune with the eternal cycle of ruin and renewal (CW 10, para.12), the creative story of mankind as a whole, rather than objective history, which is just a list of events. When he talks about trauma referring to the case studies included in the introduction to the fifth volume of his *Collected Works*, his position is clear: the contents of the psyche cannot be understood solely by theory (CW 5, pp.xxv–xxvi). For him, a wide outlook with a bigger grasp of knowledge is necessary in order to see the whole picture of a traumatised psyche. He argues that neurosis and its pathological outcomes cannot be explored solely by theory, because it medicalises the difficulty, reduces it to an illness, and misses acknowledging a soul in pain.

Jung's ideas and concepts have travelled far beyond their contexts in analytical psychology and psychotherapy. Since his death in 1961, Jung's writings have been used extensively to question, examine, and explore new areas in theology, sociology, politics, gender studies, and literature. In other words, Jungian concepts have become unconventional keys to frame and develop new research.

In this book, I adopt a similar viewpoint and I specifically apply Jungian concepts to cinematic narratives to explore the nature of grief. When people lose their job, when they lose their pet, when they divorce, when they experience miscarriage, or when they lose their health they experience grief. These experiences are all categorised under grief reactions. As it is impossible to refer to all of them in one book, I have focused on specifically one type of loss: traumatic bereavement.

Traumatic bereavement is the sudden and sometimes violent separation from a loved one. I use the word violent to refer to the etymology of the word 'bereavement'. It means 'to deprive ruthlessly or by force' in Old English. A violent separation is almost always followed by an emotional response, which can be categorised under the term complicated grief or complicated mourning. While different theorists sometimes use the words grief and mourning interchangeably, they still refer to the same complex phenomena. Complicated grief or complicated mourning is a response to losing a loved one traumatically, which may or may not match the criteria for mental disorders.

However, as Parkes and Prigerson (2010, p.4) point out, this does not mean that people who can be labelled as 'mentally ill' would really be mentally ill. Based on their observations, they argue that the majority of mental disorders are actually acceptable reactions to challenging events and situations. This means that people who suffer a traumatic bereavement, while they might engage in thoughts and actions which can be classified as psychotic, may be reacting to their individual and abnormal situation in a normal way. Their suffering may not be fully expressed and acknowledged due to a complete lack of social sympathy. In Abraham and Torok's words, their pain becomes entombed, and their losses are locked in their crypts with their entire worth and meaning:

> Inexpressible mourning erects a secret tomb inside the subject. Reconstituted from the memories of words, scenes, and affects, the objective correlative of the loss is buried alive in the crypt as a full-fledged person, complete with its own topography.
>
> (Abraham and Torok, 1994, p.130)

The key phrase here is 'inexpressible mourning'. In this book, and throughout seven films, I focus on these overwhelming, unspeakable feelings of loss and the equilibrating process taking place in each protagonist's psyche. As symbology, mythology, cryptic mourning, theoretra, and Jungian concepts are interwoven through the canvas of grief theory, the end result becomes a rich, dense, and new artistic exploration of grief.

I.1 A brief reading guide into the contents

In Chapter 1, I look at the origins and the development of grief theory. Going far back in time, I start with a Sumerian tale of loss. Linking imagination with human emotion, I mention this literary depiction of grief in order to foreshadow the main content of this book. The timeline starts with Robert Burton's study of grief in 1621 and continues with Benjamin Rush's medical inquiries in 1812. I then reference the study of Darwin into emotional expression in 1872 and the personality theory of Shand in 1914. All these studies pave the way to Freud's *Mourning and Melancholia*, which became a milestone in the main body of grief theory. I also look at Freud's contemporaries such as Helene Deutsch, Melanie Klein, and Erich Lindemann to demonstrate their indispensable contributions that helped Fairbairn and Winnicott develop the object relations theory for understanding loss and attachments. I interpret the arrival of Bowlby's attachment theory in 1958 as a big chain reaction which leads to the rise of two other significant scholars: Kübler-Ross and Parkes, who undeniably changed and shaped the theoretical understanding of modern grief theory. Following the theories of Worden and Sanders in 1981 and 1989, I look at George Bonanno, who introduced his resilience theory, which offered an alternative perspective, in 2009. I also mention more recent and emerging theories on grief, including Boddez's addiction model based on behavioural psychology. I wrap up the chapter with a short discussion on the transtheoretical aspects of Jung's theories, making two points: one, he did not write on mourning like Freud did; and two, it is possible to combine Jung's concepts with grief theory.

In Chapter 2, I look at how psychoanalytic theories and film studies came together to understand, investigate, and deconstruct cinematic narratives. To put things in perspective, I follow a timeline again. Starting with Otto Rank's essay in 1914, I trace the steps of an emerging academic field. Referring to the post-structuralism of the 1960s, I specifically mention the development of Freudian and Lacanian clusters in film studies. With the arrival of feminism, I explore Mulvey, Friedan, and the role of patriarchal society behind the images. This short history of film studies also looks at how the theories of Marx, Gramsci, and Althusser were used to explore the hegemonic relations in the cinema industry, covering scholars like Metz, Baudry, Gabbard, Žižek, and Kaplan. After I explore Winnicottian perspectives and how his transitional space concept is used in film analysis, I also present a brief history of Jungian film studies. I mention the birth of a new Jungian approach in 1979 with the publication of Don Fredericksen's article. Following this article, I trace the two main clusters of Jungian film analysis: textual and phenomenological. Building connections with a film's particular narrative, I explain how textual analysis uses symbology, mythology, and Jungian analytical psychology to create a second interconnected reading. I also look at how the theories of Husserl and Merleau-Ponty are utilised in the Jungian phenomenological cluster to investigate embodied reactions. I finish this chapter by referring to Hauke who explores a new hybridity of these clusters in his filmmaking projects, and also to the emergence of new Jungian film explorations beyond the Anglosphere.

In Chapter 3, I turn my focus to new developments in film studies, where clinical work meets cinematic fiction. I specifically mention four distinct collaborations of film and psychology: Edwards; Braswell; Gullestad; and Fox. I explain how clinical theory has been used to start innovative interdisciplinary discussions on countertransference, bioethics, sadism, and also a new neuropsychoanalytic theory of reception based on mirror neurons. In short, these examples demonstrate a new wave of film analysis where films are used as case studies. This chapter is important because it clarifies how I follow the footsteps of these scholars to develop a new theoretric medium of film analysis in this book. Referring back to Maria Torok's paper *Theoretra*, I explain how I would aim to create similar theoretric moments between the protagonists and me (as an analyst and a narrator) to demonstrate a new hybrid of clinical theory and Jungian analysis. I also point out that each analysis highlights a clear personal choice after a specific trauma.

In Chapter 4, I start examining these choices by looking at bereavement by suicide and how suicidal ideation is common in people who are traumatised by losing a loved one to suicide. I use Soderbergh's remake of *Solaris* (2002) in order to investigate the protagonist's prolonged grief disorder, combining it with Durkheim's egoistic and anomic suicide perspectives. I then apply the Jungian concepts of shadow, numinosum, union of opposites, and enantiodromia to the overall narrative arc with their symbolic depictions in the film, combining them with the research of Rosen on suicide survivors. I conclude this chapter with my final assessment of the protagonist who chooses self-destruction as a way out of his crypt.

In Chapter 5, I look at how a traumatised victim turns into a criminal due to her grief. Diving deeper into the darkness, I closely examine the violent behaviour of a bereaved woman depicted in Jordan's *The Brave One* (2007). This time I investigate the roots of the protagonist's transformation in post-traumatic stress disorder (PTSD), and again use the Jungian method of amplification to weave in visual symbols in the film that contributes to this narrative. Exploring the Jungian concepts of alchemical operations, teleological model of the psyche, and compensation, I conclude that no matter how strong the feelings of helplessness might be, violence is still a choice and in the case of *The Brave One*, it becomes another way out of a crypt.

In Chapter 6, I explore another choice deeply rooted in traumatic loss. I use Connolly's *The Bank* (2001) to highlight how bereavement can shape and fuel destructive political views that lead to nihilist actions. Developing on the theories of conscientization and embitterment, I analyse the film by applying the Jungian concepts of shadow, persona, and individuation. My concluding assessment of this case study is similar to the last two ones: even an anarchic act is a choice, and some people make this choice to get out of their intrapsychic tomb.

With Chapter 7 and onwards, I start investigating reconstructive and positive choices when it comes to traumatic loss. In this chapter, I use Tom Ford's first film as a director, *A Single Man* (2009). I identify the formation of a melancholic crypt based on the social invisibility and disenfranchised grief theory of Doka (1989) and Attig (2004). Building on this classification, I refer to the Jungian concepts of alchemical operations, union of opposites, and archetypes to explore the rich symbolic content of the film. My final evaluation of the film's ending, which is slightly different to the novel, is that choosing to form new meaningful bonds with other people can be helpful and is another way to get out of a crypt.

In Chapter 8, I continue my investigation of positive choices. As a contrast to the childhood trauma explored in Chapter 6 with *The Bank*, I look at Hancock's *Saving Mr. Banks* (2013) to examine another adult trapped in a crypt. As the only semi-biographical case study of this book, this chapter also expands on the prolonged grief disorder surveyed in Chapter 4. Through the film's narrative, I engage with the Jungian concepts of animus possession, archetypes, and enantiodromia. I specifically read the differences between the film's beginning and its ending as an abreactive ouroboric pattern. This case study ends with my conclusion that choosing to relinquish control is a way of liberating one's trapped self.

In Chapter 9, I examine the curious links between confession and forgiveness. Using Mitchell's *Rabbit Hole* (2010) as the next case study of this book, I draw parallels between the films analysed in Chapter 10 and Chapter 7 in terms of different reactions to sudden traumatic losses caused by traffic accidents. As a contrast to these two chapters, I also point out how the protagonists, now trapped in the same crypt with their three-way trauma, find their way out: by choosing to forgive. Carrying on the clinical discussion with the theories of trauma-related rumination and also expanding on PTSD, I present a real-life example similar to the events depicted in the film to underline the effect of forgiveness. This chapter engages with the Jungian concepts of alchemical operations and union of opposites through its main narrative arc. My concluding assessment is that, just like in the sacrament of penance and ideally in the relationship between a therapist and a client, admitting wrongdoing and being forgiven in return help traumatised adults come out of their intrapsychic tombs.

In my last chapter, Chapter 10, I bring together several plots from all the films and case studies examined in previous chapters. Using Barnz's darkly humoured film *Cake* (2014), I refer to all the choices I mentioned before: self-destruction; violence; anarchy; forming new bonds; letting go; and forgiving. Because all these choices are depicted in *Cake*, I argue that the film's protagonist faces these choices but ultimately decides on a different way out of her crypt. This time my clinical analysis focuses on trauma as a whole: mental; emotional; and physical. Referring to the observations of Fishbain (1999), Vastag (2003), and Levi et al. (2008), I discuss the protagonist's anguish in detail. When the Jungian concepts of shadow, alchemical operations, and compensation are applied to the overall narrative, my final assessment of this case study simply reveals itself: self-compassion is a powerful choice that leads to self-liberation and opens the way out of a crypt.

I.2 A short overview of Jungian concepts

In this book, I refer to a variety of Jungian concepts and notions within each film analysis in order to go beyond the grief theory and achieve a theoretric encounter with the protagonists. While I detail their losses and their choices, I use the following concepts: the teleological model of the psyche; dreams; alchemy; shadow; archetypes; enantiodromia; compensation; and amplification and symbols. It is important to note that I use them in accordance with each film's grief narrative and protagonist-specific situation.

Jung argues that processes in the psyche are indeed very similar to other processes in life. They follow the rules of causality and unfold with a purpose (CW 7, para.210). In other words, he says that the psyche appears to position itself towards an outcome. In the case of grief, I interpret this as an equilibrating process where the impact of loss (the cause) is balanced with a result (the effect).

In the case of a traumatic bereavement that leaves a wound in the psyche, Jung's teleological model suggests that the psyche's response to loss is to try to do something healing. It is trying to find a way of moving forward by engaging with and using the healing power of the psyche to achieve a form of homeostasis by releasing feelings, images, and symbols that provide different ways of containing the experience. That is similar to what Jung is trying to do in *The Red Book* (Jung, 2009). Using active imagination, he goes through his own personal investigation by dialoguing with his imaginary characters and making colourful paintings and drawings. The central idea is that people can use art, music, writing, and creativity in general as a healing process that will help them in times of distress. This perspective is widely accepted today, especially in art therapy. Art therapy uses images and music, especially in Guided Imagery and Music (GIM) therapy created by Helen L. Bonny. Through art and creativity, it is possible for some people to bypass the defences of their consciousness, get underneath the rational mind and access the healing powers of the psyche.[1] This therapeutic effect of writing, music, and images on grief experience is further explored in Chapter 8.

The concept of dreams and how they affect the psyche became an important discussion when Freud (1900) started exploring dreams and dream content in *The Interpretation of Dreams*. Freud was trying to decode the dream, to find out its latent and manifest content. Processes of condensation, displacement, and visualisation became the key elements of his dream work. The idea behind this was to uncover some historical trauma which revealed itself in dreams. Jung, on the other hand, argued that dreams actually look into the future, and they have a function of wish fulfilment (CW 3, para.255). A dream, then, might depict the situation as it is, but it still looks into the future where the person is trying to achieve something. Medard Boss (1957), on the other hand, argued that dreams appear as statements of a person's principal life stance or condition. In other words, the contents of a dream express that person's present condition as a whole. This curious link between grief, dreams, and their connection to present and future psychological states is especially highlighted in Chapter 7 and Chapter 10.

Jung uses alchemy, the proto-scientific method of chemical transmutations, as an over-arching symbolic argument when describing the transformation of the psyche, especially in *Symbols of Transformation* (CW 5), *Psychology and Alchemy* (CW 12), and *Alchemical Studies* (CW 13), volumes of his *Collected Works*. This deep change, as Jung describes, is not a single step of accomplishment but an ongoing process towards individuation. The chemical steps of turning base metals into gold find their psychological counterparts in Jungian analysis. Each corresponding to a specific state of the psyche, they are the steps to individuation. For example, *nigredo* refers to the dark confusion where an individual meets their own inner shadow; *separatio*, to the separation of psychic components; *mortificatio/putrefactio*, to the death and decay of fixations and fears; *dissolutio*, to the dissolving of old self to make room for the new (Hopcke, 1999).

I refer to these stages of alchemy especially in Chapters 4, 5, and 6 as they provide a new comprehension of this symbolic death and rebirth process taking place in the psyche. When the images, characters, situations, choices, actions, and their results portrayed in these films are analysed both literally and meta-phorically, especially through the lens of Jung's concept of *shadow*, namely the repressed and harmful aspects of personality every individual has (CW 16, para.470), the horrible and detrimental effect of loss and grief becomes clearer. Locked in their crypts, these characters are compelled to face their shadows during the alchemical process of *nigredo*. The symbolic transformation of their psyche is only complete when they achieve (individually perceived and unique) restorative justice at the end of their grief journey.

Jung also wrote about archetypes and their relation to the constant pro-cess of unfolding, growth, and development in the psyche, which in some way mirrors biological growth and ageing. Based on his extensive dream work, he defines archetypes as easily observable behavioural patterns which are repeat-edly depicted in myths around the globe (CW 3, para.549). In other words, archetypes (such as wise old man, hero, mother, child, etc.) are primordial images, easily perceptible and understood by the psyche because they are repeated and recreated in every culture. They become evident through their manifestations in human life. Even though an archetype is a hypothetical entity, it is funda-mentally a psychosomatic concept linking the body and the psyche, image, and instincts. I refer to archetypal content in terms of its relation to the protagonists' journeys out of their crypts specifically in Chapters 7 and 8.

Another concept of Jung that I apply to my film analyses is *enantiodromia* (CW 6, para.708). Enantiodromia, Jung argues, is a psychological rule meaning that sooner or later everything turns into its opposite. When applied to loss and grief, this concept becomes a tool to understand how death can be a gateway to a new life. One of Jung's examples is the myth of Noah in the Bible (CW 5, para.311) where the flood not only destroys but also brings a fresh beginning.

Engaging with enantiodromia, especially through the context of traumatic loss, makes it easier to see that death can also be the (symbolic) death of one part of the psyche so that something new can emerge out of it. I refer to this renewal of the psyche in every film analysis since the narratives not only por-tray the traumatic loss but also depict the beginning of a new chapter in the protagonist's lives. Therefore, the way out of the crypt becomes *enantiodromic*.

The last two concepts I will be using in this book work together: symbols and amplification. The Jungian process of amplification is different to the Freudian concept of free association. Freud developed his method of free asso-ciation while he was working on the analysis of dreams published in *Studies on Hysteria* (Freud, 1895). This method included the patient talking freely about the elements in their dreams, which led to the discovery of the chains of meaning and association between these elements. Even though the name of the method includes the word 'free', association works and follows a sequence of meaning and is certainly not that free. A simple example would be like this: classroom – teacher – authority – father. Therefore, in every step of the sequence the meaning is moving further away from the initial image (in this example, classroom).

Jung, however, defined association differently and likened it to an interconnected assemblage around a central image (CW 16, para.319). Therefore, he used amplification as a tool for further discovery and interpretation of the psyche, making connections with universal and mythic imagery. Contrary to the Freudian approach, where the gap between the image and meaning gets bigger step by step, amplification puts the image at the centre, and its links to different meanings form a web of connections. Following the same example given for Freud, a typical amplification would look like this: classroom – school, classroom – learning, classroom – wisdom. By doing this the movement involves both directions, it starts and goes away from the image then comes back to it. It enriches the image itself by connecting it to different associations. In other words, looking at parallel contexts illuminates the initial image. I use amplification in all film analyses to unearth rich layers of mythological and psychological content.

These layers, of course, are found in symbols and visual content present in the films that contribute to their overall narratives. Jung argued that symbols convey more than what the unconscious processes indicate, and their allegorical cores (which are based on universal imagery) communicate information that cannot be communicated in different or alternative ways (CW 15, para.105). His theoretical break with Freud regarding the reductionist interpretation of symbols continued here. Meaning, he argued that symbols did not always refer to libidinal content. They pointed at an impending progress in the psyche which deserved to be acknowledged. Symbols, he noted, helped people to be hopeful and positive about the future, whereas inflexible analysis and psychological data reduced individuals to fixed entities which, in return, triggered fatalism and negative thinking (CW 4, para.679).

I adopt a similar position in my analyses, and this is where the theoretric encounter with the protagonists comes into play. As I highlight and amplify the symbols in each film, the journey from trauma to relief is revealed in connection to how they contribute to this change and development in the psyche. In order to do this, I look closely at specific visual components (which function as symbols) in the narrative and draw parallels to their historical, cultural, and psychological contexts by amplifying them in relation to the protagonists' stories.

I.3 A postcard from beyond

On January 8, 2017, Meryl Streep accepted the Cecil B. DeMille award at the Golden Globe Awards ceremony. She finished her great speech with a wonderful nod to the late Carrie Fisher and to the power of art. Quoting Fisher, Streep encouraged everyone to take their broken hearts and transform them into an art form in order to move forward, to heal, to liberate themselves.

I see this book as a hybrid of academic thought and art. I have certainly taken my broken heart and turned it into a meaningful liberation, my own way out of my crypt. But this does not mean this book is a personal narrative (because it is not). It is a new, progressive, and unconventional look into cinema, grief theory, psychoanalysis, and Jungian thought. It is a transdisciplinary exploration of trauma and recovery. I sincerely hope that this book would help and inspire other survivors of traumatic loss as well as psychoanalysts, Jungian analysts, clinical psychologists, psychotherapists, actors, directors, scriptwriters, and other artists. Grief is not an illness. Traumatic loss will not define your life. You will recover. But only if you choose to.

Make that choice. Today. Now.

Filmography

The Bank (2001) Directed by R. Connolly [film]. Australia
The Brave One (2007) Directed by N. Jordan [film]. USA
Cake (2014) Directed by D. Barnz [film]. USA
Rabbit Hole (2010) Directed by J.C. Mitchell [film]. USA
Saving Mr. Banks (2013) Directed by J.L. Hancock [film]. USA
A Single Man (2009) Directed by T. Ford [film]. USA
Solaris (2002) Directed by S. Soderbergh [film]. USA

Note

1 It is also important to mention the work of Russell Razzaque (2014) here. As a psychiatrist, he argues that mental illnesses can be forms of spiritual awakening, and therapies that are designed to 'treat' episodes of mental illness should go beyond their scope and help the individual complete their spiritual journey.

Bibliography

Abraham, N. and Torok, M. (1994) *The Shell and the Kernel: Renewals of Psychoanalysis. Volume I.* Chicago: University of Chicago Press.

Attig, T. (2004) 'Disenfranchised grief revisited: Discounting hope and love', *Omega*, 49, pp.197–215.

Boss, M. (1957) *The Analysis of Dreams*. London: Rider.

Doka, K.J. (ed.) (1989) *Disenfranchised Grief: Recognizing Hidden Sorrow*. Lexington, MA: Lexington Books.

Fishbain, D.A. (1999) 'The association of chronic pain and suicide', *Seminars in Clinical Neuropsychiatry*, 4(3), pp.221–227.

Freud, S. (1895) 'Studies on hysteria', in *The Standard Edition of the Psychological Works*, Vol. 20, London: Hogarth Press.

Freud, S. (1900) 'The interpretation of dreams', in *The Standard Edition of the Psychological Works*, Vol. 4–5, London: Hogarth Press.

Freud, S. (1917) 'Mourning and melancholia', in *The Standard Edition of the Complete Psychological Works*, Vol.14. London: The Hogarth Press.

Hopcke, R.H. (1999) *A Guided Tour of the Collected Works of C. G. Jung*. Boston: Shambala.

Jung, C.G. (1960) *The Collected Works of C.G. Jung, Volume 3: Psychogenesis of Mental Disease*. Princeton: Princeton University Press.

Jung, C.G. (1961) *The Collected Works of C.G. Jung, Volume 4: Freud and Psychoanalysis*. Princeton: Princeton University Press.

Jung, C.G. (1966) *The Collected Works of C.G. Jung, Volume 15: Spirit in Man, Art, and Literature*. Princeton: Princeton University Press.

Jung, C.G. (1966) *The Collected Works of C.G. Jung, Volume 16: Practice of Psychotherapy*. Princeton: Princeton University Press.

Jung, C.G. (1967) *The Collected Works of C.G. Jung, Volume 5: Symbols of Transformation*. Princeton: Princeton University Press.

Jung, C.G. (1967) *The Collected Works of C.G. Jung, Volume 7: Two Essays in Analytical Psychology*. Princeton: Princeton University Press.

Jung, C.G. (1968) *The Collected Works of C.G. Jung, Volume 12: Psychology and Alchemy*. Princeton: Princeton University Press.

Jung, C.G. (1968) *The Collected Works of C.G. Jung, Volume 13: Alchemical Studies*. Princeton: Princeton University Press.

Jung, C.G. (1970) *The Collected Works of C.G. Jung, Volume 10: Civilization in Transition*. Princeton: Princeton University Press.

Jung, C.G. (1971) *The Collected Works of C.G. Jung, Volume 6: Psychological Types*. Princeton: Princeton University Press.

Jung, C.G. (2009) *The Red Book: Liber Novus*. 1st, Reader's ed. London and New York: W.W. Norton & Company.

Levi, Y., Horesh, N., Fischel, T., Treves, I., Or, E., and Apter, A. (2008) 'Mental pain and its communication in medically serious suicide attempts: An "impossible situation"', *Journal of Affective Disorders*, 111(2–3), pp.244–250.

Parkes, C.M. and Prigerson, H.G. (2010) *Bereavement: Studies of Grief in Adult Life*. 4th ed. London: Penguin.

Razzaque, R. (2014) *Breaking Down Is Waking Up: Can Psychological Suffering Be a Spiritual Gateway?* London: Watkins Publishing.

Vastag, B. (2003) 'Scientists find connections in the brain between physical and emotional pain', *JAMA*, 290(18), pp.2389–2390.

Wolz, B. (2019) Why *Cinema Therapy Works*. Available at: www.cinematherapy.com/whyitworks.html

Part I

From the past to the present

1 A brief history of grief theory

One of the qualities that make human beings unique is their awareness of their own temporariness: they can contemplate their own fleeting existence and their death. The first written account about this awareness goes back to 3000 BC. Being among the earliest works of literature, *The Maxims of Ptahhotep* (Lichtheim, 2006) recounts instructions on how to live a happy and fulfilled life. The author explains his reasons for writing by saying he has reached an old age and felt he had to pass on the information before he dies. *The Epic of Gilgamesh* (Sandars, 1972), however, deals with another side of this awareness. The emotional impact of the loss of Enkidu on Gilgamesh makes this ancient Sumerian poem one of the earliest literary works known to man depicting grief and the impossibility of an eternal human life following the loss of a loved one.

Death and the consequences of it are an indispensable part of oral and written literature spanning centuries. For example, in the Greek drama *The Oresteian Trilogy* (Aeschylus, 1959), Aeschylus tells how the sacrifice of Iphigenia during the Trojan War put a chain of events in motion, grief turning into a family vendetta. From the Old English heroic poem *Beowulf* (The Norton Anthology of English Literature, 1993) to *A Grief Observed* (Lewis, 2015) in 20th-century non-fiction, literature incorporates the themes of death, loss, and mourning in one form or another, and provides us countless and different examples where we gain insight into the human psyche.

While literature is rich with depictions of bereavement, and although we can trace human knowledge in anatomy, physiology, and psychology back to ancient times, research into the psychological aspects of bereavement and grief is relatively recent. The emergence and the development of grief theory in the Western world occurred mainly in the 20th century. However, its origins go back to the 17th century. In order to track its growth, I will present it in three distinct parts: pre-Freudian era; Freud and contemporaries; and post-Freudian era.

1.1 Pre-Freudian era

The term 'mourning' was incorporated into psychoanalysis in 1917 by Sigmund Freud through his work *Mourning and Melancholia* (Freud, 1917), and this term

DOI: 10.4324/9781003292630-3

has been widely used by clinicians in a broad sense to refer to a variety of psychological processes and reactions to loss ever since. Robert Burton's *The Anatomy of Melancholy* (Burton, 2001), however, dates back to 1621, and is distinctive in terms of its inclusion of grief and its association with mental health. Revised, expanded, and republished five more times in his lifetime, Burton's study was unique in terms of its scope, including extensive references to history, medicine, philosophy, literature, religion, meteorology, astrology, and even the military and navigation. Burton observed the links between mind and body within the context of grief and argued that talking about loss with other people contributed to an individual's mental and physical well-being.

Benjamin Rush is another important figure in grief theory. Prior to Freud, his book published in 1812 called *Medical Inquiries and Observations upon the Diseases of the Mind* (Rush, 1812) includes a short section on grief, describing its short and long-term characteristics, and ties it to increased risk of mortality. Although his belief that the cause of many mental problems is poor blood circulation is incorrect, he is one of the earliest founders of humane psychosocial care, later named as moral therapy.

In 1872, Charles Darwin, with his study *The Expression of the Emotions in Man and Animals* (Darwin, 1872), sought the animal basis of human mannerisms. Complete with drawings and facial illustrations, the book connects mental states to movement (hence the title, emotion), and Chapter 7 specifically focuses on sad feelings, describing grief, dejection, and despair with their revelation in body language. Although Darwin did not attempt to define the characteristics of grief, he received help especially from the British psychiatrist James Crichton-Browne during the preparation of the book (Darwin, Ekman, and Prodger, 2002). His distinct descriptions of active and passive forms of grief have become a standard in grief studies and make this work Darwin's main contribution to modern psychology. Darwin's close examination of the expression of grief in monkeys and apes also paved the way for ethological discoveries in psychology, linking grief's biological origins and significance to attachment and loss theories, especially by Bowlby (1998), Averill (1968), and Lindemann (1979).

Influenced by Darwin's theory of evolution, British psychologist A.F. Shand published his book *The Foundations of Character* (Shand, 1914) in 1914. Magai and McFadden (1995) argue that Shand's concept of linking emotions and personality is unique and different when compared to his contemporaries. Shand considered primary emotions as forces behind an individual's character, creating a causal link between the two. He wrote a lengthy discussion on the nature and the extent of grief, calling it 'the laws of sorrow'. In five comprehensive chapters, he describes different aspects of grief: how the loss of a beloved object can cause this emotion; how it can diminish when we know another person shares the same sorrow with us; how it can become stronger when kept secret; how it can strengthen or weaken the character; and how it can break the spirit. In his descriptions, he also refers to dramatic works of poetry, just like Burton did, because he thinks poets observe human nature and emotions in a superior way. Shand also categorised four reactions to loss: aggression, depression, repression, and hyperactivity. He mentioned the strength of enduring emotional bonds with the deceased, as well as the importance of social care.

1.2 Freud and contemporaries

Historically speaking, although Shand's findings were presented earlier, Freudian approach has become one of the major models in research and theory. Three years after Shand's book was published, Freud submitted his famous paper titled *Mourning and Melancholia*. Written before Freud himself experienced his own personal losses, he mainly examined the refusal of loss and how the psyche is disturbed by the loss itself. The German word he used for mourning was *trauer*, which, just like in English, means both the effect of grief and its external display. He described mourning as a reaction, either to the loss of a real person or to the loss of an abstract notion, such as freedom, national identity, and so on.

Shand and the theorists before Freud did not elaborate on the types of loss. The general concept of grief was limited to the loss of a loved person. Freud, however, expanded this concept to include the loss of abstractions that can trigger similar reactions in human beings. His main focus in this paper was on melancholia, but he continuously compared and contrasted it to mourning, which for him was the normal grief process.

Freud argued that normal mourning is a gradual, long process and that even though mourning makes people deviate from their daily routines it does not have to become a pathological condition or require medical treatment. According to him, mourning is expected to diminish naturally in the course of time, and interfering with this process can be harmful. He also noted that profound mourning contains a loss of interest in the outside world, loss of capacity to adopt new objects of love, and the rejection of anything not connected to the lost object. When the process of mourning is complete, the person will have detached from what has been lost. Most of the time, only the real loss of the loved object, mainly through death, creates mourning.

These ideas of Freud have become the basis of grief theory, which has since been both developed and challenged. It is also important to note that Freud did not make a clear distinction between bereavement, grief, and mourning. Moreover, because psychoanalysis argues that sexual energy, when not directly expressed, reveals itself in different forms whenever it finds an opportunity, the main ideas of mourning and the loss of the loved object also rest on the libidinal argument. In short, Freud brought sex and death together in examining our relationship to loss. In her reading of Freud's theories, Maud Ellmann (2005) suggests that these two forces of nature can put one's psyche out of sync with present time and create an enduring link to the past, as reality can sometimes become too much to bear.

Freud's perspective was classifying people, real objects, ideas, and notions all under the category of loved objects. His focus on the process of identification with the lost object has been referred to in all psychoanalytic theories after him. One of his biggest contributions to grief theory, however, was describing the subject of loss, and how humans cope with loss in normal and pathological ways, under the spotlight of scientific research.

Freud worked with many respectable contemporaries of his time and had many colleagues and followers who also became famous psychoanalysts. Among them was Helene Deutsch who was one of the first psychoanalysts to specialise in the treatment of women. During the course of her research, she made an interesting discovery, which she called 'Absence of Grief' (Deutsch, 1937), and published her findings in an article in 1937.

Deutsch argued that the death of a beloved person triggers a reactive expression of feeling (which she called grief), and if that response is omitted (which she called the absence) then it will manifest itself fully in an alternative form, for example, as inexplicable recurring depressions. She suggested three reasons for the absence. These were: an insufficiently developed ego to carry the burden of this loss; possibly a narcissistic self-protection mechanism; and the existence of previous conflict with the lost object.

The argument presented by Deutsch was subsequently supported by another psychoanalyst, Erich Lindemann, who noted that if the expression of grief is postponed then it might be expressed many years later (Lindemann, 1944). Sixty-six years later, Worden (2010) would be describing this phenomenon in his theoretical framework as the results of disguised grief. He noted that any supressed or disguised grief would manifest itself either as a psychosomatic problem or reckless, inappropriate deeds and manners.

While Deutsch specialised in women, another female psychoanalyst was specialising in children. Melanie Klein was the first psychoanalyst to work with young children, and it is thought that the first two children she used traditional psychoanalysis on were her own. Her research led Fairbairn (1952), Winnicott (1953), Rank (1996), and Guntrip (2018) to develop the object relations theory in response.

Klein shared Freud's views of mourning and explored the links between the mental constellations called 'paranoid-schizoid position' and 'depressive position' in infants and children, and how these positions affected individuals throughout their lives (Klein, 1940). She also made the important connection between the infant's successful relation to its mother as an object and a later ability to deal with loss as an adult. She argued if the child's early relationship with mother is not secure then the person as an adult could suffer from pathological grief.

It is also essential to mention here Lindemann's contribution to grief theory. His work provided more extensive descriptions and definitions of normal and pathological grief (Lindemann, 1944). He defined bereavement as a sudden stop or cut off from social interaction, and he sought to categorise the symptoms of normal grief (which he labelled as 'acute') from a psychosomatic perspective. In this manner, he is one of the first people to bridge body, mind, and emotions in his symptomatology. Moreover, the way he saw acute grief not as a medical or psychiatric disorder but as a normal reaction to a stressful situation brought him closer to the theories of Bowlby (1998), Kübler-Ross

(2009) and Parkes (1993). These theories have mainly formed and influenced the post-Freudian era.

1.3 Post-Freudian era

Being a psychologist, psychiatrist, and a psychoanalyst, John Bowlby is one of the most important figures in grief research due to his revolutionary work on attachment theory. Originally submitted to the British Psychoanalytical Society as three separate papers in 1958, 1959, and 1960, his theory completely rejected the psychoanalytical view of forming attachments. In return, the British Psychoanalytical Society not only rejected his theory but also banished him. Bowlby's attachment theory, however, which combines data from ethology, control theory, cognitive psychology, neurophysiology, and evolutionary biology, and which was a result of his dissatisfaction with existing theories of his time, has become an indispensable aid in understanding emotional bonds, relationships, and social development.

Bowlby formulated his theory to show the inclination of human beings to form bonds with the people around them and the strong emotional reactions shown when these bonds are at risk or broken. He also argued that the stronger these bonds are, the more powerful, intense, and varied the reactions will be when they are broken. Ultimately, Bowlby applied all his observations about attachments to grief and bereavement, covering infant, toddler, and adult reactions under the same theory.

Bowlby's theory is divided into four phases (Bowlby, 1998). He suggests that, when a loss occurs, grief is a normal adaptive response. This response, which is determined by the person's psychology and their environment, can be observed in four phases, which are neither precise nor sequential, because a person can move back and forth between them. During the first phase, a fluctuation between two emotional states (feeling numb or angry) and a state of instability can be observed. The second phase is shaped by deep longing, which can last for years. The third phase brings disorder and hopelessness. Only during the fourth and the last phase does a sense of recovery become apparent.

The starting point for the theories that came before Bowlby was always a sick patient. These theories, either by choice or underestimation, excluded the fact that grief can be an intensely painful response for a healthy person as well. The weakness of these theories, which only included diagnosing, labelling, and categorising patients and looking at grief as an illness, was thoroughly exposed through Bowlby's work.

Understanding grief itself, as opposed to using it as a label to understand an illness, is an approach also used by Colin Murray Parkes and Elisabeth Kübler-Ross. Kübler-Ross, however, handled the concept of bereavement and grief from another perspective, namely people who are dying. First published in 1969, her book *On Death and Dying* (Kübler-Ross, 2009) included her interviews with dying patients at the University of Chicago. Through these interviews, Kübler-Ross was able to develop her stage theory of grief, which has become highly influential as a way of explaining responses to not only death and dying but also any major life change.

Kübler-Ross was visited by Bowlby's colleague Parkes during the data collection phase before the publication of her book (Bretherton, 1992). Bretherton (Ibid.) suggests that due to this visit she was influenced by Bowlby's idea on four phases of mourning, and she developed her 'Five Stages of Grief' theory (Kübler-Ross, 2009), which documented the stages that dying people go through as they approach death.

Although Kübler-Ross studied these stages closely, her research and her book did not have the aim to expand the boundaries of grief theory. Instead, it was mainly observations based on some of the common reactions expressed by dying people. As she wrote in the preface of her book, her study was simply to acknowledge and describe patients as human beings. But because it has revealed so much about human nature – the comprehensive array of human emotions and thought – the theory has transcended its original context, which was limited to dying people, and become widely accepted, applied, and referred to in grief theory as a whole.

Kübler-Ross named her first stage as 'Denial and Isolation'. This stage is expressed in sentences like 'No, it cannot be true' and 'Leave me alone'. The second stage is called 'Anger', and it finds its expression in sentences such as 'God is a disappointment, and my faith feels shattered with his plan for me and my loved one'. The third stage is 'Bargaining', and the feelings are conveyed in statements like 'Please, God, let me fall asleep and wake up realising this was all a dream. I will do anything to have her back'. The fourth stage is called 'Depression', and in this stage an individual may find everything pointless. The fifth and the last stage is 'Acceptance', and it neither includes depression nor anger. It is a stage of inner calm.

Acting like a bridge between Bowlby and Kübler-Ross, Parkes is also an essential figure in grief theory. Including his works with Bowlby on attachment and loss, for more than 20 years he has integrated extensive research in resilience, neurophysiology, cellular chemistry, and immunology with his own research in psychiatry. He was also the first person to set up bereavement assistance in hospice care in the UK. Parkes's theory on grief is that it is a psychological and a social transition. Because change is inevitable in every aspect of life, social bonds that human beings form cannot escape this simple law of the universe. This change, especially when it brings loss and becomes a life-altering force, grows into a transformative process which human beings adapt to. What makes Parkes go a step further than the theorists before him is his description of grief, in which he underpins the individuality of loss. He argues that grief highlights the difference between the real world and how an individual wants that real world to be. While researchers find it easy to observe the real world, that individual's perceptions of and hopes about that real world become more allusive and difficult to observe.

Parkes suggests that not only do people have to adapt to the external world, which the now-lost bond has no connection to, but they also have to accept and adapt to the change happening in the internal world, in which this bond had the most intense and meaningful relevance. Therefore, grief, as an emotion, is a double-layered process. While people are coming to terms with the reality of the loss in social life, their internal realm of emotions, which was whole before the loss, is trying to adjust to being less-than-whole due to the severed tie.

For decades following Kübler-Ross and Parkes, the main body of grief theory aimed to help the individual, both as a human being going through a loss and as a patient seeking professional help. The popularity of Kübler-Ross's stage theory, even though it received criticism on its methodology and lack of evidence (Kastenbaum, 2009), paved the way for two distinct theories, namely Sanders's phases (Sanders, 1989), and Worden's tasks (Worden, 2010).

Sanders (1989) argued that people suffering a loss inevitably go through six distinct phases, which, in total, form their psychological, mental, and physical response. Her research-based approach is different to Kübler-Ross's clinical observations and also highlights the individual responses to loss to expand the discussion on the context of grief. The six phases of Sanders are: 'Shock'; 'Awareness of Loss'; 'Conservation-Withdrawal'; 'Healing'; 'Renewal'; and 'Fulfilment'.

Worden (2010), on the other hand, reshaped Kübler-Ross's stages and turned them into four distinct tasks, which a counsellor needs to encourage a client to take on, and therefore introduced a new perspective towards fine-tuning the help that professionals offer. These tasks are put together to help and guide psychotherapeutic interventions. They are simply described as: coming to terms with the separation; working with the pain of separation; finding ways to adapt to a new chapter in life; and forming a new, meaningful bond with the departed without spoiling the joy of living.

Contrary to Bowlby, Kübler-Ross, Sanders, and Worden, who describe grief as an experience that is handled in phases, stages, or tasks, clinical psychologist George A. Bonanno (2009) offered an alternative perspective. Mirroring Bowlby's courage in challenging canonical theories, Bonanno conducted his research in different parts of the world and showed that the resilience people display when they are faced with a major loss is an important and natural element of reactions to loss. He pointed out that no matter how big a traumatic loss can be, people still showed one of three patterns.

Bonanno named his first pattern as 'prolonged grief'. In this situation, individuals suffer for years and never seem to get any better. Prolonged grief is seen in about one in every ten bereaved people. The second pattern is called 'recovery pattern'. Individuals suffer intensely but get over the loss quickly. Although they begin to act like the person before the loss, they still hurt even years later. Together with prolonged grief, the people that show recovery pattern make up one-third of all bereaved people. The third pattern is called 'resilience' and is observed in between one-third and two-thirds of all bereaved people. Individuals suffer and struggle with their loss, but with calmness and composure. They are able to maintain their daily routines while they manage to cope with the loss. They accept it and move on.

Bonanno's introduction of the idea of resilience to grief theory was received as controversial, because it was a direct challenge to what all the theories were saying since Freud. This was especially the case when Bonanno demonstrated scientifically that some practices in grief and trauma counselling (such as asking people to talk or cry about a loss) can be harmful. He also challenged the very idea of crying after a loss by showing that genuine laughter can be as helpful and protective as a good cry.

It is important to note that in the post-Freudian era of grief theory, there are several other academic engagements with loss and recovery. Some of them are: Stroebe and Shut's (2001) 'dual-process model', which introduces the idea of oscillation between facing and avoiding grief as a coping mechanism; Rando's six-stage model, called 'Six R's of mourning' (Rando and Nezu, 1993); Klass, Silverman, and Nickman's (1996) 'continuing bonds' theory, where there are no steps, phases, or tasks; Berger's (2009) 'identities of grief' approach, where every individual follows a pattern of creating meaning after their loss; describing grief as a pathological condition and searching for solutions within science and medicine (Neimeyer, 2005); comparing it to addiction based on behavioural psychology (Boddez, 2018); and suggesting that grief needs to be discussed more widely and openly in society in order not to turn a normal part of life into a clinically labelled and treated illness (Collier, 2011).

The ongoing research, however, has not fully changed the positioning of grief theory within the field of modern psychology today. As Granek (2010) points out, the principles of modernism, namely scientific observation and rationality, reason and goal orientedness, functionality and efficiency, are still the shaping forces in constructing grief as a pathological condition that requires clinical intervention in order to speed up the healing process for the bereaved. Plus, modern life requirements, employment systems, and general expectations in today's society affect how theoretical paradigms in grief theory are shaped. Grief is perceived as an obstruction in the way of a productive and effectively functioning society. Therefore, it needs to be processed in tasks, stages, or phases as efficiently and as quickly as possible through therapeutic interventions and grief work in order for the bereaved to return to normal (Stroebe et al., 1992).

1.4 Jung and grief

Carl Jung himself did not specify a conceptual framework around bereavement, grief, or mourning as Freud did in *Mourning and Melancholia*. He, however, wrote extensively about death, loss, and regeneration in connection with religious and mythological stories and iconography that span centuries of human history both in the Western and the Eastern worlds. Even though it is not possible to find a section in his Collected Works specifically outlined for grief and mourning, his transtheoretical approach to human suffering and healing can be applied to grief theory.

This is because Jung's ideas and concepts travel beyond their contexts in analytical psychology and psychotherapy. Since his death in 1961, Jung's writings have been used extensively to question, examine, and explore new areas in theology, sociology, politics, gender studies, and literature (Young-Eisendrath and Dawson, 1997). In other words, Jungian concepts have become unconventional keys to unlock new fields of research. Another example of this collaboration is the application of Jung's ideas in film and media studies in order to decipher new levels of meaning and comprehension regarding life and human nature.

Bibliography

Aeschylus (1959) *The Oresteian Trilogy*. London: Penguin Books.

Averill, J.R. (1968) 'Grief: Its nature and significance', *Psychological Bulletin*, 70, pp.721–748.

Berger, Susan A. (2009) *The Five Ways We Grieve: Finding Your Personal Path to Healing after the Loss of a Loved One*. Boston: Trumpeter Books.

Boddez, Y. (2018) 'The presence of your absence: A conditioning theory of grief', *Behaviour Research and Therapy*, 106, pp. 18–27.

Bonanno, G.A. (2009) *The Other Side of Sadness: What the New Science of Bereavement Can Tell Us about Life after Loss*. New York: Basic Books.

Bowlby, J. (1998) *Loss: Sadness and Depression*. London: Pimlico.

Bretherton, I. (1992) 'The origins of attachment theory: John Bowlby and Mary Ainsworth', *Developmental Psychology*, 28(5), pp.759–775.

Burton, R. (2001) *The Anatomy of Melancholy*. New York: New York Review of Books.

Collier, R. (2011) 'Prolonged grief proposed as mental disorder', *Canadian Medical Association Journal*, 183(8), pp.439–440.

Darwin, C. (1872) *The Expression of the Emotions in Man and Animals*. London: John Murray.

Darwin, C., Ekman, P., and Prodger P. (2002) *The Expression of the Emotions in Man and Animals*. Oxford: Oxford University Press.

Deutsch, H. (1937). 'Absence of grief', *The Psychoanalytic Quarterly*, 6, pp.12–22.

Ellmann, M. (2005) 'Introduction', in Phillips, A. (ed.) *On Murder, Mourning and Melancholia*. London: Penguin Modern Classics, pp.vii–xxviii.

Fairbairn, W.R.D. (1952) *Psychoanalytic Studies of the Personality*. London: Routledge.

Freud, S. (1917) 'Mourning and melancholia' in: *The Standard Edition of the Complete Psychological Works of*, Vol.14. London: The Hogarth Press.

Granek, L. (2010) 'Grief as pathology: The evolution of grief theory in psychology from Freud to the present', *History of Psychology*, 13(1), pp.46–73.

Guntrip, H. (2018) *Schizoid Phenomena, Object-Relations, and the Self*. Abingdon: Routledge.

Kastenbaum, R. (2009) *Death, Society, and Human Experience*. Boston: Allyn and Bacon.

Klass, D., Silverman, P.R., and Nickman, S. (1996) *Continuing Bonds: New Understandings of Grief*. London: Routledge.

Klein, M. (1940) 'Mourning and its relation to manic-depressive states', *International Journal of Psycho-Analysis*, 21, pp.125–153.

Kübler-Ross, E. (2009) *On Death and Dying*. 40th ed. Oxon: Routledge.

Lewis, C.S. (2015) *A Grief Observed: Reader's Edition*. London: Faber & Faber.

Lichtheim, M. (2006) *Ancient Egyptian Literature: A Book of Readings*. Berkeley: University of California Press.

Lindemann, E. (1944) 'Symptomatology and management of acute grief', *American Journal of Psychiatry*, 101, pp.141–148.

Lindemann, E. (1979) *Beyond Grief: Studies in Crisis Intervention*. New York: Jason Aronson.

Magai, C. and McFadden, S. (1995) *The Role of Emotions in Social and Personality Development: History, Theory, and Research*. New York: Plenum Press.

Neimeyer, R. A (2005) 'Defining the new abnormal: Scientific and social construction of complicated grief', *Omega: Journal of Death and Dying*, 52, pp.95–97.

The Norton Anthology of English Literature (1993) 'Beowulf'. London: W.W. Norton & Company, pp.21–67.

Parkes, C.M. (1993) 'Bereavement as a psychosocial transition: Processes of adaptation to change' in Stroebe M.S., Stroebe W., and Hansson R.O. (eds). *Handbook of Bereavement: Theory, Research and Intervention*. Cambridge: Cambridge University Press, pp.91–101.

Rando, Therese A. and Nezu, Christine M. (1993) *Treatment of Complicated Mourning*. Research Press.

Rank, O. (1996) 'The genesis of the object relation' in Kramer, R. (ed.) *A Psychology of Difference: The American Lectures*. Princeton: Princeton University Press, pp.140–149.

Rush, B. (1812) *Medical Inquiries and Observations upon the Diseases of the Mind*. Philadelphia: Kimber & Richardson.

Sandars, N.K. (ed.) (1972) *The Epic of Gilgamesh*. London: Penguin Books.

Sanders, C. (1989) *Grief: The Mourning After – Dealing with Adult Bereavement*. New York: Wiley.

Shand, A.F. (1914) *The Foundations of Character: Being a Study of the Tendencies of Emotions and Sentiments*. New York: Macmillan and Co.

Stroebe, M., Gergen, M.M., Gergen, K.J., and Stroebe, W. (1992) 'Broken hearts or broken bonds: Love and death in historical perspective', *American Psychologist*, 47, pp.1205–1212.

Stroebe, M. and Schut, H. (2001) 'Models of coping with bereavement: A review' in Stroebe M., Hansson R., Stroebe W., and Schut H. (eds) *Handbook of Bereavement Research*. Washington, DC: American Psychological Association, pp.375–403.

Winnicott, D.W. (1953) 'Transitional objects and transitional phenomena—A study of the first not-me possession', *International Journal of Psycho-Analysis*, Issue 34, pp.89–97.

Worden, W.J. (2010) *Grief Counselling and Grief Therapy*. Hove: Routledge.

Young-Eisendrath, P. and Dawson, T. (eds) (1997) *The Cambridge Companion to Jung*. Cambridge: Cambridge University Press.

2 A brief look at the intersections of psychoanalysis, film theory, and Jungian studies

Even though the emergence of psychoanalysis and cinema does not perfectly align chronologically, they broadly coincided in the 1890s. Their arrival can be located in the post-Darwin world where a backward-looking society was suddenly coming to terms with evolution, new developments, and the myth of progress. Western society began to become more advanced via mechanisation and industrialisation. A completely different perspective of seeing the world was taking shape, a new vision where the world was not necessarily seen as fallen from grace. In this post-Darwin world, there was already plenty of optical entertainment before the arrival of cinema: photography; phénakisticope; the movie magic lantern shows; diorama with its optical effects and illusions; and of course, phantasmagorias (Warner, 2006). Therefore, the cinema did not emerge out of nowhere. While questioning or rejecting different traditions, the scientific, political, and cultural developments of the era influenced the form, content, and production of art and its status within a rapidly changing world.

2.1 Psychoanalysis and film

The roots of psychoanalytic film studies go back to Freud and his encounter with the *fotoreclami* in 1907. In the letter to his family, later published in 1961, he wrote how he was spellbound with the reaction of the crowd as he observed them (Freud, 1961). Even though he wrote to Ferenczi in 1925 to say that he did not wish to be involved with any film (Falzeder and Brabant, 2000, p.222) and he did not believe in general that psychoanalytic ideas could be represented by cinema (Sabbadini, 2012), his followers had completely different views. Starting with Münsterberg's study of the similarities between the conscious mind and cinematic experience in 1916 (Münsterberg, 1970), followed by Otto Rank and his analysis in 1925 regarding the cinematic representations of the psychological problems within man's relation to himself, condensed in essay *The Double* (Rank, 1971), and Sachs's ideas on Freud's theory of parapraxis (Sachs, 1929), psychoanalysis and film interacted in ways Freud did not anticipate.

Starting in the 1960s, different clusters of theoretical orientation employed psychoanalytic perspectives in their interpretation of films. With the development of post-structuralism in the late 1960s, Lacan's writings paved the way to

DOI: 10.4324/9781003292630-4

discussions of Freudian theory (Julian, 1994). While Freud focused on human sexuality as a tool to investigate the human psyche, Lacan looked at language and the subject. Lacan's two important focal points in psychoanalysis were the concepts of *manque* and *stade du miroir*. The former referred to the feeling of being unsatisfied even when one gets what they want (meaning desire is impossible to fulfil), and the latter was based on the Wallon's mirror test in 1931, where an infant facing a mirror recognises its own body from the reflected image, which then forms the basis of a representational understanding of an illusory medium (Roudinesco, 2003). Through his study of psychoanalysis, Lacan argued that the unconscious has a language of its own, a structure of symbolic exchanges, and the unconscious is the medium where these symbols achieve independence and become more real than themselves. This key difference created the main two strands of psychoanalysis in film studies: Freudian and Lacanian. These two strands so far have primarily engaged with three focal points: the textual analysis of the film through psychoanalytic concepts; the relationship between the film text and the spectator; and fantasy as a conscious expression of desire.

Following Lacan, film scholars like Metz (1982) and Baudry (1974) positioned themselves in theories representing point-of-view and the ideological nature of films. As Laura Mulvey (1989) pointed out, film and screen theory around the 1970s and 1980s was not really a psychological theory. What the screen theory was primarily interested in doing was not engaging with the psychology of the moving image but engaging in a process of deconstruction, revealing the hegemonic power relations that are invested inside the images, films, and the industry. The camera and editing made cinema become an instrument for the transmission of dominant cultural values. Derived partly from the theories of Marx (1979) on base (finance, or the economic base of society) and superstructure (the socio-cultural sphere that surrounds the base), which postulate that film as a medium would be reliant on money and therefore would be controlled by the base, and partly influenced by Gramsci's hegemony (Adamson, 1980) and Althusser's interpellation theories (Althusser, 2014), the theorists of this era focused on how cinematic apparatus constructed film viewers' positioning and determined the actual meaning and significance of a film. Similar connections between film, popular culture, and critical theory in the context of psychoanalysis and unconscious mental processes, plus specific angles of filmmaking (such as mise-en-scène, screenplay, camera work, etc.) are further reflected in the works of other theorists such as Heath (1985), Žižek (1992), Kaplan (1990), and Copjec (1994).

The fellowship of psychoanalysis and film theory continued when Miller (1966) introduced his idea of *suture* to Lacanian theory, and it intensified the discussion around the relationship of cinema with its audience and the techniques used in film to make the viewer forget that there is a camera that is doing the actual 'looking'. Psychoanalytic concepts such as regression (the dark environment of a theatre becoming a symbol for womblike experience), voyeurism (the viewers' desire to see certain acts on the screen), and fetishism (film actors being worshipped like gods) were woven/stitched into film studies, combining socioeconomic and cultural phenomena. Especially after Betty Friedan's book *The Feminine Mystique* (Friedan, 1963), where she argued that the American psychoanalysts used Freud's theory of penis-envy in order to label women as irrational if they rebelled against their prescribed role in society as housewives, feminist theory found a strong voice in film scholars such as Mulvey (1989), Lauretis (1984), and Doane (1987), who discussed the role of the male voyeuristic gaze in cinema towards women as fetish objects in terms of sexuality and gender stereotyping, and provided new perspectives on the intersections of film, semiotics, and psychoanalysis.

It is important to mention that film theory also benefited from another psychoanalyst: Donald W. Winnicott. His two concepts, namely *mirroring* and *transitional space*, helped film scholars forge new theories for reading and understanding cinematic narratives. Winnicott's mirroring concept is comparable to the Lacanian mirror stage, and it refers to the exchange of gazes between a mother and her baby, which assist the gradual formation of an awareness of personal identity in the baby (Winnicott, 1967). His transitional space concept, on the other hand, refers to the illusory half-way between the baby and another person where internal and external realities are independent but connected (Winnicott, 1953). Film scholars applied these concepts to cinema and discussed fresh perspectives, such as: using film as an example to elaborate on the Winnicottian theory of 'pathological character formation as an outcome of environmental failure' (Newman, 1996, p.787), especially due to faulty mothering; spectatorship and the creatively fluid space between reality and fantasy (Konigsberg, 1996); how psychoanalysis helps our understanding of 'looking' into images (Lebeau, 2009); and also cinema as the shared space of creators and consumers where the creativity of the creator meets the wish of the consumer in a playful way (Kuhn, 2013).

2.2 Jungian film studies

In *Civilization in Transition*, Jung pointed out the similarities between literature and cinema, and he likened it to a detective story (CW 10, para.195). He argued that cinema, similar to reading an exciting thriller, allowed people to experience fantasies, delights, fears, and adventures without getting harmed. His main point was, of course, the psychological impetus behind this safe wish-fulfilment. This perspective of looking at cinema as an avenue to perceive and explore the unconscious has become one of the key points of Jungian film studies, which gradually established itself and introduced new psychological perspectives into film analysis.

Hauke and Hockley (2011) trace the birth of a Jungian approach in film studies to the article of Don Fredericksen published in 1979. His article on Jung, symbols, and film was a new route deviating from the popularity and the influence of Freudian and Lacanian criticism which had defined the field and become the norm. Fredericksen argued that the established notions of meaning within film studies make things limited, and a new reading using Jungian concepts would encourage a more open mind and vision. His main point was to indicate the variation between Freudian and Jungian perspectives, showing the difference between the reading of signs/metaphors in film narratives and the interpretation of symbols and their meanings in films. He specifically noted that the interpretation of symbols in films can lead to a new and fertile ground in film analysis.

Following Fredericksen, many academics have contributed to Jungian film studies over the years, and they have produced distinct ways of analysis through textual, phenomenological, and 'film as experience' avenues. By incorporating psychoanalytic concepts and, in particular, ideas from analytical psychology in reading and analysing films, Jungian film studies have gone beyond Jung's 'detective story' description of cinema and, rather, evolved into a (symbolically) archaeological research field with a strong symbiotic relationship with film theory, unearthing and discovering new things beneath the visible and exterior layers of films. As Bassil-Morozow and Hockley (2017) put it:

> In understanding what lies beneath the surface of films, Jungian film theory relies on the deep mycological transmission of psychological ideas and concepts to permeate the work at an almost chemical and subterranean manner, and in so doing to suffuse the soil and earth of our film theory.
>
> (p.6)

2.2.1 Jungian textual analysis cluster

The textual analysis cluster of Jungian film studies includes scholars like Izod (2001), Beebe (2001), Waddell (2006), and Bassil-Morozow (2012). They concentrate on the main composition of a film and the layers of meaning based on the symbols embedded in it, connecting them to several Jungian terms and ideas such as archetypes, collective unconscious, shadow, and synchronicity. Their readings of films open up new discussions on the reciprocal relationships between stories, myths, personal identity, and how media reflects both the internal situation of individuals and the society they live in. This cluster of analysis illustrates how Jungian theory can pave the way for a new understanding of psychological richness and depth in films.

This close textual film reading finds its roots and cause in the late 1970s, when Barthes and Derrida were pointing out the pluralities in a text, which signalled the paradigm shift from the central formula of Saussure on the nature of the linguistic sign (Saussure, 1959). As Saussure laid the foundations of structuralism and argued that the linguistic sign is a two-sided psychological entity, namely 'signifier' (object) and 'signified' (concept), the concept of text became easier to break down and decode if one had the right methodology and hermeneutic approach. With the arrival of post-structuralism, the relationship between linguistic signs and texts in the way Saussure described became more complex and fluid. Barthes (1978) pointed out how a text extended to other texts as the 'signified' surfaced in a network of concepts. In his essay originally published in 1979, Derrida carried this idea further by arguing that a text is never finished because it forever refers to other texts (Derrida, 2004).

This group of Jungian film studies investigates cinematic texts in this spirit, looking at the complex web of meaning networks that is more than the sum of its parts. Miller (2018, p.11) defines cinematic text as an interlocking grid where different narrative layers (scene arrangements, props, clothing, sound and music, camera work, etc.) come together and create a richer storytelling. In examining this interwoven and dense narrative, the images, their positions, and boundaries are described precisely (within a film's own ecosphere) utilising technical terminology if necessary. Creating chains of meaning within a film's narrative, this parallel reading is further expanded through: amplification by showing its connections to mythological, historical, and cultural latitudes (Samuels, Shorter, and Plaut, 2005); restatement by highlighting the words' synonymous or metaphorical content (Miller, 2018); and analogy in order to open up the text further.

2.2.2 Jungian phenomenological cluster

The phenomenological and cinematic experience clusters of Jungian film studies stand close to each other, and they tend to cross-pollinate. Husserl's theory of *noesis* (the act of apprehending) and *noema* (the object apprehended) (Smith, 2003) blends with Merleau-Ponty's argument on the formation of meaning and the precognitive capacity of the human body (Merleau-Ponty, 1962), and finds its echo in the Jungian understanding of the relationship between a therapist and a client, or rather the meeting zone, where the conscious mind and cognition meet the unconscious and the embodied reactions. Scholars such as Hockley (2007; 2014), Barker (2009), and Singh (2014) focus on a number of questions including: the process of meaning-making; the intra-sensory stimulation of films that go beyond the visual and aural; the therapeutic effect of films; identification with images; and how cinema is able to mimic an individual's relationship with the everyday world. Hockley's particular phenomenological approach explores the space between the screen and the viewer, and how this space is filled with a fusion of the image on the screen with the personal perception and response to that image. The result of this fusion provides clues to the process of making/creating meaning and how individuals are affected by films. These clues are interpreted further in relation to Jungian terms and ideas including association, amplification, projection, and introjection.

2.2.3 A new Jungian hybridity

Hauke (2014) argues in a way that bridges both narrative and phenomenological aspects. He not only explores how films are made through his own filmmaking projects but also writes about cinema. He argues that cinema becomes a three-dimensional space and morphs into a vessel where human psyche is aroused and comes to life. Even though an individual's inner journey towards self-discovery might be painful, cinema can become a medium where certain experiences for the individual can be easier to accept and process. This sounds similar to Jung's understanding of cinema as a detective story[1] where repressed desires are lived through.

2.2.4 Emerging clusters in Jungian film studies

The marriage of Jungian thought and film theory proves to be productive. This field of research is still expanding today and embraces new approaches such as Ashman (2018) and Yama (2018) that go beyond the Anglophone cinematic sphere, and also the contemporary presence of digital media on computer and mobile screens, which takes the idea of image into previously uncharted and unexplored territories of film and psychology now investigated in the works of Balick (2018) and Fuery (2018).

Note

1 Hauke has also taken this detective story angle further by being the psychology con-sultant and content creator for the iOS game *The Craftsman*. Launched in 2013 by Portal Entertainment, this Apple iPad-based experiment combines fiction, cinema, and online gaming in an immersive fashion where each user/player creates their own unique way into the adventure by interacting with the game's storyline in different ways by responding to on-screen prompts during the day, even when they are not playing.

Bibliography

Adamson, W.L. (1980) *Hegemony and Revolution: A Study of Antonio Gramsci's Political and Cultural Theory*. Berkeley: University of California Press.

Althusser, L. (2014) *On the Reproduction of Capitalism: Ideology and Ideological State Apparatuses*. London: Verso Books.

Ashman, A.L. (2018) 'The han cultural complex: Embodied experiences of trauma in new Korean Cinema', in Hockley, L. (ed.) *The Routledge International Handbook of Jungian Film Studies*. Oxon: Routledge, pp.229–241.

Balick, A. (2018) 'Cinema without a cinema and film without film: The psychogeography of contemporary media consumption', in Hockley, L. (ed.) *The Routledge International Handbook of Jungian Film Studies*. Oxon: Routledge, pp.387–400.

Barker, J. (2009) *The Tactile Eye: Touch and the Cinematic Experience*. Los Angeles: University of California Press.

Barthes, R. (1978) 'From work to text', in Heath, S. (ed.) *Image – Music – Text*. New York: Farrar, Straus & Giroux, pp.155–64.

Bassil-Morozow, H. (2012) *The Trickster in Contemporary Film*. Hove: Routledge.

Bassil-Morozow, H. and Hockley, L. (eds) (2017) *Jungian Film Studies: The Essential Guide*. London: Routledge.

Baudry, J-L. (1974) 'Ideological effects of the basic cinematographic apparatus', *Film Quarterly*, 28(2), pp.39–47.

Beebe, J. (2001) 'The anima in film' in Alister, I. and Hauke, C. (eds) *Jung and Film: Post-Jungian Takes on the Moving Image*. London: Routledge, pp.208–225.

Copjec, J. (1994) *Read My Desire: Lacan against the Historicists*. Cambridge, MA: MIT Press.

Derrida, J. (2004) 'Living on', in Bloom, H. (ed.) *Deconstruction and Criticism*. London and New York: Continuum Publishing Company, pp.62–142.

Doane, M.A. (1987) *The Desire to Desire: The Woman's Film of the 1940s*. London: Macmillan.

Falzeder E. and Brabant, E. (eds) (2000) 'Letter of 14 August 1925' in *The Correspondence of Sigmund Freud and Sándor Ferenczi, Vol. 3, 1920–1933*. Cambridge, MA: Belknap Press.

Freud, E.L. (ed.) (1961) 'Letter of 22 September 1907' in *Letters of Sigmund Freud, 1873–1939*. London: Hogarth Press.

Friedan, B. (1963) *The Feminine Mystique*. London: Penguin Books.

Fuery, K. (2018) 'The unlived lives of cinema: Post-cinematic doubling, imitation and supplementarity', in Hockley, L. (ed.) *The Routledge International Handbook of Jungian Film Studies*. Oxon: Routledge, pp.436–449.

Hauke, C. (2014) *Visible Mind: Movies, Modernity and the Unconscious*. Hove: Routledge.

Hauke, C. and Hockley, L. (eds) (2011) *Jung and Film II: The Return*. Hove: Routledge.

Heath, S. (1985) *Questions of Cinema*. Bloomington: Indiana University Press.

Hockley, L. (2007) *Frames of Mind: A Post-Jungian Look at Cinema, Television and Technology*. Bristol: Intellect Books.

Hockley, L. (2014) *Somatic Cinema: The Relationship between Body and Screen – A Jungian Perspective*. New York: Routledge.

Izod, J. and Dovalis, J. (2015) *Cinema as Therapy: Grief and Transformational Film*. Hove: Routledge.

Julian, P. (1994) *Jacques Lacan's Return to Freud: The Real, the Symbolic, and the Imaginary*. New York: New York University Press.

Jung, C.G. (1970) *The Collected Works of C.G. Jung, Volume 10: Civilization in Transition*. Princeton: Princeton University Press.

Kaplan, E. A (ed.) (1990) *Psychoanalysis and Cinema*. London: Routledge.

Konigsberg, I. (1996) 'Transitional phenomena, transitional space: Creativity and spectatorship in film', *The Psychoanalytic Review*, 83(6), pp.865–889.

Kuhn, A. (ed.) (2013) *Little Madnesses: Winnicott, Transitional Phenomena and Cultural Experience*. London: I.B. Tauris & Co.

Lauretis, T. de (1984) *Alice Doesn't: Feminism, Semiotics, Cinema*. London: Macmillan.

Lebeau, V. (2009) 'The arts of looking: D.W. Winnicott and Michael Haneke', *Screen*, 5(1), pp.35–44.

Marx, K. (1979) *A Contribution to the Critique of Political Economy*. Intl Pub.

Merleau-Ponty, M. (1962) *Phenomenology of Perception*. London: Routledge & Kegan Paul.

Metz, C. (1982) *The Imaginary Signifier: Psychoanalysis and the Cinema*. Bloomington: Indiana University Press.

Miller, C. (2018) 'A Jungian textual terroir', in Hockley, L. (ed.) *The Routledge International Handbook of Jungian Film Studies*. Oxon: Routledge, pp.7–25.

Miller, J-A. (1966) Suture (Elements of the Logic of the Signifier). Available at: www.lacan.com/symptom8_articles/miller8.html

Mulvey, L. (1989) *Visual and Other Pleasures*. London: Macmillan.

Münsterberg, H. (1970) *The Film: A Psychological Study – The Silent Photoplay in 1916*. Dover.

Newman, K.M. (1996) 'Winnicott goes to the movies: The false self in ordinary people', *The Psychoanalytic Quarterly*, 65(4), pp.787–807.

Rank, O. (1971) *The Double: A Psychoanalytic Study*. Chapel Hill: University of North Carolina Press.

Roudinesco, E. (2003) 'The mirror stage: An obliterated archive' in Rabaté, J-M. (ed.) *The Cambridge Companion to Lacan*. Cambridge: Cambridge University Press, pp.25–34.

Sabbadini, A. (2012) 'Psychoanalysis and film' in Gabbard, G.O., Litowitz, B.E., and Williams, P. (eds) *Textbook of Psychoanalysis*. Arlington: American Psychiatric Publishing, pp.537–550.

Sachs, H. (1929) 'Zur psychologie des films', *Die Psychoanalytische Bewegung*, 1(2), pp.122–126.

Samuels, A., Shorter, B., and Plaut, F. (2005) *A Critical Dictionary of Jungian Analysis*. London: Routledge.

Saussure, F. de (1959) *Course in General Linguistics*. New York: The Philosophical Library.

Singh, G. (2014) *Feeling Film: Affect and Authenticity in Popular Cinema*. Hove: Routledge.

Smith, A.D. (2003) *Routledge Philosophy GuideBook to Husserl and the Cartesian Meditations*. Oxon: Routledge.

Waddell, T. (2006) *Mis/takes: Archetype, Myth and Identity in Screen Fiction*. Hove: Routledge.

Warner, M. (2006) *Phantasmagoria: Spirit Visions, Metaphors and Media into the Twenty-first Century*. New York: Oxford University Press.

Winnicott, D.W. (1953) 'Transitional objects and transitional phenomena—A study of the first not-me possession', *International Journal of Psycho-Analysis*, Issue 34, pp.89–97.

Winnicott, D.W. (1967) *Playing and Reality*. London: Tavistock.

Yama, M. (2018) '*Spirited Away* and its depiction of Japanese traditional culture', in Hockley, L. (ed.) *The Routledge International Handbook of Jungian Film Studies*. Oxon: Routledge, pp.254–262.

Žižek, S. (1992) *Enjoy Your Symptom! Jacques Lacan in Hollywood and Out*. New York: Routledge.

3   New perspectives in mental health through film analysis

While there is no specific film genre that can be called 'psychoanalytic', many films can be read with a psychoanalytic lens due to their representation of psychologically credible characters (where they are not purely good or bad), exploration of psychoanalytic themes (such as pathological behaviour, voyeurism, or mourning), and depiction of the psychoanalytic profession itself. In this context, Freud's way of using psychoanalysis as a tool to examine literature and anthropological texts becomes the norm in film analysis to refine, deepen and clarify cinematic narratives.

The collaboration of film and psychoanalytical theory today is expanding further towards clinical work. The growing interest in how the human psyche and its states (both socially acceptable and psychopathological) are portrayed in films, and how these portrayals can enrich the theoretical knowledge and the clinical work of psychoanalysts, is an emerging research field. As Sabbadini (2012) points out, exploring films and their narratives in detail can lead to new ways of understanding the human psyche. He argues that films and character studies have untapped potential for psychoanalysts and therapists because they portray a vast array of complex situations, personalities, and psychological material.

This creative approach of combining cinematic narratives with clinical theory helps film analyses to offer an enhanced understanding of both healthy and unhealthy aspects of human psyche. In this chapter, I would like to present four interesting examples.

3.1 Countertransference

Edwards (2010) uses the film *Morvern Callar* (2002) as a teaching tool to create the proto-experience of countertransference in pre-clinical students. By focusing on the main character Morvern and her unemotional and detached behaviour following her boyfriend's suicide, she uses the film's narrative to make links with primarily Kleinian psychoanalytic ideas about schizoid states, saying a client's repression of trauma might trigger feelings of helplessness and despair in clinicians because there seems no internal or external way for the client to engage with the reality of loss. Edwards argues that watching and

DOI: 10.4324/9781003292630-5

analysing this film in an academic setting might become a new way for future clinicians to experience how their feelings can be projected towards a client.[1] Examining emotional responses to cinematic narratives and then linking them with theoretical concepts can indeed bring a better comprehension of certain notions in psychotherapy and psychology.

3.2 Bioethics

Similarly, Braswell (2011) introduces psychoanalysis to clinical bioethics and shows how cinematic representations can help clinical thinking in a new way. Referring to Gilman's (1998) psychoanalytic model where representations become the site of conflict between sickness and health, he uses the film *Million Dollar Baby* (2004) to clarify his point when he discusses scenes of assisted suicide, the route from paternalistic behaviour to showing respect to one's autonomy, and their importance in a wider discussion of bioethics. Braswell argues that critics who read into these conflicts might open a new window into a more comprehensive understanding of both physical and psychological trauma. The father–daughter dynamic represented in the film is also a common theme in Jungian theory. Samuels (1986) gives examples of the influence of fathers on the psychology of their daughters: a woman can become independent; she can find a male authority figure and serve him; and she can fail to separate from her father and become a substitute wife, etc. Braswell's description of personal autonomy (and parents' respect to it), in this sense, shares common ground with Jung's individuation process, a synthesis of both conscious and unconscious elements, happening especially in the second half of one's life.

3.3 Sadism

Gullestad (2011) is another scholar who explores the intersections of film and psychoanalysis. She looks at sadism and separation anxiety in the film *Antichrist* (2009) to highlight the contribution of psychoanalysis to the interpretation of art, namely illuminating feelings and actions in a film that can be shocking and baffling to viewers. She specifically adopts the Freudian view of pleasure experienced through sadistic actions in explaining some of the dreadful scenes that take place between a mother, a father, and a child. Focusing on the cine-matic representation of satisfaction that depends on the suffering or humiliation inflicted upon others, Gullestad uses psychoanalysis to penetrate the characters' minds and illuminate the motives behind their seemingly instinctual actions in the film.

3.4 Neuropsychoanalysis

Coming from a neuroscience perspective, Fox (2016) introduces a new neuropsychoanalytic theory of reception by referring to the discovery of mirror neurons.[2] He draws attention to neuroscientists' estimation that only 10 percent of the processes of the mind can be known while conscious, and the rest of its workings are deeply hidden and happening beyond the awareness zone. He then aims to formulate a new understanding of the process of spectators' reception and reaction to a work of fiction, based on neuroscience's current ability to develop a hypothesis about an embodied response centred around how mirror neurons in the brain work and respond to the sight, sound, and the imagination of an action. Talking about the limitations of the cognitivist attempts to explain cinematic representations, especially the post-structuralist approach where meaning is subjectively and discursively produced, he argues that these attempts underestimate the unconscious processes embedded in the creative arts. Fox, therefore, calls for a wider, more expansive psychoanalytic model, specifically surpassing the works of Freud and Jung, in order to merge what is known about the brain today with the creative and receptive functions of the unconscious.

3.5 Engagement with Jungian concepts

On the Jungian side of film studies, several psychotherapists and Jungian analysts have delved into fresh thinking that married clinical approaches with the practice of filmmaking and the individual experience of watching films. Some of these names are already mentioned in Chapter 2. When it comes to engaging with grief theory and film, however, Jungian-oriented scholars are still surprisingly shy. For example, Izod and Dovalis (2015) look at its transformational value, how the characters accept or reject their loss. Through a series of different films, they engage with the phases of grief, attempts at restoring the feelings of loss, and how the cinematic medium can become a new door for transpersonal aspects of healing. However, there are several unexplored perspectives in Jungian thought, including: the absence of grief; pathological and complicated mourning; the help, hindrance, or limits of grief counselling; group response to loss; disenfranchised grief; or grieving in specific types of losses like suicide, abortion, or AIDS. In this sense, Jungian perspectives can be easily applied to films to advance the discussion around trauma and recovery to new and unconventional territories.

3.6 A new transdisciplinary approach and a short guide into Part II

This book is certainly aiming to be an example of this advancement. In the coming section, Part II, I adopt the role of an analyst, and let the narratives and the visual content of the films reveal what the protagonists are unable to verbalise. Through this process not only are their crypts defined, but also how these traumatised characters find their way out. Crossing the boundaries of symbology, mythology, clinical theory, and Jungian thought, hidden layers of narrative in each film are uncovered in a holistic manner. As I analyse seven different films with seven different stories, they ultimately become seven unique case studies, depicting different responses to traumatic loss.

In order to present a quick and straightforward example of a Jungian concept, the union of opposites, I group these films into two different categories: destruction and reconstruction. The reason is simple: every path out of an intrapsychic tomb is unique to both the trauma and the individual, and therefore the choices can be negative or positive.

The link between loss and destructive urges is repeatedly associated with feelings of anger and depressive states in grief theory. As this is an observed and established fact, I am expanding it further in order to examine entirely negative examples that are generally regarded as taboo or difficult to discuss. I present three different types and levels of destruction, all tied to traumatic loss, which demonstrate the choices protagonists make to come out of their crypts. These are:

- suicide (or self-destruction)
- murder (or destruction of another person)
- anarchy (or destruction of an institution).

It is important to note that on each level, the fallout after a traumatic loss is getting bigger. The escape hatch of the crypt presents itself as a choice, starting with self-destruction, moving on to killing other people, and ending up at the biggest level, the obliteration of an organisation that itself is a part of a bigger establishment. These examples are not to be taken as inspiring answers to trauma, but rather as accounts of theoretric moments between a client and an analyst without condoning or condemning. They are here to serve a good purpose: to inform and to demonstrate the negative paths out of intrapsychic tombs.

Of course, traumatic loss does not always lead to destructive choices. Different models of psychotherapeutic interventions aim to help the bereaved acknowledge their trauma and move beyond the painful state to a more healthy and balanced existence. Just like I am doing with the destructive aspects of grief, I am expanding this approach to give constructive examples as choices that the protagonists make to come out of their crypts. I categorise these choices under four headings:

- human connection (or forming new bonds)
- letting go (or releasing negative attachments)
- forgiveness (or replacing negative emotions with positive ones)
- self-compassion (or acknowledging oneself).

In these examples, the emotional weight of traumatic loss lends itself to a conscious reparative choice, rather than a damaging or retaliatory form of action. It is also important to note that while I do not present these examples with a prescriptive motivation, I do acknowledge their power in psychological healing and recovery. Again, these categories are here to spell out and to validate the positive paths out of intrapsychic tombs.

It is now time to turn to the cinematic components of this book and present the film analyses chapters. Even though they look at fictional situations and choices, their narratives are universal in terms of human suffering. The overall range of analyses includes Egyptian and Greek myths, Christian iconography, Kabbalah, Tarot, mathematics and chaos theory, medical conditions such as hemoptysis and chronic pain, DSM-5, quantum theory, and parallel universes. Therefore, they are rich, multi-layered, and kaleidoscopic.

The first analysis is on *Solaris* (2002), and it brings two people who love each other to the edge of an abyss. In the next chapter, I will explore the aftermath of a suicide and how a clinical psychologist is driven to suicide due to his trauma.

Filmography

Antichrist (2009) Directed by L. von Trier [film]. Denmark
Million Dollar Baby (2004) Directed by C. Eastwood [film]. USA
Morvern Callar (2002) Directed by L. Ramsay [film]. UK
Solaris (2002) Directed by S. Soderbergh [film]. USA

Notes

1 This argument also demonstrates her theoretical journey from her earlier focus on Kleinian theory (Edwards, 2005) to her growing exploration of other perspectives including mathematics, chaos theory, ethnology, and sculpture (Edwards, 2019).
2 These neurons were discovered accidentally in 1992 while neuroscientists were working with macaque monkeys and observing their brain activities (Di Pellegrino et al., 1992). The mirror system of neuroanatomy showed that a neuron fires in the brain both when an animal acts and when a second animal observes the same action performed by the first. The neuron in the second animal mirrors the action of the first even though the second one is only observing. This theory created new implications and triggered new theories about cognition, language acquisition, and autism in humans. This discovery also led to fresh applications in film theory under the term 'neurocinematics' (Hasson et al., 2008) in relation to embodied responses while watching films. It simply argues that viewers feel what the character in a film is doing on screen because the action is triggering the same sensations in them.

Bibliography

Braswell, H. (2011) 'Taking representation seriously: Rethinking bioethics through Clint Eastwood's *Million Dollar Baby*', *Journal of Medical Humanities*, 32(2), pp.77–87.
Di Pellegrino, G., Fadiga, L., Fogassi, L., Gallese, V., and Rizzolatti, G. (1992). 'Understanding motor events: A neurophysiological study', *Experimental Brain Research*, 91(1), pp.176–180.
Edwards, J. (2005) 'Before the threshold: Destruction, reparation and creativity in relation to the depressive position', *Journal of Child Psychotherapy*, 31(3), pp.317–334.
Edwards, J. (2010) 'Teaching and learning about psychoanalysis: Film as a teaching tool, with reference to a particular film, *Morvern Callar*', *British Journal of Psychotherapy*, 26(1), pp.80–99.

Edwards, J. (ed.) (2019) *Psychoanalysis and Other Matters: Where Are We Now?* London: Routledge.

Fox, A. (2016) *Speaking Pictures: Neuropsychoanalysis and Authorship in Film and Literature.* Bloomington: Indiana University Press.

Gilman, S.L. (1998) *Disease and Representation: Images of Illness from Madness to Aids.* Ithaca: Cornell University Press.

Gullestad, S.E. (2011) 'Crippled feet: Sadism in Lars von Trier's *Antichrist*', *The Scandinavian Psychoanalytic Review*, 34(2), pp.79–84.

Hasson, U., Landesman, O., Knappmeyer, B., Vallines, I., Rubin, N., and Heeger, D.J. (2008) 'Neurocinematics: The neuroscience of film', *Berghahn Journals*, 2(1), pp.1–26.

Izod, J. and Dovalis, J. (2015) *Cinema as Therapy: Grief and Transformational Film.* Hove: Routledge.

Sabbadini, A. (2012) 'Pyschoanalysis and film' in Gabbard, G.O., Litowitz, B.E., and Williams, P. (eds) *Textbook of Psychoanalysis*. Arlington: American Psychiatric Publishing, pp.537–550.

Samuels, A. (1986) *Jung and the Post-Jungians*. London: Routledge.

Part II

Tales of loss and recovery

4 Suicide and *Solaris*

I watched *Solaris* (2002) in February 2003, nearly three years before my partner's suicide. Having read the novel and seen the earlier film adaptations, I was simply blown away by the candid portrayal of grief, the weight of a broken, damaged relationship, and the unendurable sorrow of holding on to that memory. In hindsight, I can openly say that the film was somehow an eerie training for me and my future trauma. While I was grieving, there were moments when I remembered scenes, music, and dialogue, and I felt like I embodied a fictional character. This film, well and truly, got under my skin. Therefore, I was somewhat compelled to write about it.

So, what is so special about this film? First of all, it is an adaptation from a science-fiction classic with the same name. Written by Polish writer Stanisław Lem (1987), its main narrative is a thought experiment in which humans try to interact with a sentient planet called Solaris. In other words, it is a full-blown alien encounter. Soderbergh's Hollywood adaptation in 2002, while it remains faithful to this central theme, also focuses on the nature of human relationships that are delicate and fragile. He specifically puts the problematic relationship of its two main characters at the front: Chris and Rheya. This is exactly where the trauma happens and where Chris gets trapped in his crypt due to losing his wife Rheya to suicide.

The storyline of the film is linear, with a few flashbacks as dream sequences. Chris Kelvin (George Clooney), a clinical psychologist, is asked to travel to a remote space station in order to investigate the sudden break in communications. He reluctantly agrees to go. Shortly after his arrival, he understands what the problem is: the planet Solaris taps into the memories of the scientists while they are asleep, creates what the scientists have lost, and sends them in physical form to the station. In Chris's case, it is his wife Rheya (Natascha McElhone), and, via flashbacks, the narrative reveals how they met, how she killed herself, and how Chris was traumatised and never got over it. The narrative after this point becomes independent and follows a different trajectory compared to the novel.

In the film, Chris Kelvin is not only inconsolable but also unable to help himself as a trained mind in human psychology. Therefore, his helplessness has a dual quality: mental and emotional. His melancholic intrapsychic tomb fits in with the definition of Abraham and Torok (1994). He has lost the hope of being

DOI: 10.4324/9781003292630-7

acknowledged, and therefore he denies not only his loss but his love as well. As the planet forces him to face this loss in the flesh again and again, he gradually realises that he cannot continue his life in denial and decides to stay on the space station, which is about to crash into the sentient planet.

This chapter not only looks into the inner workings of Chris's suicide, but also explores the theory of prolonged grief disorder, with its ties to self-destruction after a traumatic loss. I specifically interpret Chris's final destination as a transition to a higher plane of existence, which is what the ending of the film suggests. Therefore, the way out of his crypt becomes mystical and beyond human understanding. As I apply Jungian concepts to the analysis, I tie the film's finale with the research of Rosen (1975), who interviewed several people after they jumped off the Golden Gate Bridge in San Francisco.

4.1 Choices are the answers

There is a short but important dream sequence in *Solaris*. In this sequence (60:00) a cryptic conversation takes place between Chris Kelvin and his deceased ex-colleague, Gibarian (Ulrich Tukur). Gibarian simply tells Chris that he may not find the answers he is searching for, because only choices are important. This short yet crucial sentence provides insight to the different steps and the end of Chris's grief journey which is the focus of this chapter.

Lem's novel stands as a philosophical thought experiment where human beings discover, observe, try to study, and understand an intelligent but mysterious planet. Their ambition is only matched by their failure as the novel ends with a defeated Kris on a tiny island on the planet confessing humanity's inability to comprehend such a majestic extra-terrestrial entity.

Tarkovsky's (1972) compelling cinematic adaptation with the same name incorporates most of Lem's philosophical musings on celluloid, but it also shifts the focus from alien contact to love and human relationships. However, Soderbergh, with his version, takes this approach one step further and puts Chris and Rheya's relationship at the heart of the film, where the attempt to understand a new intelligent being becomes a minor problem.

The pointlessness of the attempt lies in the fact that human beings, specifically the ones portrayed in the film, are depicted in numerous scenes where they are unable to communicate or understand each other properly. Communicating with a godlike being, therefore, becomes a trivial and impossible endeavour when one cannot even understand one's own species. This is surprisingly in tune with Lem's original intentions in the novel, even though he hated both cinematic interpretations.[1]

As Soderbergh muses on love and loss, Chris's attempts to come to terms with his traumatic loss and his struggles to recover become the main storyline. From the very first scene to the very last one, the director never deviates from Chris's suffering, which ultimately leads him to a deliberate choice (and sacrifice) that comes at the end of the film.

In order to examine the film's narrative closely, the rest of this analysis is structured in three parts: the first part looks at the symbolism embedded in the film; the second part looks at the intersections of grief theory and Jungian analysis; and the last section focuses on Chris's choice. Before delving further into Chris's psychological journey, I will discuss some of the key symbols in the film and how they contribute to the major and necessary shift in Chris's psyche.

4.2 Close encounters with the past

The word Solaris is linked to the Sun in Latin. It basically means 'pertaining to the Sun'. The Sun, as an astronomical object, is the source of light, heat, and life, and its rays have penetrated all the layers of the Earth since its formation as a planet. Ever since Babylonian times, it is symbolically associated with a powerful Sun god/deity as a destroyer of evil and darkness. In Christian iconography, Jesus Christ is a chronocrator and therefore triumphant over time. As his birth is celebrated every year, he brings light and warmth to humanity as the cold and dark days of winter reach an end with the solstice in the Northern Hemisphere. Psychological symbolism depicts the Sun as the cosmic intellect that shines and illuminates the deepest recesses of mind, body, and soul. Hindu writers attribute the beginning and the end of all things to the Sun, which is symbolised by the Sun deity, Savitri (Chevalier and Gheerbrant, 1996c). In Lem's and Soderberg's case, it is not so far away from this belief either. Solaris appears as the creator, or the source of the doppelgangers (called 'visitors') on the space station, and that is where they return to when they are killed by a high-energy proton accelerator.

Solaris, however, is not a star. It is a planet. Planetary symbolism goes back to prehistoric ages, and it is the sign of belief in the symbiosis of Heaven and Earth. Linking the movements of the planets (celestial) and their effects on humans and the Earth (terrestrial) is another concept Jung has looked into (CW 15, para.82; CW 8, para.875; CW 8, para.987). Chevalier and Gheerbrant (1996b), in their planetary list of the Kabbalistic system of correspondences, explain how the Sun is linked to one of the operations of the spirit, namely will. In this context Solaris, as a sentient planet, becomes the embodiment of will, which denotes capacity, ability, and undeniably, choice. The planet does not provide any answers to human curiosity and questions, and the observers on the space station bend to the planet's will. This is similar to how an individual is said to be influenced by the aspects of planets on his/her astrological natal chart. Chris is compelled to make a choice due to Solaris's effect on his psyche. This is something he did not foresee and did not expect, as it was buried deep in his unconscious until he came face to face again with Rheya.

Pauli, in his interpretation of Kepler (Jung and Pauli, 1955), talks about circular motion and the image of the circle as functions and faculties of the soul: ratiocinatio, reflection, and logical conclusion. Solaris, depicted in the film as a perfect circle with changing colours from blue, pink, and magenta, suggests the fluxes in Chris's grief journey, his rationality, his relation to his past with Rheya, and his inevitable decision at the end of the film.

Another interesting point in the film is that the spaceship that brings Chris to the doomed space station orbiting Solaris is called Athena (08:06). Continuing the mythological connection, the space station in orbit is called Prometheus.[2] These two Greek gods, even though they differ in their mythological origin, symbolism, and relations to human beings, share one unique characteristic. They both offer help to humans to transform their way of life. While Prometheus brings fire and triggers technological progress, Athena offers wisdom and truth to alter consciousness. Chris's journey through the film is a change of consciousness in itself because he realises that he will neither be happy nor complete if he goes back to Earth.

When one looks at the symbolism of the name Rheya, which is a derivative of the name Rhea, things get even more interesting. Greek mythology makes only a tiny distinction between Gaia and Rhea. In fact, Rhea seems to be a continuation of the Gaea/Mother Earth myth (Guirand, 1996, p.150). Mythologically speaking, Rhea parallels Gaea in terms of her pregnancy and her husband's demise. Guirand also adds that the Egyptian goddess of Nut lies at the source of Rhea. In the film, Rheya's blatant rejection of the idea of having a child is evocative of the punishment of Ra, who forbids Nut from having a child. Nut eventually gives birth to the solar god Horus. She is also the guardian of the dead as she is frequently depicted as carrying dead people in her arms. All this heavy and multi-layered symbolism makes the union of Chris and Rheya at the end very significant in terms of death, dying, grief, and rebirth.

The name Chris is of course a derivative of Christ and comes from its Greek origin, meaning 'carrier of Christ'. With this unbreakable connection, the name brings all the religious references, connotations, imagery, and symbolism of Christ, including (but not limited to) Saviour, Redeemer, ascension/descension, man's suffering and redemption, banishment of death, resurrection, and sacrifice/sacrificial death. According to Jung, Christ becomes an archetypal symbol of self (CW 9ii, para.68–126; CW 11 para.226–33), alpha and omega, and ouroboros (CW 14, para.423), wholeness (CW 9ii, para.73), alchemy of Sol and Luna (CW 16, para.355), dying and self-transforming god (CW 11, para.146).

The relationship between Rheya and Chris is intertwined with door, gate, and lock imagery. The sequence of these images starts with Chris's fridge door (03:21) at his home on Earth, which is shown again at the end of the film. The second one is the doorknob scene on the train (21:34), which is the first time they see each other and which marks the beginning of their journey together. Door/lock imagery appears on the space station too. The first-visitor Rheya is sent off to outer space after Chris ejects her by closing the shuttle door. Before the arrival of second-visitor Rheya, Chris locks himself in his room to prevent her possible return. Once she arrives, however, he refuses to let her go and locks the door again.

Gateways and doors symbolise the actual passing from one state, from one world to another, or from a known realm to an unknown one. They indicate a threshold that must be crossed in order to initiate a voyage to somewhere beyond human understanding, definition, and limits. Chris's actual shutting of doors, in this sense, implies his denial and inability to come to terms with the passing and transformation. The fridge door, which is shown at the beginning and at the end of the film, is deeply symbolic in itself too. A fridge is used to keep things cool, chilled, or frozen, to preserve them. It is an item that is accessed daily and several times. Chris's almost empty fridge at the beginning, without the photo of Rheya on the fridge door, implies his frozen state of grief (and emotions), which he is aware of even though the door on it is shut.

The imagery of *torana*, a Hindu gateway symbol associated with Kala the Devourer, is also important to mention here. It is depicted as the monster's mouth and symbolises not only the route from life to death, but also from death to transformation, the cyclical process of beginnings and ends. Chevalier and Gheerbrant (1996a, p.289) also mention the 'kālamukha' as the symbol of a consistent pattern in the universe where growth and decline follow each other, which can be both scary and calming at the same time.

With all these recurring symbols embedded in the film, it is also significant to note the choice of DBA (the fictional space administration) to send Chris to Solaris. Their rationale is briefly explained when two officers show up at Chris's house at the beginning of the film. For reasons they do not know, the on-board instrumentation is still working, but the scientists aboard the space station avoid communicating with the command centre on Earth. In order to guarantee their safe return, a psychologist is needed in order to identify and solve the human element of the problem. This request puts Chris in a powerful but difficult position, which is similar to a misconception regularly observed in therapist–client relationships, where the therapist is asked and expected to know everything and provide a quick solution when asked. Lévy-Leboyer (1998) describes this situation as a catch-22. She mentions the strange paradox that when psychologists require research to deliver answers and offer their guidance following the findings of that research, they are sometimes disregarded as well. This predicament for Chris becomes the gist of his argument with Gordon (Viola Davis) later on in the film. As he cannot explain or understand (and becomes frustrated with his failure to comprehend) Rheya's appearance and the motives of Solaris, his suggestion to study his visitor further is quickly and aggressively rejected by Gordon.

In a nutshell, the film focuses on Chris's reminiscence of his dead wife, his inability to move on emotionally after her suicide, his dull and mechanical life on Earth after his loss, and how things get complicated when he is forced by Solaris to face and deal with his grief in the present. Soderbergh includes many of Lem's linguistic and symbolic choices, but deliberately changes the angle of how the human–god connection is portrayed with the film's enigmatic ending. With this decision, he makes *Solaris* an intriguing and innovative examination of human suffering and healing in terms of Jungian analysis. The next section will look at the concept of grief within the context of its representation in the film.

4.3 A life in anguish – prolonged grief disorder

Hans Schaer (1951) likens Jungian psychology to a big planet with lots of undiscovered territories and mysteries, a place where everything is possible. This description becomes a key to decipher how Solaris is portrayed in the film. With its vast ocean, everything that makes Solaris is liquid and dissolved, creating a completely unknown domain. The source (or the limits) of its powers, intelligence, and consciousness is not only lurking beneath the surface but is also made tangible and magnified to a universal scale. It defies human understanding, calculation, and reason. In Chris's case, however, it creates the battleground of his grief and leads him to his encounter with the numinous.

At the beginning of the film Chris Kelvin's cool, calm, and calculated life as a psychologist is set within the first few minutes. He organises group therapy sessions and discusses the individual personality traits and their links to sessions with a client on the phone. He then tries to cook a dinner for only himself, his loneliness reflected in the frugal fridge. Apart from his commute on the train and his clients, there is no sign of anyone significant in his life, no friends, no significant other. He leads a lonely and a distant private life. He is deep in this seemingly safe routine, and he shows resistance to the DBA officers' suggestions that he is the right person to go.

The opening shot of the film shows raindrops hitting the window and Chris sitting on his bed safely guarded from the rain looking tired, silent, and despondent. As Rheya's voiceover is heard, it appears as if he has blocked the whole world out and is absorbed in his own mind. The second scene shortly depicts a group therapy session where Chris's status is ambiguous. It is not clear whether he is the facilitator or a participant. In either case, he is still completely silent. The dialogue in this scene highlights and foreshadows the events that will happen on Solaris. The male participant mentions how the traumatic memories of his wife are so easily triggered and how anything can set his wife off and make her return to that vulnerable place. The female participant, on the other hand, complains about seeing images and not feeling anything, thinking they are less than real every time she sees them.

These two descriptions of how memories and images can trigger anxiety in the present or alienate a person from reality completely match how Chris and Rheya are portrayed in the film. With Rheya's first visit on Solaris, Chris is instantly thrown off balance emotionally. His deep wish to enjoy Rheya's presence once again is conflicted with the knowledge that what appears as Rheya in front of him is not her. As a responsible psychologist and a rational person, he has to accept the fact that she is dead. Therefore, he lets go of the first-visitor Rheya and sends her off to space (33:23), unable to contain his emotions for the loss of his wife for the second time, feeling helpless and duty-bound, because he has failed to save her again.

Rheya, on the other hand, during her second appearance on the space station as a visitor, starts to realise that her memories have a fake quality to them. In a form of depersonalisation, she remembers them as images and events, but she clearly describes (47:07) how she feels not having lived them. This contrast is reminiscent of Schaer's (1951) interpretation of Jung. He argues that there is an unbreakable link between our outer and inner experience, and physical reality ultimately liberates the contents of the psyche. In the film, Solaris releases what Chris has been ignoring and freezing all along. It creates Rheya out of Chris's psyche, which is why Rheya's memories feel manufactured. Chris, in return, is forced to sense, perceive, and experience his grief as well as everything connected to Rheya that was suppressed, buried in his intrapsychic tomb, but is now in front of him in corporeal form, as a perfect replica.

Gibarian's short speech about how humans essentially search for mirrors in the universe disguised in the act of discovery takes its most serious form in the case of visitors. Solaris, as a planet, not only reflects back what is most wanted but also what is most hidden and reproduces loss as tangible entity. When Chris desperately wants to know if Rheya will come back or not (35:10) after he jettisons his first visitor into space, his question to Snow (Jeremy Davies) illustrates how deeply rooted his grief is. His pining for his wife starts to overwhelm his rational mind, and this powerful yearning would eventually defeat his thinking self.

Suicidal ideation after a traumatic bereavement, and suicide as a solution for grief, is not uncommon (Parkes, 1970). It not only provides a radical shortcut for achieving a reunion with the deceased, but also delivers a deeply craved relief from the feelings of abandonment, alienation (both self and social), desolation, and hopelessness. The snowball effect of these feelings offers the grieving person a simple and practical solution to an exceptionally complex problem, which the conscious mind can neither cope with nor contain any more. Jung describes this as *abaissement du niveau mental*, the weakening of an individual's will-power, which leads to decreasing levels of self-control and grip upon circumstances, moods, and thoughts (CW 3, para.521). The sense of a negative future then becomes sufficient to eat away at the survival instinct. The notion that suicide can also deliver altruistic, anomic, or egoistic results (Durkheim, 2002) supports the attraction an individual feels towards self-destruction.

The systematic studies of Prigerson et al. (1999) and Horowitz, Bonanno, and Holen (1993) into prolonged grief disorder identify several characteristics that Chris displays. These are: empty sense of self or confusion after the loss, or feeling that a part of oneself has died as a result of the loss; avoidance of reminders of the loss; extreme difficulty moving on with life; absence of emotion; and also, feeling life is empty and the future bleak without the deceased.

In the brief opening scenes of the film, Chris is seen without any reminders about Rheya. There is neither one single photo together as a couple or of Rheya individually, nor is Chris shown wearing his wedding ring. The memory of Rheya and her suicide is carefully repressed, even though its effects are visible in Chris's depressed state by the bed. He does not smile or cry at all until the first-visitor Rheya appears in the film. Just before Chris embraces the idea of death, towards the end of the film, it is revealed by him, in a flashback/

flashforward sequence, how he felt empty, hopeless, and unable to heal after Rheya's death on Earth.

In different ways and for different reasons, Chris and Rheya unite and agree on the idea and the act of suicide. Rheya, physically abandoned and rejected by Chris after her abortion (50:25), cannot cope with the idea and the feelings of losing her husband. Hers is an egoistic suicide triggered by a deep sense of unbelonging. Her suicide results from a sense of deep personal failure as she realises that she is responsible for not meeting Chris's expectations of her and that Chris has stopped loving her. Chris's choice to stay on the space station, which is about to crash into Solaris, however, appears as an anomic suicide. With the death of Rheya, he loses his deepest personal and meaningful connection. He also feels guilty, as his decision to abandon Rheya so abruptly paved the way for her death. His loneliness, isolation, and estrangement with society feeds into his sense of meaninglessness. The reasons behind the despondent, mostly silent, and mechanical scenes of Chris at the beginning of the film are revealed towards the end where his psyche steps out of the boundaries of time, connecting past, present, and future in a perfect Jungian synchronicity. He perceives time not as past, present, and future, but in one singular moment. He knows that it was, it is, and it will continue to be unbearable to deal with Rheya's suicide on Earth. His meaningful life ended with Rheya's death and there is absolutely no way of recovering a piece of that happiness which is now lost. This realisation, as he stands by the door of the spaceship Athena ready to cross another threshold to go back to Earth with Gordon, triggers his choice to embrace death. In this scene (80:33) Soderbergh lets Chris express his thoughts in a voiceover, and Chris reveals how his perception of time and human relationships changed. He describes that his loss transformed him into being a quiet imitator rather than an authentic person, mimicking the gestures of other people in order to continue living. As he tells how he could not go back to being in tune with the rhythm of his life before Rheya, he also confesses that he is deeply bothered by the possibility of his failure in remembering and doing everything correctly.

These words are important because they expose Chris's limitations as a psychologist. As a professional, he is expected to convey his knowledge and expertise in order to help people/clients deal with the outside world and its shortcomings. Here, however, he muses about how he has become a shell of himself, devoid of any emotion and unable to make a meaningful, loving connection. As he confesses his conscious efforts to look as if he is an ordinary human being, he describes his deliberate attempts to 'study' human behaviour in order to mimic them in the best possible way. In other words, he finally has his realisation that if he goes back to Earth after losing Rheya for the fourth time he would not be able to live a real, fulfilling life. He would be forever trapped in an exogenous depression fuelled by guilt and grief. The life that awaits him now is a copy, a facsimile of his past life and past self, just like Gordon's description of the visitor Rheya. He is aware that he has become a stranger not only to himself but also to life on Earth, which he finds unfamiliar. In a different way, he describes how Erica Bain in *The Brave One* (2007) dealt with her grief. His loss has forced him to become someone else and transformed him from within. The power of loss is so strong that his expertise in human psychology can only help him become a shell, but not heal and move on. All that knowledge leads to him being an unenthusiastic mimicker of a real person, a puppet of his own self. This realisation happens as he watches Gordon launching the return journey to leave the space station, just before he makes his last conscious choice as a human being. After losing Rheya for the fourth time, he now does not expect or hope for anything. He is consumed by what Hillman (1997) calls an 'analytical despair'. He chooses to stay on the space station, fully knowing that the station is going to crash into the planet and that he will die.

Chris's suicidal ideation is implied via his fascination with Dylan Thomas's famous poem titled 'And death shall have no dominion' (Thomas, 2016). In the film it is mentioned three times: first, it is revealed as Chris's favourite while he was dating Rheya; second, when Chris finds a torn page containing the poem in – now dead – Rheya's hand back on Earth (53:30); and third, when this memory of Chris was revealed to the visitor Rheya in the aftermath of her suicide on the space station (75:58).

Freud's concept of the death instinct postulates a wish to dissolve and obliterate oneself, a struggle towards the diminution of opposing tensions in the psyche to zero-point. Jung, on the other hand, considers death as an end to a former way of life, especially in the relationship between the first and the second half of a life of a person, which Jung describes as a circular motion. It is a cyclic form of transcendence from a separated, differentiated ego from the self to a better, a wiser unification of the ego and the self. This can be achieved as one gets older and closer to the end of their life. In the poem, Thomas argues that death has no control over the human soul. Equally, death, which is the natural end of all things, is the ultimate dissolver of all human conflicts, dilemmas, and separation, including the ego and the self.

In Chris and Rheya's case, the separation can only be reversed, and Chris's perpetual grief can only be dissolved by death and in death. Chris's suicide decision comes after his realisation that his personal tragedy was the result of events that include his personal mistakes, and the effects of these events will continue to haunt him even beyond Earth. Paired with his yearning for Rheya, death loses its fear factor and becomes an escape hatch.

Zanardo (2011) interprets the result of Chris's choice as being overrun by his imagination and needs. He argues that Chris has failed to acknowledge Rheya as an imaginary product of his own mind due to his deep yearning to be with her. In other words, Chris traps himself in another crypt in outer space for eternity. My interpretation of the film's mystical finale is that Chris experiences *numinosum*. In the scene where the space station slowly (and loudly) falls into the planet, he reaches out and grabs the hand of Solaris, which now appears to him as a child. In this crucial scene (89:35), the visual reference to *The Creation of Adam* by Michelangelo, the famous fresco from the Sistine Chapel, is unmistakeable. But Soderbergh does not make the index fingers touch. This time a defeated, grief-stricken man surrenders and holds on to a godlike being. In other words, Chris opens up to receive celestial help and strength as he dies.

With his direct contact with a cosmic entity, Chris's experience of his personal numinosum and transformation begins. According to Jung, the numinosum cannot be conquered. One can only open oneself to it. It alters the consciousness completely and forever as it transcends the current reality. He describes numinosum (CW11, para.6) as an experience that is caused by an object's quality or by a mystical force independent and external to the person.

When Chris surrenders to Solaris, his symbolic (and probably literal) death finally unites him with his wife and ends his suffering. Rheya's calm and sympathetic reply to Chris's question whether he is alive or dead in the last scene (90:58) is crucial. She suggests that they do not have to indulge in binary thinking. He is now beyond time and space, where all conflicts between life's opposites are diminished. This is given to him by Solaris, which mirrors the help of the Greek gods, Athena and Prometheus. It is finally revealed that his last choice has enabled him to live in a perpetual blissful state, making second-visitor Rheya's wish in her suicide note come true: he can now live truly in a feeling forever.

4.4 Entering the void

Even though Lem uses his character Kris to illustrate how it is impossible for humans to understand a higher form of intelligence and being, and ends his novel with a feeling of futility, Soderbergh chooses to push the envelope further by giving Chris the freedom to be a part of a bigger, deeper understanding, a higher wisdom, a quantum consciousness where simple dichotomies like life and death do not matter. All polar opposites are neutralised because they cancel each other out. There is no more residual tension trying to marry opposites. His psyche is dissolved in Solaris and recreated by Solaris. His rejection of a meaningless, loveless, joyless, guilty existence without Rheya, coupled with his realisation that his expertise and knowledge in human psychology cannot and will not help him move on, takes him to a higher domain of consciousness, a super-unification with an entity, a complete immersion into the great unconscious, which is symbolised as Solaris's massive ocean. The major themes and defining qualities of Christianity, which are sacrifice and redemption, become intertwined with Chris as a person and his ultimate choice.

Solaris, from its bleak beginning to its mystical end where everything seems to be forgiven, is a 92-minute meditation on death, as well as its many forms and reasons. When Chris arrives at the space station, the first thing he finds is a group of dead bodies in a cooling unit. After the first-visitor Rheya is sent off, it is revealed that people are coming back from the dead. Gordon's visitor is never shown but she describes how she got rid of it using the proton accelerator, which is another example of death and murder. Snow, on the other hand, revealing he is actually the visitor Snow (79:37) and not the real person, describes how he killed his original in self-defence just because he wanted to survive. Death, as a concept, takes different forms on Solaris, either embodied or embedded in action.

Freud takes *Thanatos* (*Todestrieb*) as a drive, a theoretically generalised impulse towards destruction and death. Common human behaviours such as rejection, aggression, and denial form the basis of this urge. In all the cases displayed in *Solaris*, we see one or a combination of these factors playing in the background: Chris's furious reaction to Rheya's abortion leads to Rheya's suicide; this, in turn, feeds into Chris's grief, his rejection and off-screen destruction of first-visitor Rheya, and finally his suicide; Gordon refuses to share the same space with her visitor and destroys it completely; Snow attacks his own self/copy in a moment of madness and aggression. When Solaris acts as the great mirror, everything hidden, rejected, denied, and buried in the psyche becomes visible and tangible. Jung's shadow archetype (CW 16, para.470) reaches its maximum capability when the negative memories and qualities these characters try to conceal break their hold, get reflected in Solaris's mirror, and overwhelm the characters' seemingly well-ordered egos and lives.

Chris's heartbreakingly honest confession to second-visitor Rheya (68:22), when he says he does not see anything else but her, sums up how he is now beyond the sensible, reasonable, controlled, rational (but utterly lifeless) Chris shown at the beginning of the film. In Kübler-Ross's (2009) terms, he is unable to break the loop between two stages: denial and depression. In other words, he is stuck between two impossible situations. If he lets Rheya go, he will forever be mourning her loss and never heal. If he rejects everything and everybody else, he will be clinging on to something that is not the real Rheya, a fake but preferable reality.

Parkes and Prigerson (2010) believe that calm and careful evaluation of traumatic experiences has the potential to help people develop a realistic understanding about their current situation. Grief work, in this sense, is a way of creating meaning and making sense of a seemingly pointless but painful event. The repeated appearance of Rheya as the embodied form of Chris's trauma, however, swings his mind to the opposite. The fact that he has not moved on, not processed his grief both as a suicide loss survivor and a psychologist, now reduces his mind to an obsessed, almost infantile stage of pure want and need.

The small but philosophical statement of Chris that comes just before this confession (67:49) is a good example of a psychologist trying to help a client overcome their difficulty in breaking out of a negative cycle. He says that the past does not have to determine the future and people have the will and agency to change things. Chris is desperately trying to convince the visitor Rheya that she can resist her impulses to kill herself over and over again. Sadly, however, it also foreshadows his own destruction because it is the only viable option left to break his vicious emotional cycle as a tragic hero.

To understand the longstanding literary concept of tragic hero one must look at Greek drama. Aristotle (1996) lists *peripeteia* (reversal, a situation changes into its opposite), *anagnorisis* (discovery), *pathos* (catastrophe, misfortune) and *praxis* (action, doing) as characteristics of a tragedy. Chris's grief journey, in this sense, mimics a Greek tragedy because it reverses his situation, brings back his unfortunate past, and pushes him towards the shocking, sad, but inevitable conclusion where he discovers there is no hope but a choice to die.

In Greek tragedies, however, there is also the concept of catharsis, and this resolution is sometimes achieved by divine intervention. Soderbergh delivers Chris's much-needed healing and liberation in the form of a *deus ex machina*: Solaris takes the role of Athena and Prometheus and brings sweet relief to a psyche trapped in misery. On the one hand, it is possible to say that it is another easy and sugar-coated Hollywood ending to an impossible problem: the lovers unite in their perfect little heaven called home; Chris does not have to feel guilty for Rheya's suicide anymore because everyone and every act is pardoned; they do not even have to think about death any longer. In short, all is well that ends well.

On the other hand, this appears as Chris's only salvation. Solaris makes him get in touch with his archetypal self or, rather, the realisation of his destiny as an individual. Chris, then, brings his alpha and omega together and closes the circle like an ouroboros. In the eternal cycle of life and death, his guilt, loss, and grief are finally purged. The cessation of his life brings no harm, and it is not a source of duality or conflict anymore. This is shown in the repeated but now altered scene where he cuts his finger and it instantly heals (85:57). Solaris resurrects him in a state of wholeness and a complete, indivisible sense of fulfilment, a perfect whole in harmony with Rheya where there is no more separation. The fact that he is resurrected in his own house is also a symbol of his eternal homecoming. He has now returned to the starting point of his grief journey, but in an idealised form of timeless happiness. He has emerged in a higher form of existence, in the mind and thoughts of a god.[3]

This remarkable shift in Chris's psyche is another form of bringing opposites together, as he bends the straight line of belief and forms a circle. During the dinner scene (44:36) where Chris, his friends, and Rheya discuss the notion of god, Chris claims that the appearance of humans in the universe is just a statistical probability and there is nothing mystical or a mysterious all-powerful being behind the scenes. Ironically, his complete and true healing is provided by a mystical and mysterious entity that he surrenders himself to. From a complete atheist to a true believer, his grief journey forces him to bring two opposites together, cross the threshold he refused to take, and open the symbolic door he kept locked. This brings him to what he rejected, denied, ignored, and suppressed.

The release of negative and destructive thoughts and emotions through suicide, or at least the attempt of a suicide, is not a new concept among Jungian analysts. In his study of people who survived jumping from the Golden Gate Bridge in San Francisco, Rosen (1975) explains how these individuals describe the same thing: their self-destructive impulses have subsided, a mysterious force took over and they survived, and a new identity in them emerged after yielding to something bigger than themselves. He labels this as a psychotic suicidal depression which brings forth a transformative religious experience that fills the individual with joy and takes the depression away (Rosen, 2002).

Chris, in this case, shares similar characteristics with these individuals. They have all made a choice to end their lives without the certainty of an afterlife.

Their last choice, however, soothes their mental and emotional anguish, dissolves their depression, and gives them a fresh start. This does not mean that suicide is the correct go-to solution for impossible problems. But for some people like Chris, it seems like the only choice left to break out of a cycle, and they are not afraid to make that decision. As Rosen showed, in some instances suicide seems to allow these individuals to purge their destructive drive and experience the cycle of life and death internally.

It is also possible to observe a commonality between Claire Bennett's courage to face death in *Cake* (2014) and Chris's in *Solaris*. Burdened by losses they cannot erase from their lives, they choose to erase themselves out of the equation and out of their current predicaments. In Chris's case, he finds solace in his surrender to death (and god) and he is given a healing that he is unable to achieve in real life, a healing he longs for and deserves.

When Singer (1973) describes the Jungian concept of individuation, she notes that individuation is ultimately a rebellious act because it requires the refusal of established norms and attitudes in society that most people live by. Chris does not find his healing in the therapy room and certainly not in the theories of psychology he represents. He rejects these conventional approaches completely. Consumed by loss, he becomes an example of a trained mind unable to fix its own problems. He, however, finds his completion, reunion, and healing beyond time and space boundaries, in a unique oneness with an entity bigger than himself. This does not make his healing any less important, valuable, or complete than a healing achieved by working through grief with a professional. On the contrary, it makes it even more profound.

4.5 From suicide to murder

As a survivor of bereavement by suicide, I understand Chris Kelvin's choice without condoning or condemning. Suicide is always a permanent solution to a temporary problem. In Chris's case, the feelings of loss and love he buried so deep in his crypt are excavated by Solaris and thrown in front of him. He tries to stop this by sending the first-visitor Rheya into deep space. Then the second-visitor Rheya appears, and this is where his defence mechanisms, both as a human being and as a clinical psychologist, fail. She dies twice: first, by killing herself after learning the fate of the first visitor; and second, by asking to be disintegrated by the proton accelerator. In short, Chris is forced to deal with Rheya's death four times. Nobody can fully and easily recover from such a complex traumatic loss. Therefore, his wish to end his unbearable pain is understandable, no matter how unpalatable or how horrible it may sound.

I also have to acknowledge the fact that he has been shown an extraordinary compassion by the planet. Solaris, even with its own alienness, even though it is beyond human comprehension, responds to Chris's pain with care and delivers him the enantiodromic change he needs. It puts him in a new mystical dimension and helps him reunite with Rheya without the fear of further injury or death. Via this completely unique ending, which defies both the novel and Tarkovsky's film version, Soderbergh says something extremely important: Chris is not unhappy anymore, he is not in pain. What does this suggest in terms of his prolonged grief disorder? If Chris had been able to consider even for a moment that Rheya's unhappiness ended with her suicide, he might not have been trapped in his crypt, and he might not have chosen the same route to end his pain.

Solaris, both as a novel and a film, raises a lot of interesting questions about the nature of the universe and man's place in it. Soderbergh certainly pushes the boundaries of science fiction into new realms where our limited (scientific) knowledge is unable to come up with satisfying answers. That is why Gibarian's sentence that I mentioned at the beginning sums up the film: there are no answers for humans, but only choices to make.

In the next chapter, I will look at a different destructive choice: murder. This time I present another traumatic loss which also forces the survivor to change from within. Here is the primary query: what happens if there is no hope of justice and suicide is not an option?

Filmography

The Brave One (2007) Directed by N. Jordan [film]. USA
Cake (2014) Directed by D. Barnz [film]. USA
Solaris (1972) Directed by A. Tarkovsky [film]. Soviet Union
Solaris (2002) Directed by S. Soderbergh [film]. USA

Notes

1 Lem admitted he had not seen the film (but only read the reviews) and was not planning to watch either. He defended his novel by saying that he did not write it as a love story. On the contrary, he imagined it to be an encounter with a mighty alien being that cannot be comprehended by the human mind.
2 Its name is never mentioned in the film, but in the film's script, which can be found in DVD extras, the name of the space station is specified.
3 The symbolic connection between a god and man goes further. Rheya hugs Chris in a final, everlasting embrace similar to Nut carrying a dead body as the guardian of the dead. Besides, just like Rhea, she has driven Chris to his unhappy end and become the sole reason of his self-destruction.

Bibliography

Abraham, N. and Torok, M. (1994) *The Shell and the Kernel: Renewals of Psychoanalysis. Volume I.* Chicago: University of Chicago Press.
Aristotle (1996) *Poetics.* London: Penguin.
Chevalier, J. and Gheerbrant, A. (1996a) 'Devourer' in *The Penguin Dictionary of Symbols.* London: Penguin.
Chevalier, J. and Gheerbrant, A. (1996b) 'Planet' in *The Penguin Dictionary of Symbols.* London: Penguin.

Chevalier, J. and Gheerbrant, A. (1996c) 'The Sun' in *The Penguin Dictionary of Symbols*. London: Penguin.

Durkheim, E. (2002) *Suicide*. London: Routledge.

Guirand, F. (ed.) (1996) 'Gaea, Rhea and Cybele' in *The Larousse Encyclopedia of Mythology*. London: Chancellor Press.

Hillman, J. (1997) *The Soul's Code: In Search of Character and Calling*. New York: Warner Books.

Horowitz, M.J., Bonanno, G.A., and Holen, A. (1993) 'Pathological grief: Diagnosis and explanation', *Psychosomatic Medicine*, 55, pp.260–273.

Jung, C.G. (1960) *The Collected Works of C.G. Jung, Volume 3: Psychogenesis of Mental Disease*. Princeton: Princeton University Press.

Jung, C.G. (1966) *The Collected Works of C.G. Jung, Volume 15: Spirit in Man, Art, and Literature*. Princeton: Princeton University Press.

Jung, C.G. (1966) *The Collected Works of C.G. Jung, Volume 16: Practice of Psychotherapy*. Princeton: Princeton University Press.

Jung, C.G. (1969) *The Collected Works of C.G. Jung, Volume 8: The Structure and Dynamics of the Psyche*. Princeton: Princeton University Press.

Jung, C.G. (1969) *The Collected Works of C.G. Jung, Volume 9, Part 2: Aion: Researches into the Phenomenology of the Self*. Princeton: Princeton University Press.

Jung, C.G. (1970) *The Collected Works of C.G. Jung, Volume 11: Psychology and Religion: West and East*. Princeton: Princeton University Press.

Jung, C.G. (1970) *The Collected Works of C.G. Jung, Volume 14: Mysterium Coniunctionis*. Princeton: Princeton University Press.

Jung, C.G. and Pauli, W. (1955) *The Interpretation of Nature and the Psyche*. London: Routledge & Kegan Paul.

Kübler-Ross, E. (2009) *On Death and Dying*. 40th ed. Oxon: Routledge.

Lem, S. (1987) *Solaris*. New York: Harcourt.

Lévy-Leboyer, C. (1988) 'Success and failure in applying psychology', *American Psychologist*, 43(10), pp.779–785.

Parkes, C.M. (1970) 'The first year of bereavement: A longitudinal of the reaction of London widows to the death of their husbands', *Psychiatry*, 33, pp.444–467.

Parkes, C.M. and Prigerson, H.G. (2010) *Bereavement: Studies of Grief in Adult Life*. 4th ed. London: Penguin.

Prigerson, H.G., Shear, M.K., Jacobs, S.C., Reynolds, C.F., Maciejewski, P.K., Davidson, J.R.T., Rosenheck, R., Pilkonis, P.A., Wortman, C.B., Williams, J.B.W., Widiger, T.A., Frank, E., Kupfer, D.J., and Zisook, S. (1999) 'Consensus criteria for traumatic grief: A preliminary empirical test', *British Journal of Psychiatry*, 174(1), pp.67–73.

Rosen, D.H. (1975) 'Suicide survivors: A follow-up study of persons who survived jumping from the Golden Gate and San Francisco-Oakland Bay Bridges', *The Western Journal of Medicine*, 122(4), pp.289–294.

Rosen, D.H. (2002) *Transforming Depression: Healing the Soul through Creativity*. York Beach: Nicolas-Hays.

Schaer, H. (1951) *Religion and the Cure of Souls in Jung's Psychology*. London: Routledge.

Singer, J.K. (1973) *Boundaries of the Soul: The Practice of Jung's Psychology*. London: Victor Gollancz.

Thomas, D. (2016) *The Collected Poems of Dylan Thomas*. London: Weidenfeld & Nicolson.

Zanardo, A. (2011) 'Love, loss, imagination and the 'other' in Soderberg's *Solaris*', in Hauke, C. and Hockley, L. (eds) *Jung and Film II: The Return*. London: Routledge, pp.49–66.

5   Murder and *The Brave One*

In this chapter, I look at the inner workings of a traumatised woman named Erica Bain and how she zigzags between two opposite states due to her loss: being a victim and being a criminal. In *The Brave One* (2007), the destructive impulse is not directed at the self. It follows an outward trajectory. Erica does not want to kill herself like Chris Kelvin or Rheya, even though she is as devastated as they are, and her feelings of helplessness are similar. On the contrary, she wants to kill the people who caused her trauma. Here, in terms of her crypt, there is a dual lock: Erica is trapped not only because of her traumatic loss, but she also starts killing people with a steely determination that further complicates her suffering. Therefore, she can find solace neither as a victim nor as a criminal. Within the context of Abraham and Torok's (1994) theory of intrapsychic tomb, she is haunted by two ghosts: grief and guilt.

This analysis, just like the chapter on *Solaris* (2002), brings together several different elements, covering clinical knowledge and universal imagery. While I look at Erica's post-traumatic stress disorder, I also highlight its connections to the visual components of the film, such as clothes, objects, and places, by applying the Jungian concept of amplification. In this difficult tale, there is also an interesting and visible theoretric moment between a criminal and a police officer. This final twist brings about the necessary change for Erica and helps her find the way out of her crypt.

5.1 The world of *The Brave One*

In the pilot episode of ABC's legal thriller TV series *How to Get Away with Murder* (2015), Annalise Keating (Viola Davis), who is a professor of law, explains to her students the three-step strategy to win a murder case in court: discrediting the witnesses; introducing a new suspect; and burying the evidence. Even though *The Brave One* does not include or depict a court case scene, the director Neil Jordan uses an alternative strategy in order for his heroine to get away with murder: colluding with law enforcement.[1]

The Brave One tells the story of a radio host named Erica Bain (Jodie Foster), who is forced to transform within and become a vigilante after she, her fiancé, and her dog were violently attacked in Central Park, New York. Following the

DOI: 10.4324/9781003292630-8

death of her fiancé and the trauma of the attack, her feelings of loss, fear, and helplessness give way to the emergence of a merciless killer in her, which she describes as 'the stranger' who has no resemblance to her old self. As she tries to find the three men who attacked her, she starts to kill any and every man who dares to threaten her (or others). This unstoppable serial killing makes her path cross with detective Sean Mercer (Terrence Howard) who not only befriends her but also figures out that she is the suspect. Even though detective Mercer is bound by law and serves the law, he is also feeling helpless and severely frustrated by the legal loopholes criminals exploit. This inner ambivalence reaches its end during the final act of the film where he understands that, in order to stop the killings and bring Erica back from her inner hell, he needs to go beyond the standard definition of right and wrong, and help Erica take her revenge and kill her attackers.

On the surface, Jordan tells a straightforward story where crime meets punishment. Also, in terms of the depiction of revenge and violence, he does not actually say or show anything new. The main philosophical problem about punishment is that because it involves the infliction of harm in some way, murder/ death as punishment transgresses the ethical boundaries around the preservation of human life and requires a different ethical justification. Retributory violence, or simply revenge in this case, becomes the main framework and justification of Jordan's tale, which is used tediously many times in cinema.

The list of films that focus on the 'eye for an eye' aspect of (perceived) human justice is quite long. The ones that stand out with their depiction of 'good guys/girls going bad', where irredeemable characters meet their well-deserved slaughter, are also like *The Brave One* in terms of their straightforward narrative. The protagonists in *The Big Heat* (1953), *Straw Dogs* (1971), *The Last House on the Left* (1972), *Thriller: A Cruel Picture* (1973), *Death Wish* (1974), *I Spit on Your Grave* (1978), *Ms .45* (1981), *The Crow* (1994), and *Oldboy* (2003) share similar qualities with Erica Bain. They suffer from random and senseless cruelty, which motivates them to obtain justice and closure for themselves by resorting to violence.

Jordan's violent New York story, however, is not just a single person narrative. While it certainly focuses on Erica's grief, alienation, and character transformation, it also touches on concepts like miscarriages of justice, ineffective policing, and social decay, through Mercer's character. His helplessness and frustration within the system not only echo Erica's loneliness but also resemble the idealistic judge character called Steven Hardin (Michael Douglas) in *The Star Chamber* (1983), who does not hesitate to join a secret group of judges hiring an assassin to get rid of criminals. In this sense, Jordan creates a rather combustible and volatile mix of ideas that are woven through the film, which makes *The Brave One* a complex example in a long list of revenge films where the psychological transformation of protagonists is either basic or underdeveloped.

While this complexity might be regarded as positive, the film also portrays shallow, almost cartoonishly simple, violent male characters who are either of colour, or misogynistic, or both. It is unknown whether this directorial choice is deliberate or not, but it certainly makes Erica's killing spree fall into a rather stereotypical box. Even though Mercer is a black detective who helps Erica both physically and psychologically, his redeeming male presence in the film is not a great and strong contrast when compared to the trail of dead male bodies[2] Erica leaves behind. While Jordan includes other favourable characters of colour, like Erica's fiancé David Kirmani (Naveen Andrews) and her female neighbour Josai[3] (Ene Oloja), who tends to Erica's wounds, the depiction of their helpful and loving nature (not to mention their quite short screen time) also pales in comparison to the clichéd depiction of black thugs on the subway and the gangsters in Spanish Harlem (who, unsurprisingly, all get killed by Erica). This strange and unbalanced snapshot of New York's sociological structure adds to the reasons behind several disapproving reviews of the film. *The Times* film critic A.O. Scott (2007) argues forthrightly that the film glorifies lynching so well that even liberal-minded people can enjoy it without guilt.

Even though *The Brave One* makes statements on race, justice, gun ownership, and a law enforcement system under strain, it does not examine any one of these in detail. Instead, it focuses on Erica's inner transformation and the intricate relationship between her and Mercer (which not only sustains its tension until the very end but also mollifies the bitterness of both in unusual ways). In order to explore the film's psychological complexity, I will focus on this transformation in three parts: the first part will look into the symbolic content that is embedded in the film; the second part will examine Erica's feelings of loss and their connections to violence, using grief theory; the last part will investigate Erica's healing with references to Jungian concepts of shadow, compensation, and alchemical operations.

5.2 Explosive potency

From its light, soft, and calm opening to its dark, rough, and bloody ending, *The Brave One* is a tough story, which holds the concept of transformation at its core. This transformation, which is both physical and psychological, is presented through several different visual and aural clues scattered throughout the film. These are: mirror/reflection; sound/silence; gun; tunnel; dog; fly; eagle; and fish.

The film opens with cold, greyish reflections of New York on glass. As Erica is shown, in intercutting scenes, walking, recording sounds of the city, and broadcasting her radio show, these reflections slowly slide and blend into several new visual forms of patterns and shapes, mixed with city views from New York. She tells several stories about the old stuff in New York slowly disappearing (or already disappeared) before the eyes of city residents, sounding nostalgic. Her monologue about how the city is losing its pieces that once were a part of its life and history foreshadows the loss that awaits Erica.

Mirrors and reflective surfaces appear several times during the film as visual metaphors. As changes in New York reflect society's transformation (both good and bad), Erica's inner and outer metamorphosis is also told through her reflections in the mirror. After the attack in Central Park, she looks at her own bruised and bloody face, first, as a victim. Following her first murder, she – several times throughout the film – examines her face as a perpetrator, both fascinated by her inner change and curious to examine this new stranger looking back at her. This behaviour is best observed in the bar toilet scene (48:30) after she kills the two black men on the train. The mirror is also cracked in this scene, and Erica's distorted reflection visually represents her psyche cracking under the weight of grief and anger, giving way to the emergence of a fearless killer living within.

Erica's fascination with her own mirror image stems from her curiosity to learn about the stranger inside her. Mirrors ultimately symbolise the awe, the wonder, and the perception of a new reality which is beyond the two-dimensional reflection looking back at us (Ronnberg and Martin, 2010d). Chevalier and Gheerbrant (1996a), on the other hand, mention the truth-revealing aspect of mirrors and draw parallels to the enlightenment and wisdom that can be gained through the Dharma (Buddha's teachings) which is also called *The Mirror of Dharma*.

Straight after her first murder and in a monologue, Erica describes her encounter with a stranger in herself who has her arms, legs, and eyes (37:21). In this sense, her reflections in the mirror contribute to her estrangement to and knowledge of what is changing inside her. The person she sees in the mirror looks like her, but in fact, she is completely alien to the old Erica who was irrevocably and permanently changed after David's violent death. Her reflection now shows the cause of her actions in her own words: a stranger who does not sleep, who is restless, and who keeps on walking day and night.

Erica's transformation is also depicted by sound. At the beginning of the film, Erica, as a successful radio host, is shown as a woman deeply in love with New York, who walks around the city with recording equipment capturing the sounds of the city. She is talkative and has a soft, friendly voice. Right after the attack, her ability to talk and to express herself diminishes, which is depicted in the second live broadcast scene where she falls silent for a full minute, unable to speak. Her voice becomes raspier, and her general speech/attitude becomes more confrontational. The fact that she is unable to talk to anybody about her trauma and grief openly throughout the film contributes to her feelings of becoming an invisible and deadly stranger. This extreme change is effectively depicted at the end of the film when she kills her last remaining attacker: her scream[4] as she pulls the trigger is now like a wild animal killing its prey (108:37).

Sound has a complex symbolism. It is a transmitted disturbance perceived by ears. It comes before the creation of light and the universe as a symbol of (spoken) divine power. Knowledge, human or holy, can be seen but also heard, too. Silence, on the other hand, sometimes denotes that something is better left unsaid. Erica's silence comes partly from being unable to confess her vigilante acts and partly from being unsupported by friends or professionals. The film neither shows any close friends supporting her grief process nor includes scenes of psychotherapy. In a way, the grieving Erica and the angry murderer Erica are both condemned to a silence that seems to block her ways of getting help. This perpetual state of inner anguish finds its outlet and transmission in one of the most disturbing and loudest ways possible: a gun.

'Gun' combines two forces in the psyche: fear, which triggers aggression, and the desire to protect oneself from danger (Ronnberg and Martin, 2010c). It is also inherently masculine due to its explosive, penetrative, and forceful qualities. As Jordan turns the classic male vigilante formula on its head in his film, he depicts a woman becoming as violent as a man and lets Erica express her pain and aggression through her gun. The depth of her trauma is so big she symbolically penetrates every man she kills[5], making sure their wounds are deep too. In this sense, her gun appears not only as a totem of her emerging inner stranger but also as her way of protecting herself from further physical and psychological dangers that seem to lurk around every corner in Jordan's New York.

Another symbol that highlights Erica's trauma and inner transformation is the tunnel. It is not only the actual location near Strangers' Gate in Central Park where she and her fiancé get attacked, but also a dark place in her mind, a place she cannot come out of. The symbolism of enclosed and dark passageways almost always indicates rites of initiation in several traditions, including Egypt, Mesopotamia, and pre-Colombian America, linking the realms of the living and the dead (Chevalier and Gheerbrant, 1996b). The attack scene clearly shows that Erica lost her consciousness in the tunnel. This physical helplessness contributes to her feelings of fear and being trapped even when she visits the same place the second time (but cannot come out the other end). Her sudden exposure to darkness, violence, and death, without a chance to escape, becomes the starting point of her painful transition from a calm radio host to a furious killer. In this sense, tunnel imagery fits in with Erica's fluctuation between two psychological states, both equally disorientating and restricted. Ronnberg and Martin (2010e) also add that the way tunnels are used in art and fiction highlight how this symbol appears as a narrative representation between opposite themes of human experience.

Erica eventually walks through the tunnel she is attacked in, having taken her revenge, conquered her fears, and shown an act of grace. The very last scene of the film shows her progression into a new state and her reconciliation, not only with the stranger that harbours within but also with the weight of her grief. As she admits in her monologue that there is no going back to her old self, her kidnapped dog Curtis finally joins her as she comes out of the tunnel.

Throughout history, dogs have become powerful and rich symbols in myths and belief systems. Several symbology authors dedicate hundreds of pages to dogs, covering almost every culture, continent, and time period in wondrous detail. Anubis, Asclepios, Cerberus, Xolotl, and Garmr (or even Fenrir) are all different manifestations of a powerful canine associated with destruction but also with protection. As loyal friends but also as guards to ward off evil, dogs have been considered to have healing qualities. Some alchemists refer to the purification process of gold by using antimony as a wolf consuming a dog. The complexity of dog symbology, however, boils down to a singular combination of opposites: life and death.

Erica's dog Curtis appears only at the beginning and at the end of the film, connecting two different situations: the attack in the tunnel that ends with David's death, and the revenge that starts Erica's new life as a transformed woman. Curtis not only joins Erica during the very last scene as she walks out of the tunnel, but also guides her to the remaining two attackers in Spanish Harlem and helps her murder them in the previous scene. As a symbolic living link to her old life with David, and as the third victim of the same attack that altered Erica, Curtis appears again not only to help her destroy her enemies but also to comfort her with his presence after the violent conclusion of the film. As Erica completes her mission as an irreversibly changed person and kills her attacker in front of Mercer, she also destroys what is left of the old Erica only to be understood and forgiven by him, giving her inner stranger the right to exist and heal.

The emergence of Erica's inner stranger is also symbolically depicted in the film. After the attack she wears three different t-shirts with three different animals printed on them: while she is at home recovering there is a big fly on her chest (21:03); after her subway murders she wears a t-shirt with an eagle on it (52:53); the last animal, fish, appears during her hospital visit (82:18) to Chloe (Zoë Kravitz), the woman she rescued from the hands of the drug dealer/pimp she killed.

The fly symbol carries all the negative associations one can think of (Biedermann, 1996b). Parasitic, unclean, and seen as harbingers of disaster and disease in religious contexts, the fly is seen as an unholy creature which suggests malicious situations and deeds. Quoting the Talmud, Ronnberg and Martin (2010a) point out how evil spirits resemble flies, bringing unwanted influences. Even though a similar creature, the butterfly, is associated with beautiful trans-formations, the symbolic connections of the fly are reduced to death and putre-faction. In this sense, Erica's fly − which literally covers her heart − indicates her almost parasitic inner stranger slowly poisoning her mind and body. Her bruised body and face reflect the decay of old Erica, unable to contain/hide the physical and emotional impact of the attack, becoming alien to everyone and everything she loved in the past.

This alienation gradually transforms Erica into a ruthless predator as she conquers her fear of New York, and the random violence it contains, with the gun she carries around. This inner change is fully reflected in the eagle symbol[6] on her t-shirt, which is shown after she kills the thugs on the subway, carrying it like a proud emblem of a pest controller. She is now fully aware of her inner stranger's powers and not afraid to use them when necessary.

As an apex predator, the eagle blends two opposite worlds: the powers of the sky and the underworld in one singular image. Considered as the king of birds, eagles can roam the sky freely, their sharp vision is unparalleled, and, according to several legends, they can look into the Sun without blinking. Sea eagles can dive in waters to catch their prey with unflinching precision. As a devotee and a vehicle of Vishnu, the protector of the good and the universe, Garuda hunts and destroys serpents and evil. In Vedic scriptures, Garuda is depicted as an eagle and a solar bird.

The inner struggle of Erica trying to stop this emerging killer in her, while never hesitating to kill when required, is also depicted in the film when she shows up at a police station with the intention to confess. After her third live show, when she hears the public support and hybristophilia for the vigilante, she looks distressed and emotional, unable to understand why the police cannot connect the dots and arrest her. Her predatory behaviour fuelled by grief clashes with her wish to stop herself from killing more men who seem to appear less like humans and more like vermin to her. She is trapped between compulsion and repulsion.

These two opposing forces of psyche are further symbolised by the fish. When Erica is invited by Mercer to visit Chloe at the hospital, she turns up wearing this symbol, ready to get arrested by Mercer following Chloe's expected testimony. She even encourages her discreetly to tell the police what really happened that night, counting on Chloe to stop her from killing more people. In other words, she appears ready to surrender her inner stranger for the common good as the emotional toll of this transformation is unbearable to her. Ronnberg and Martin (2010) note the similarity between the astrological symbol of Pisces (two fish facing opposite directions) and the theories on the conscious and the unconscious psyche (as opposing forces). They also mention how early Christians called themselves little fish (*pisciculi* in Latin) following Jesus for his teachings and his pastoral care (*cura animarum* in Latin)

The fish, on the other hand, is cold-blooded by nature. Plus, there are cultural links between fish symbolism, Christian baptism practices, and rebirth (Biedermann, 1996a). Even though Erica appears to kill with unflinching intent, especially in the second half of the film, she is also carefully depicted as a lost soul who cannot seem to accept herself either as an invisible victim or as a cold-blooded killer. Her *cura animarum* (cure of the soul), however, is delivered when she fully reveals her inner stranger in front of Mercer who represents law and order. As she finally takes her revenge and is fully forgiven by him, she is reborn and earns the spiritual mastery and control over her destructive side.

Even though *The Brave One* looks like a typical revenge tale on the surface, the lengths it goes to depict and examine deeply psychological and philosophical problems concerning grief, justice, and forgiveness makes it a complex example among other Hollywood productions. The next section will focus on Erica's experience of bereavement through the prism of grief theory and how this experience turns a victim into a criminal.

5.3 Becoming someone else – PTSD

In *I Walk the City*, the short documentary about the making of the film included in the DVD release, screenwriter Roderick Taylor explains the origins of the film's name. He argues that revenge is not driven by courage but by hatred and anger. He claims that even though Erica does not seem to want to live anymore after being traumatised and hurt so deeply, there is a stronger desire in her to rebuild her life and turn things around positively. It is what he calls true courage and that is why the film is called 'The Brave One'.

While these sentiments sound constructive, they neither reflect realistically what is happening in the film nor describe the way it is written or directed. Erica is never depicted as suicidal; therefore it is impossible to imply she does not want to live. On the contrary, it is shown several times that she actually kills men with relish[7], only to feel guilty of this pleasure when she comes back to her senses. Whatever she is shown to be reconstituting internally as a victim is not due to a wish to live. Her psyche produces an impulsive and blood-thirsty predator who is trying to evolve and counterbalance the physical and psychological damage Erica has suffered.

Erica's predicament is an example of *psychischer konflikt* (psychical conflict), which occurs when opposing wishes and emotions in the psyche create considerable pressure for the subject. While she, as a bereaved woman, is clearly struggling to deal with David's death, she also becomes very much aware of a clogged and inefficient justice system in her first visit to the police station. Her helplessness in this scene, both as a victim and a voiceless mourner, triggers her desire to protect herself by buying a gun. Even though her first murder is a kill-or-be-killed situation and can be classified as self-defence, the murders that follow reveal more about her growing inner conflict. She knows she is doing something wrong and illegal, but she distributes justice with her own hands. She is not feeling helpless anymore when she does that. She feels right and content.

In Jungian terms, Erica is on a similar path with her encounter with the shadow archetype, just like Chris Kelvin in *Solaris* (2002), and Jim Doyle in *The Bank* (2001). The negative, destructive, and primitive side of her nature, namely her shadow, appears to manifest after the loss of her fiancé and is fighting for existence in Erica's psyche. Trapped in a neurotic battle, Erica is swinging between right and wrong, light and dark. Samuels, Shorter, and Plaut (2005) also note that an internal conflict with shadow is expected in anybody as it is impossible to eliminate it.

Erica's descent into darkness after David's death is almost inevitable due to the way David died. As a result of a random and meaningless act of evil, Erica is trapped between a yearning for justice and a desire for destruction. Jung argues that this dilemma is impossible to avoid, because evil causes evil in return (CW 10, para.410). He also notes that good, innocent people can become so furious due to being a victim, they can deliver the punishment for the wicked like a sword commanded by fate (Ibid.).

In this sense, the whole film is about Erica's struggle to come to terms with her shadow in a violent and illegal way, becoming the sword of judgement because of a fateful encounter, yet hating the fact of becoming one. Failed by the police, the justice system, and her immediate social circle, she attempts to deliver justice not only for herself but also to other victims like Chloe. That is why the gradual shift in her depiction, from being a peaceful radio host waxing lyrical about New York, blissfully oblivious to crime and brutality, to a ferocious killer who cannot stop hurting inside is both difficult and sad to watch. Difficult and sad, because Erica's visible struggle with both her grief and the loss of meaning has many characteristics of a complex disorder that affects many bereaved people in real life. This condition is called post-traumatic stress disorder, or simply PTSD.

While DSM-5 and ICD-11 differ in describing and selecting criteria for a comprehensive definition of PTSD (Stein et al., 2014), the core elements of this disorder are the same. PTSD manifests after a traumatic event such as accident, natural disaster, war, rape, murder, etc., and its signs can include hypervigilant behaviour, apathy, or a pervasive psychological detachment, and sometimes intense fear and shock responses (Reber, Allen, and Reber, 2009). Especially following the event of a manslaughter, PTSD is induced almost inevitably due to the unexpected, dreadful, and untimely death of a loved one. The shock of this loss after such an aggressive and forceful separation can also evoke extreme rage, because it has the power to damage one's trust in others, including friends, family, law enforcement, and other legal structures (Parkes and Prigerson, 2010). While Rynearson (1994) points out how the appetite for retribution can be a defence mechanism to deal with bereavement, Worden (2010) also adds that traumatic losses not only lead to complicated mourning, but also destroy survivors' self-esteem, trust in others, and their ability to express their emotional turmoil.

Erica's jarring inner transformation, which bridges victimhood and criminal behavior, embodies PTSD from start to finish. After the attack, she first displays symptoms of agoraphobia as she feels she is unable to leave her apartment (20:18). When she succeeds in her second attempt, her hypervigilance is visible as she is startled even by the sound of the footsteps of other people (22:40) on her way to the police station. Her delicate condition is further intensified at the station when she witnesses how the police treats each case with the same empty courtesy and indifference (23:06). Unable to get help or express her complex emotions of anger, grief, and fear, she then resorts to the only choice left available for her: protecting herself with a gun.

The film does not dwell on the absence of psychotherapeutic interventions. It is unknown whether Erica has been offered support by the police or not, or why she did not seek help herself. However, research focusing on female victims of criminal assault and rape shows that it is a common occurrence to detach from others and even to ignore pain when a violent attack triggers pathological dissociative experiences (for example, an alteration in one's sense of identity), which make PTSD even more complicated (Dancu et al., 1996). While the current literature on the psychopathology of homicidally bereaved individuals is inconclusive and has gaps of knowledge (Denderen et al., 2013), it points to the link between grief and PTSD, revealing that women experience complex grief (Kersting et al., 2011) and PTSD (Komarovskaya et al., 2011) more than men. Erica, in this sense, is in a similar situation to Chris Kelvin in *Solaris* (2002), displaying symptoms of *abaissement du niveau mental*. Jung uses this term to describe psychic phenomenon where split-off fragments of personality are produced, normal trains of thought are hindered, ego's responsibility and reactions are decreased, and inadequate emotional reactions are given (CW 3, para.510).

The film also depicts Erica as a victim of a rather slow and inefficient justice system. Even though the police are shown to be working on the case actively, this is partly due to Mercer's growing friendship with Erica, indicating a situation of prioritising and favouritism working in the background. The inefficiency of the system is further explored in the scene where Erica interviews Mercer (55:38). As he candidly talks about his powerlessness in arresting criminals like Murrow (Gordon MacDonald), he admits (and immediately regrets saying) that there is nothing legal he can do about it. While this confession makes Erica feel that she is not the only person feeling unsatisfied with the justice system[8], it also feeds her inner narrative that she can achieve personal justice and closure herself through illegal means, which further complicates her grief process.

Another social factor that makes Erica's grief journey even more problematic is her radio show. Originally created to entertain and inform listeners about several aspects of New York that might go unnoticed, the show is forced to change its content and style by Erica's manager Carol (Mary Steenburgen). This happens after Erica suddenly goes silent mid-sentence on her first live show after the attack. As she recovers from this after a minute and unexpectedly shares (with everyone listening) her feelings of fear and how she has changed, the show becomes a hit. Carol sees this as an opportunity to boost the radio's publicity and asks Erica to take phone-ins about the vigilante killings. In other words, instead of offering support as a colleague and as a woman, she attempts to benefit from a terrible personal experience as a manager due to Erica's growing fame.

Erica's live phone-in show comes straight after her third murder and disturbs her already damaged psyche even further. She opens the show with a quote from D.H. Lawrence (69:32), saying that the American soul is isolate, stoic, and a killer, describing her situation discreetly. While the male callers support the vigilante and the idea of vengeance in general, the female callers go one step further as one of them finds the vigilante sexy. Erica's distress is visible in this scene as she realises in real time how her loss and grief have been reduced to a piece of entertainment for people, victimising her further. This entertainment value of her trauma is underlined again later in the film when she discovers the video recording of her attack and David's death, which was kept by her attackers as a token of achievement, pushing her further towards a point of no return. She appears as an individual who not only has lost a loved one but also the ability to make or appreciate a meaningful human connection, just like George Falconer in *A Single Man* (2009).

The absence of human connection in Erica's life is a key factor in her transformation. The film depicts a clear-cut distinction between her old and new life. Her social life with her friends completely disappears after the attack, adding to her loneliness and helplessness. However, her truly life-changing and meaningful connection appears to be the one she has with Mercer, who is as world-weary, disillusioned, and lonely as she is, from witnessing, as a police officer, the corruption and the collapse of social fabric. Therefore, these two jaded souls gradually form an unexpected bond that transgresses the basic cat-and-mouse game between a detective and a criminal: they see each other's weariness, bear each other's burden, and help each other out. This is not because of a sneaky motivation to avoid or derail a murder court case, but due to a genuine human need of closure.

In this context, Erica's journey through extremes, from a victim to a murderer, is a slow and tortuous process beset by grief both unvoiced and unheard. However, Erica finds her state of temperance, her way out of swinging between compulsion and repulsion with the help of Mercer who, by showing mercy and compassion to a completely broken and hurting woman, becomes a catalyst to her healing. The next section will explore this act of grace and how it helps Erica's grief to become more tolerable.

5.4 Coming out of the tunnel

The Brave One depicts a bereaved woman feeling trapped and zigzagging between two opposite psychological states. These states are equally unsustainable for Erica. She neither can accept nor can live with the feeling of being a victim, therefore this becomes an internal force of change that pushes her psyche to the other extreme. What awaits her on the other side is equally unacceptable and unpalatable, as becoming a murderer only adds to an already complicated mourning process. It is important to remember the dark tunnel imagery here. In Jungian terms, Erica has encountered her shadow. In terms of alchemical operations, she is at the *nigredo* stage, the dark night of the soul when chaos reigns in an individual's psyche due to the collision of their conscious and unconscious (CW 9ii, para.304). She is going through a transformation forced by grief and she is in the midst of an intense psychological change, or rather simply a tunnel.

What makes Erica's position interesting is that she is not totally unaware of her transformation. As represented by the fish symbol, she is a semiconscious soul in need of *cura animarum*. This becomes particularly clear midway through the film. When she answers Mercer's simple but incredibly important question, asking how she survived after the attack, she tells the truth. She says she did not survive, she became someone else (59:15), indicating her restricted position between opposites. Of course she survived the attack physically, but what she really means is that she did not move on, she did not get over the trauma, and she stayed as a victim. But this victimised state gave birth to an unexpected stranger within, and she became someone else as a murderer.

The last fifteen minutes of *The Brave One* bring another unforeseen twist: a powerful release of grief, anger, and helplessness coming together in an act of violent revenge where Erica kills her third and final attacker in front of and with the help of Mercer. This twist is especially interesting, because up until this point in the film Erica's grief and the ways she responds to her loss have almost constantly been examined against a fixed position of right and wrong through the character of Mercer, who represents law, justice, and order. When Mercer steps outside the ethical boundaries of crime and punishment, he also acknowledges and mirrors Erica's impossible situation and struggle with her shadow. In other words, two different people with two distinct positions of helplessness, namely Erica's shadow triggered by grief and Mercer's shadow as a jaded policeman, who strives for justice but cannot always get it in the way he wants, truly and transparently meet.

Probably the most unfortunate aspect of this scene is the fact that it plays out very quickly. Therefore, it is possible to miss the intricate parallel processes here. Erica not only commits her last murder in front of Mercer but also immediately asks him to arrest her, accepting the guilt and the punishment she deserves, ready for redemption. Mercer, however, not only witnesses the crime and the criminal's pain as a man of law but also chooses to assist that criminal who is struggling both to forgive and to be forgiven.

This unforeseen encounter becomes the catalyst of Erica's progress towards bridging her two extreme states, her integration of loss and liberation, and her healing. It goes without saying that murderous revenge is not the correct way to heal grief and loss. However, it is also crucial to remember Jung's view of neurosis. He not only sees neurosis as a (short-lived) consequence of an overwhelmed psyche that cannot self-adjust, but he also underlines its teleological orientation (CW 7, para.54). Meaning, even when there is an unmanageable conflict in the psyche, it is still trying to achieve balance and trying to heal itself.

Erica's psyche, in this sense, is striving to reach that equilibrium between victimhood and criminality. Her multi-layered helplessness, physical, emotional, social, and legal, is compensated through becoming a ruthless killer. While Jung sees compensation as stabilising and correcting (CW 6, para.693), he also conceives it as a self-adjusting mechanism of the psyche (CW 6, para.694). He adds that compensation is triggered following an incident which is shockingly evil or wrong, and this compensatory process[9] can defy the law and social norms (CW 10, para.250). This is why Erica's murderous inner stranger goes against law and order, desperately trying to achieve a balance in her psyche regardless of the cost.

However, therein lies the rub: a missing piece in this compensatory attempt to heal. Erica can neither forgive her attackers as a victim nor fully forgive and accept herself as a murderer. Frozen in trauma and pain, she is unable to move beyond two conflicting states of suffering. As stated earlier, her *cura animarum*, the missing piece that helps her break through her vicious circle, comes from Mercer in the form of forgiveness and compassion.

The moment where Mercer becomes a witness to Erica's grief, anger, helplessness, and pain in its rawest form is also the moment where he decides to help her. His dilemma, however, is not easier than Erica's. He certainly can arrest Erica's attacker, knowing this choice would expose Erica, in her already broken state, further to long and arduous legal battles where the attacker might eventually use a loophole to avoid punishment just like Murrow. But this choice would also reveal Erica's earlier murders and exacerbate her suffering as a victim of fate. Alternatively, he can help Erica take her revenge and kill a man who is beyond any remorse or redemption, not only stopping Erica's uncontrollable killing spree but also eliminating the possibility of her fully becoming this homicidal stranger, showing her that she cannot distribute justice on her own and with a gun forever.

Hence, Mercer makes the difficult choice by stepping out of his law enforcement role. He gives Erica his own gun and lets her kill her attacker. Because, after all, she is the one who needs saving; she is the real victim. Mercer also does something quite unique and unconventional here. In order to set the murder scene right and help both get away with it easily, he asks Erica to shoot him so that it would look like self-defence. Apart from the legal advantages of this set up, it also gives her a strong ethical inhibitor as it literally shows Erica that if at any point in the future she goes back to her vigilante ways she might have to shoot good men as well, either by mistake or willingly.

This is where the real meaning of the film's title emerges. Even though the whole story is about Erica experiencing grief as affect and the impasse she finds herself in, she is not the brave one, not for getting a gun to face her fears and certainly not for becoming a murderer. Mercer is the real brave one here, for perceiving, understanding, and forgiving Erica, even when she cannot understand and forgive herself. Therefore, out of this unpretentious act of clemency, Erica's true and much-needed healing begins. In other words, Mercer brings *lapis philosophorum* to Erica's *nigredo* and transmutes her impasse. Jung describes this alchemical, but ultimately psychological operation as achieving intrinsic wholeness (CW 14, para.779) which renews the bond between the conscious and the unconscious, altering both in a positive, expansive way.

Even though the film's final scene does not show this wholeness literally, it does depict it symbolically. Erica, having taken her revenge and been forgiven, walks to the tunnel in Central Park where the attack took place. This time she does not stop at the entrance, she walks through it and comes out the other end. Her dog Curtis also joins her. She is not alone or scared any longer. She is a transformed woman who is neither solely a victim nor a murderer but a woman reborn out of a horrible experience, who is more than both of those combined. Maybe not yet fully healed, but certainly on the right path to healing and self-acceptance.

5.5 From murder to chaos

The Brave One throws a lot of difficult subjects into the mix, including race relations, the reasons and the results of gun ownership, and unemphatic and insufficient law enforcement. Even though the director Neil Jordan does not deal with them as efficiently and as delicately as one might have hoped, he excels in sliding under the skin of a grieving woman and shows what the loss of a loved one can change her into. His, at times, convoluted storytelling is a bit tricky to decipher, but his unconventional approach in showing the deep psychological connections between grief, destruction, and mercy makes *The Brave One* a good example among other revenge films.

Following *Solaris* (2002), *The Brave One* points at the significance and the consequence of a destructive choice. Erica, even though she is traumatised, is always conscious of and perceptive about her internal shift from a victim to a killer. She, again and again, chooses to walk down a dark path. Just like Chris Kelvin, she is aware of where this path leads to: (literally or figuratively) the end of a previous life. Again, just like Chris, she is saved by another party. But this time, there is nothing mystical. It is generosity, compassion, and human forgiveness. I will revisit this perspective on forgiveness in the chapter about *Rabbit Hole* (2010).

The next chapter builds up on the query of *Solaris* and *The Brave One*. This time the destructive capabilities of a person go one level up and affect society as a whole in a rather positive way. This interesting film from Australia – *The Bank* (2001) – combines grief with corruption, and it certainly has a political agenda. However, I focus on the two intertwined tales of trauma, which drive two men to two different ways of dealing with loss. The question this time is: what would happen if suicide was not an option, and if justice could not be achieved by violent means?

Filmography

The Bank (2001) Directed by R. Connolly [film]. Australia
The Big Heat (1953) Directed by F. Lang [film]. USA
The Brave One (2007) Directed by N. Jordan [film]. USA
The Crow (1994) Directed by A. Proyas [film]. USA
Death Wish (1974) Directed by M. Winner [film]. USA
I Spit on Your Grave (1978) Directed by M. Zarchi [film]. USA
The Last House on the Left (1972) Directed by W. Craven [film]. USA
Ms .45 (1981) Directed by A. Ferrara [film]. USA
Nocturnal Animals (2016) Directed by T. Ford [film]. USA
Oldboy (2003) Directed by P. Chan-wook [film]. South Korea
Rabbit Hole (2010) Directed by J.C. Mitchell [film]. USA
A Single Man (2009) Directed by T. Ford [film]. USA
Solaris (2002) Directed by S. Soderbergh [film]. USA
The Star Chamber (1983) Directed by P. Hyams [film]. USA
Straw Dogs (1971) Directed by S. Peckinpah [film]. USA
Thriller: A Cruel Picture (1973) Directed by B.A. Vibenius [film]. Sweden

TV Series

How to Get Away with Murder (2015) Directed by M. Offer [TV show]. ABC, USA

Notes

1 This strategy is replicated in Tom Ford's second film *Nocturnal Animals* (2016) for different reasons and with different – but equally powerful – results. His exploration of grief, which started in *A Single Man* (2009), continues as he charts the dark paths between loss and murder.
2 The final kill count is seven.

3 The fact that her name is never mentioned in the film makes Jordan's motivations and choices even more opaque. The viewers are left to think that it is perfectly alright for Erica not to know/say the name of an immigrant neighbour who offers help and stitches her wounds.

4 It is also possible to argue that this is the first and the only time she gives voice to her wounded self in the way she really felt and expresses the hurt and anger she has been hiding from everyone.

5 This penetrative assault continues even when she does not use a gun. When she kills Murrow (Gordon MacDonald), the suspect Mercer cannot arrest due to his wealth and army of lawyers, she makes sure the crowbar is lodged in his skull.

6 Bald Eagle is also the national symbol of the United States, the place where the film takes place and where gun ownership is constitutionally protected by the Second Amendment.

7 This is especially obvious during the scene where Josai stitches Erica's wound. She asks if Erica killed the guy because he hurt her. Erica's reply is dark and blunt. She says she would have killed Murrow anyway.

8 In spite of the belief that participation in the criminal justice system may impact emotional and cognitive recovery of victims, Kunst, Popelier, and Varekamp (2014) point out the lack of research on this topic.

9 Jung also invites other scholars to research into the processes of compensation in criminals (CW 8, para.1138).

Bibliography

Abraham, N. and Torok, M. (1994) *The Shell and the Kernel: Renewals of Psychoanalysis. Volume I.* Chicago: University of Chicago Press.

Biedermann, H. (1996a) 'Fish' in *The Wordsworth Dictionary of Symbolism.* Hertfordshire: Wordsworth Editions.

Biedermann, H. (1996b) 'Fly' in *The Wordsworth Dictionary of Symbolism.* Hertfordshire: Wordsworth Editions.

Chevalier, J. and Gheerbrant, A. (1996a) 'Mirror' in *The Penguin Dictionary of Symbols.* London: Penguin.

Chevalier, J. and Gheerbrant, A. (1996b) 'Tunnel' in *The Penguin Dictionary of Symbols.* London: Penguin.

Dancu, C.V., Riggs, D., Hearst-Ikeda, D., Shoyer, B., and Foa, E., (1996) 'Dissociative experiences and posttraumatic stress disorder among female victims of criminal assault and rape', *Journal of Traumatic Stress*, 9(2), pp.253–267.

Denderen van, M., Keijser de, J., Kleen, M., and Boelen, P. (2013) 'Psychopathology among homicidally bereaved individuals', *Trauma, Violence, & Abuse*, 16(1), pp.70–80.

Jung, C.G. (1960) *The Collected Works of C.G. Jung, Volume 3: Psychogenesis of Mental Disease.* Princeton: Princeton University Press.

Jung, C.G. (1967) *The Collected Works of C.G. Jung, Volume 7: Two Essays in Analytical Psychology.* Princeton: Princeton University Press.

Jung, C.G. (1969) *The Collected Works of C.G. Jung, Volume 8: The Structure and Dynamics of the Psyche.* Princeton: Princeton University Press.

Jung, C.G. (1969) *The Collected Works of C.G. Jung, Volume 9, Part 2: Aion: Researches into the Phenomenology of the Self.* Princeton: Princeton University Press.

Jung, C.G. (1970) *The Collected Works of C.G. Jung, Volume 10: Civilization in Transition*. Princeton: Princeton University Press.

Jung, C.G. (1970) *The Collected Works of C.G. Jung, Volume 14: Mysterium Coniunctionis*. Princeton: Princeton University Press.

Jung, C.G. (1971) *The Collected Works of C.G. Jung, Volume 6: Psychological Types*. Princeton: Princeton University Press.

Kersting, A., Brähler, E., Glaesmer, H., and Wagner, B. (2011) 'Prevalence of complicated grief in a representative population-based sample', *Journal of Affective Disorders*, 131, pp.339–343.

Komarovskaya, I.A., Loper, A.B., Warren, J., and Jackson, S. (2011) 'Exploring gender differences in trauma exposure and the emergence of symptoms of PTSD among incarcerated men and women', *Journal of Forensic Psychiatry & Psychology*, 22, pp. 395–410.

Kunst, M., Popelier, L., and Varekamp, E., (2014) 'Victim satisfaction with the criminal justice system and emotional recovery', *Trauma, Violence, & Abuse*, 16(3), pp.336–358.

Parkes, C.M. and Prigerson, H.G. (2010) *Bereavement: Studies of Grief in Adult Life*. 4th ed. London: Penguin.

Reber, A.S., Allen, R., and Reber, E.S. (2009) 'Post-traumatic stress disorder' in *Penguin Dictionary of Psychology*. 4th ed. London: Penguin.

Ronnberg, A. and Martin, K. (eds) (2010a) 'Fish' in *The Book of Symbols: Reflections on Archetypal Images*. Cologne: Taschen.

Ronnberg, A. and Martin, K. (eds) (2010b) 'Fly' in *The Book of Symbols: Reflections on Archetypal Images*. Cologne: Taschen.

Ronnberg, A. and Martin, K. (eds) (2010c) 'Gun' in *The Book of Symbols: Reflections on Archetypal Images*. Cologne: Taschen.

Ronnberg, A. and Martin, K. (eds) (2010d) 'Mirror' in *The Book of Symbols: Reflections on Archetypal Images*. Cologne: Taschen.

Ronnberg, A. and Martin, K. (eds) (2010e) 'Tunnel' in *The Book of Symbols: Reflections on Archetypal Images*. Cologne: Taschen.

Rynearson, E.K. (1994) 'Psychotherapy of bereavement after homicide', *The Journal of Psychotherapy Practice and Research*, 3(4), pp.341–347.

Samuels, A., Shorter, B., and Plaut, F. (2005) *A Critical Dictionary of Jungian Analysis*. London: Routledge.

Scott, A.O. (2007) 'Packing heat after a coldhearted crime', *The New York Times*, 14 February. Available at: www.nytimes.com/2007/09/14/movies/14brav.html

Stein, D., McLaughlin, K., Koenen, K., Atwoli, L., Friedman, M., Hill, E., Maercker, A., Petukhova, M., Shahly, V., van Ommeren, M., Alonso, J., Borges, G., de Girolamo, G., de Jonge, P., Demyttenaere, K., Florescu, S., Karam, E., Kawakami, N., Matschinger, H., Okoliyski, M., Posada-Villa, J., Scott, K., Viana, M., and Kessler, R. (2014) 'DSM-5 and ICD-11 definitions of posttraumatic stress disorder: Investigation "narrow" and "broad" approaches', *Depression and Anxiety*, 31(6), pp.494–505.

Worden, W.J. (2010) *Grief Counselling and Grief Therapy*. Hove: Routledge.

6 Nihilism and *The Bank*

The third and the last film that not only deals with change after trauma but also a deliberate act of destruction is *The Bank* (2001). *The Bank*'s fictitious storyline is complex and intertwines like a double helix. It includes two fathers and two sons who are all affected by the same deceitful and ruthless financial institution, named Centabank. One of the fathers kills himself and his son decides to destroy Centabank, sacrificing his whole career. The other son tragically dies trying to save his father from the bank, and his death pushes his father to the brink of violence. I approach this multi-layered, interlocked tale using Abraham and Torok's (1994) crypt theory specifically for the protagonist's position.

The crypt is revealed in a flashback almost at the end of the film, before the main character Jim Doyle (David Wenham) deploys his fictional mathematical formula in the bank's mainframe, which basically makes it go under. This flashback shows that Jim's father hanged himself due to his debts to Centabank and little Jim discovered his body. Out of this terrible trauma, a lonely and vengeful mathematical genius is born. As a helpless child, Jim gets trapped in his crypt unable to express his loss, anger, and bitterness. He releases these feelings completely and comes out of his crypt only years later (and as an adult) by destroying the bank, knowing fully what the consequences are.

Similar to Chris Kelvin and Erica Bain, Jim Doyle deliberately chooses a destructive path in order to deal with his trauma. This chapter explores the roots of this choice and the results it brings as a way out of the crypt. I divide the analysis into three parts. The first part describes the political agenda of the film. The second part investigates Jim's trauma with its connections to the theory of embitterment. The third part unearths the Jungian content of sacrifice and transformation.

6.1 The route to lawlessness – *The Bank*'s politics

In his novella *The Ladybird*, first published in 1923, D.H. Lawrence (2000) wrote about the interesting relationship between man and law, expressed in a simple question and answer. The dialogue between Count Dionys and Lady Daphne starts on a nice spring day. Disparaging towards life and his country, Count Dionys expresses his disappointment about England, how trapped he feels, and

DOI: 10.4324/9781003292630-9

how he wishes he could be free from the law. Then he suddenly asks Lady Daphne how one gets outside the law. The answer is short, wise, and maybe a bit enigmatic. She says the only way to get outside the law is to go inside oneself.

Seventy-eight years later, Robert Connolly's first film *The Bank* (2001) follows Lawrence's observation on human nature by depicting two different but intertwined stories of grief and how people change and step outside the law due to loss. Bringing an eccentric mathematician, named Jim Doyle, and a grieving father, named Wayne Davis (Steve Rodgers), together, Connolly delivers an anti-business story, which appears as a cautionary tale. It depicts acts and events full of lies and deceit, corporate mischiefs, ruthless business procedures, market manipulation, and stockholders conspiring to decimate the competitors for profits at the expense of society.

The Bank is an interesting and complex revenge story, and it revolves around four main characters and their interactions with each other, which reach their explosive climax at the end of the film: Simon O'Reily (Anthony LaPaglia) appears as the greedy and ruthlessly realistic CEO of the fictitious Centabank; Jim Doyle as the genius mathematician who is hired by Simon to perfect his formula[1], using the bank's computing resources to predict the next global market crash; Wayne Davis as the grieving father who suffers the loss of his business and his son due to the unscrupulous methods of Centabank; and Michelle Roberts (Sibylla Budd) as the mildly romantic interest of Jim who works in the customer services of the same bank and is critical of her boss Simon's business activities.

The revenge angle of the story is two-fold, which brings Jim's past and Wayne's present together with the same intense purpose: to bring down the bank. While these two characters' actions come together during the finale and achieve their shared aim, they follow different routes to reach that stage and continue on different trajectories after they succeed. Connolly puts traumatic loss and grief as the main initiator behind the desire of revenge and shows how these two bereaved men move outside the law in different ways when they had no choice left but to transmute under the heavy pressure of loss.

Wayne's and Jim's stories of grief and loss are intertwined by the bank itself. Due to a loan Wayne and his wife took in a foreign currency at Centabank, they become insolvent. Tragically, their young son drowns trying to hide the eviction notice he has been delivered irresponsibly by the bank. The couple sue the bank on the grounds that they were not informed properly about the risks of a loan in foreign currency. When Simon demands a proof of loyalty from Jim, asking him to give a false statement in court that Wayne Davis was sufficiently informed when taking out the loan, Jim does not hesitate to do it as he has an ulterior motive: to appear loyal until he makes the bank go under. As the couple lose the case, Wayne, incensed with grief and anger, goes to Simon's mansion to kill him, only to decide not to at the last minute. During this intense confrontation at the mansion, Jim is at the headquarters of the bank and finally deploys the formula he has perfected using the mainframe. As the bank loses 50 billion dollars in a matter of seconds by being devoured by the stock market from whose demise it wanted to profit, it is finally revealed why Jim was so hellbent on destroying the bank: he is simply avenging his father who hanged himself years ago due to his debts to Centabank.

The portrayal of corporate shenanigans is an established topic in films, either as fiction or real-life documentary. *The Bad Sleep Well* (1960), *Trading Places* (1983), *Wall Street (1987)*, *Enron: The Smartest Guys in the Room* (2005), *Margin Call (2011)*, *The Wolf of Wall Street* (2013), and more recently *The Big Short* (2015) contribute to a bigger narrative canvas where greed is applauded in different contexts[2] and show the extent of both individual and corporate corruption.

Even though Connolly adopts a similar perspective in constructing his film, he also brings in a heavily political discussion into the mix. Connolly describes *The Bank* as a thriller with a political angle (Cordaiy, 2001), and his camera and intentions have certainly all the highly charged political reasons behind the writing and the production of the film. In this interview, he discusses the function that banks play in Australian society and culture at the beginning of the new millennium. He argues that individual struggles against these big corporations are akin to the Biblical account of David and Goliath. However, due to the way he engages with these concepts, the film steps out of its local position and becomes a much larger contemplation on the nature of losing/loss, gaining/settling of scores, obtaining a sense of justice and renewal out of chaos and on the intricacies of all these notions.

According to the same interview, Connolly's main impetus for making the film was the growing effect of globalisation. It is important to note that the film was made during the dot-com crash between 2000 and 2002, but before the big economic crises and market crashes of the 21st century, including the financial crisis between 2007 and 2009, and the European debt crisis of the 2010s. Therefore, it fits in well within the historical context of the constantly evolving and recurring economic problems of the world that came before and after the film.

Connolly also reveals that he established his film's political angle on the ideas of J.R. Saul (1997), and Naomi Klein (1999), combining the dangers of corporatism[3] and the unawareness of populations that contribute to these dangers. He also talks about how he mixed these ideas with alchemy, fractal theory, and the swift computerisation of business, as he presents a tricky question: 'what do you do as an individual when you are faced with something that is far greater and more powerful than your government and isn't as regulated and as answerable?' (Cordaiy, 2001). The answer he provides is volatile and evokes the ideas of Pierre-Joseph Proudhon (1876): anarchy.

The main political statement of the film that Connolly is trying to make is depicted and sprinkled over a few scenes, especially where the scenes include short monologues from Simon making bold, brash, and brutal observations about human nature, society in general, and the mechanisms of the corporate world and banking: 'The bank is so powerful financially we can buy anything, public or not. [...] We can force IMF or any country to behave in a certain way because we hold the monetary power'; 'The world has entered the age of corporate feudalism. Bankers are the new princes'; 'I cut 20% of the workforce, shut down 15% of the factories, and I get applauded for doing that, called a genius. My life is dull and I want to do something extraordinary. I want to blow people's minds away'; 'Most people live their lives in quiet desperation, they struggle from birth till death and they don't achieve anything. Society crushes their hopes and aspirations. History forgets them' (*The Bank*, 2001). In short (and in his own words), Simon describes himself as the better dressed version of God and appears as the slick, charming big bad guy of the film. Therefore, his contrasted placement against both Jim and Wayne makes the film's political position appear almost as black and white. However, Connolly (2001) argues that the futures traders who have financed this film think he has not even portrayed the banks and the boardrooms half as bad as they are in reality.

Banking and economy, of course, are strictly tied to mathematics and numbers. This is where Connolly's alchemy analogy emerges for the viewer. Connolly sees and portrays Jim as the alchemist who finds the holy grail of mathematics, the *lapis philosophorum* that turns metals into gold, the elusive principle that governs everything in the universe, even chaos itself. The film's depiction of and allusion to the power and symbolism of numbers and mathematical formulas begin with the opening scene, which portrays Jim as a child at school. In this scene, a representative from Centabank is telling the students in a classroom the importance of saving money and having a bank account.

This scene has a layered quality. Firstly, it looks like an innocent portrayal of conveying ideas on monetary systems and how each person's life is dependent on having a sound relationship with earning, spending, and saving money. As the representative cheerfully explains the concepts of having a car, a house, and then having enough money left over for retirement, it becomes a sinister indoctrination as the children are taught to think that money is extremely important. They are simply treated as customers at a very early age and the idea of having more money is carefully implanted/reinforced in their minds by the wombat piggy banks sitting in front of them. Chevalier and Gheerbrant (1996b) examine the historical links between the pig symbol and the insatiability of humans. They argue that pig is a common symbol in several myths representing a joy in being dirty, lustful, and greedy.

Ron Goulart (1970), in *The Assault on Childhood*, talks about a specific risk. He says children learn very quickly from adults, and if they start adoring expensive physical things too early, then all they will expect from life will be monetary power. He expresses his concerns about teaching children that their future and personality can be defined by the possession of things and describes the easiest way to do it: reinforcing this impression by frequent repetition.

This opening scene, which comes before the computer-generated main titles, actually has two parts, and the beginning of the film shows only the first part, where Jim encounters the banking system for the first time, which appears as a helpful instrument of life. The second part of this scene plays at the end of the film where Jim comes home from school and finds his dead father hanging from a tree, revealing the destructive effect of the same system. Connolly hides this crucial information/trauma, which shaped Jim's personality, until the end of the film in order to create the maximum emotional effect in his story. The point he is making is simply this: as a child, Jim could have been converted into a good, obedient consumer if his father had not killed himself and opened Jim's eyes to the strong links between social structures and the individual. In other words, the shock of bereavement derails the indoctrination process of Jim and creates the basis for conscientization.

Pedagogy of the Oppressed (Freire, 1970) was a revolutionary study in terms of coining the term *conscientization* – in other words, becoming conscious. What Freire meant by this was the process of people recognising how social policies impact their daily lives and how they discard their previous understandings due to this awakening. According to Trifonas (2018, p.367), he voiced his opposition to 'the hegemony of what he called "banking education" and the transmission of knowledge from teacher to student in a master/slave dialectic that created the dyad of oppressor and oppressed'. Students' early internalisation of this dyadic structure, Freire argued, limited their thinking and freedom in the long run. He defined conscientization as becoming aware of social, economic, and political conflicts that are entrenched in a given society, and learning to take the necessary steps to challenge and change them. In other words, this term describes the transformations in one's consciousness that help the person to view their reality under a new light and question that reality if necessary. Liberation and breaking free of the master/slave dialectic, therefore, is earned through questioning and resistance, through struggle against the established social structures and mechanisms that disregard, subjugate, and disempower individuals, groups, or classes. The intention of and the determination for resistance eventually overcome the fear of freedom.

The conscientization of Jim and Wayne follow the same formula in the film. They both lose a loved one directly related to Centabank and its practices. These losses change their relation to the world, the society they live in, and the norms they are expected to follow. Wayne's feeling of helplessness is portrayed throughout the film. Firstly, when he and his wife learn the reason why it is so difficult to find a solicitor to represent their case against the bank: because the majority of the solicitors are actually working for the bank on different cases and therefore there is a conflict of interest. This also shows the extent of influence of the bank over the legal system in general. Access to justice in dispute resolution, especially for the poor, is a significant problem. If paths to an appropriate court case are inaccessible or increasingly difficult to access[4], the disputes are often resolved by power and not rule of law. Meaning, the resources of opposing parties in a dispute determine the outcome. This, of course, adds to the perceived injustice felt by the losing party. As a result of Jim's perjury, the couple lose the court case, and the additional trauma of losing their business and the tragic death of their son is understandably intensified. In this context, Wayne's desire to force the bank to admit its wrongdoing is naïve, and in the banking world there is no room for naïveté. Connolly, therefore, portrays a couple becoming conscious of an economic and a legal system working together to create a burning injustice that these systems were supposed to alleviate or remove altogether in the first place.

Jim's conscientization is a bit more ambiguous. The film does not clearly show when and how his awareness of social power imbalances came to be. While it is somewhat safe to say that it is deeply rooted in his childhood trauma, this awareness is further verified and strengthened by his interactions with Simon. Simon's condescending and arrogant behaviour towards him is best portrayed during the scene where he mocks Jim's liberal views due to his naïve wish to use the formula for the benefit of the society.

It is, therefore, no surprise that Jim, after being traumatised by his father's suicide years ago and after witnessing the real inner mechanisms of Centabank in the present, wants to bring an absolute end to the existence of a financial institution that brought death and destruction to the lives of ordinary people through its daily activities. In other words, the anger at the death of his father is played out in his desire to 'murder' the patriarchal bank. His awakening, or rather conscientization, starts with the death of his father and reaches its zenith with his interactions with Simon and Wayne. To achieve his sense of justice, he lets his inner turmoil, destruction, and chaos out by formulating and executing his plan carefully to make the bank collapse. In a way, two chaotic worlds overlap: his world filled with grief and loss, and the world of the stock market. However, this time the unpredictability of an individual, like a butterfly effect, creates the perfect storm and brings universal balance, like a divine intervention, to the earthly domain, affecting both the individual and society in general. In other words, Jim steps outside the law by being consumed by grief, and, by adding his inner anarchy into the chaotic and unjust world of global finance, he manifests his sense of order and fairness, just like an alchemist creating gold.

The multidimensional links between loss and justice, chaos and order are mirrored by a similar dual but contrasting arrangement in the film. Even though their paths bring them together momentarily, the grief journeys of Jim and Wayne depict two different men expressing their loss and coming to terms with their loss in two different ways. The next section will look into this contrast and the varieties of grief.

6.2 The gravity of revenge – embitterment

The complex attachment and mourning processes of individuals have been well-documented and analysed, and become the backbone of many grief theories to this day. While the story of *The Bank* mainly focuses on the greed and the corruption of a financial institution, the opposing force to that corruption finds it roots and focuses on the losses of two individuals: Wayne and Jim. In order to develop this perspective, Connolly shows four deaths in these converging storylines: one real death in the present (Wayne's storyline), one real death in the past, and one symbolic death in the present (Jim's storyline). The combined consequence of these deaths then brings the figurative death of Centabank.

The grief journey of Wayne starts with the death of his son, Roger (Joshua Jay). While Roger's death affects Wayne and his wife Diane[5] (Mandy McElhinney) as a couple, Connolly takes Wayne's response further and depicts it as an antithesis to Jim's response. The way Wayne deals with Roger's death follows a certain trajectory: from a depressive state to murderous aggressiveness, and finally to a painful and difficult acceptance. There are three key scenes that overlap with this story arc. The first scene is where Diane and Wayne meet their solicitor Stephen O'Connor (Mitchell Butel) for the first time. In this scene (35:02), Wayne is distant, quiet, sad, and not engaged with the conversation. His puffy eyes, red face, and lack of body language highlight his depressive state further. In the second scene, Wayne is in the courtroom. After the false testimony of Jim, he cannot contain his emotions anymore and calls Jim a liar with visible and bubbling anger. This anger continues to define Wayne's actions and becomes the main emotion behind his choice to go and kill Simon, especially triggered after seeing Simon on TV telling a reporter that the court case was 'a waste of time' (75:30) (*The Bank*, 2001). His aggressive instinct, his wish to destroy the person who he thinks is responsible for Roger's death, makes him step outside the law. In the third scene, where Simon confronts Wayne with the reality and consequences of his choice, his rage dissolves into an agonising acknowledgement of the situation.

According to Parkes and Prigerson (2010), blaming and the expressing of irritability are common in bereaved people, because the loss is perceived as a harmful attack that needs to be named and blamed. In Wayne's situation, there is an added complexity. He considers Simon as the lawbreaker and the murderer of Roger. In other words, Wayne sees Roger's death as manslaughter, and not as a tragic accident or suicide.[6] This fuels his anger and leads to his attempt to kill Simon in order to avenge Roger's untimely death. The role Wayne plays within the main cause and effect narrative of the film and his psychological state are supported by research into the grief reactions of parents of murdered children. Wickie and Marwit (2000) argue that parents whose children are murdered are forced to deal with a multitude of stressors: such as the breakdown of societal rules and bonds, which they once thought were protecting them; deep anger towards the criminal; feelings of powerlessness; and re-traumatisation due to police investigation and court cases. In short, these parents' perception of the world shifts from joy to misery.

Seeing Simon as the main criminal, having been let down and discarded by the justice system, and being ridiculed by Simon on TV, Wayne unleashes his anger, helplessness, and anguish in an intense, confrontational scene. Even though Simon tries to turn the situation around by offering Wayne cash several times, he makes it clear that he is not particularly scared by the death threat; in fact, he is increasingly annoyed by the grieving man in front of him who neither goes ahead and kills him nor lets him warn his colleagues about Jim's plan. In other words, Simon's sense and position of power does not shift. This leads to an interesting and brutal reality check for Wayne (85:44) where Simon describes Wayne's irresponsible and irrational position:

WAYNE: [...] This is his picture.
SIMON: Look... .it's Wayne, isn't it? This is all very touching but...
WAYNE: Look at it... .I want you to look at him... .It's beautiful, isn't he?
SIMON: Yeah, he's a doll.
WAYNE: Oh, you're fucking dead!
SIMON: Nothing, there's nothing you can do to make me give a fuck! Do you understand that? Nothing! Nothing you can do to turn your situation around! Because he is gone! Do you understand that? Your son is gone! And if I could bring him back I would! If there was something I could do I would do it, but I cannot! You cannot! You will die with this fucking misery in your heart. Now, your killing me would just put you in prison for the next twenty years, hurt your wife, fuck up the rest of your life as humanly as possible. Now, I just want to make a phone call. After that, you can beat me, barbecue me, fuck me up the ass, I don't give a shit, just let me make that call.

(*The Bank*, 2001)

It is only after this cruel but factual explanation that Wayne realises his impossible situation. Killing Simon would not only not bring back Roger in any way, but also not help him heal, as things would become much worse because his life would be completely derailed. In a matter of a few seconds, Simon makes Wayne understand how much he has gone inside himself and how much further he is about to go outside the law. As Wayne slowly acknowledges his grim reality, his rage slowly fades away and he leaves Simon's mansion without killing him. Connolly does not give any more clues on how Wayne finds his inner strength to let go, but in the very last scene of the film he is shown smiling with Diane who is now pregnant, clearly indicating that he has chosen to rebuild a new life while moving on from the horrors of his past.

In Jungian terms, Wayne had a clear encounter with his 'shadow'. Described by Jung as the dark side of one's personality (CW 16, para.470), shadow is a term for the negative qualities in the psyche that are repressed and hidden from others. Being pushed to his limits by events and people beyond his control, Wayne unleashes his shadow in a state of rage. Jung describes this state as shadow possession (CW 9i, para.222) which compels one to be confrontational, hostile, and destructive. Wayne's emotionally bruising encounter with Simon, therefore, disrupts this possession. It brings his rationality back as he, in a matter of a few minutes, comes to terms with the death of his son, his wish to kill and the consequences of acting on this wish. In a weird twist of fate, Simon actually not only helps Wayne to become aware of his shadow but also to break free from its short but compulsive hold.

The concept of shadow and shadow possession certainly plays a part in Jim's narrative arc as well, especially in terms of his unwavering, cold-blooded passion to avenge his father and destroy the bank. But what is more interesting about Jim is that he portrays an intriguing example of a fusion with *persona*. Originally used to describe the mask that actors used on stage, persona, according to Jung, is the main personality people present to others. It is the 'I' that is visible in social interactions. Jung sees persona as an outer shell, a mechanism to adapt to the world (CW 6, para.801) which is ultimately fake but perceived as genuine both by oneself and the others (CW 9i, para.221).

Connolly keeps the information on Jim as a persona hidden until the climax of the film. While Wayne confronts his shadow and Simon, Michelle discovers not only that Jim Doyle is an invented/adopted persona but also that his real name is Paul Jackson. These revelations are presented in a three-way drama that unfolds in three different locations, but most importantly on three different timelines. Just before Jim hits enter on his keyboard and starts the live deployment of his formula on Centabank's mainframe, which is connected to the world markets, he remembers (as young Paul) coming back from school and finding his father dead. In this scene everything comes together for Jim in one singular moment where Connolly depicts a complex, multi-layered destruction: the death of Jim's father; the destruction of the bank that drove Jim's father to death; and the elimination of any future for Jim under the name of Jim Doyle, namely the destruction of his persona, his symbolic death.

The main impetus behind the creation of the persona called Jim Doyle lies in the suicide of Paul's father, David Jackson, 24 years ago. Conveyed briefly through the newspaper articles Michelle looks at, this information reveals the length of suffering Jim/Paul has gone through. Traumatic loss that stays silent, undiscovered, and unresolved is common among people who are bereaved by suicide. Stepakoff (2009) argues that the silence around trauma needs to be broken if people want to heal. Referring to the influential book of Christopher Lukas and Henry Seiden called *Silent Grief*, she describes how survivors of suicide stay quiet about their pain due to the fear of becoming an outcast. For these survivors, giving a form or a voice to that pain is essential for recovery:

> In order for healing to occur, it is necessary for the bereaved to move from a state of formless anguish to one in which the pain can be symbolized or represented, either in words or in non-verbal media such as drawings, music, and dance. It is also necessary to move beyond self-imposed or socially enforced isolation into a state of meaningful contact with at least one other human being.
>
> (Ibid., p.105)

Throughout the film, Jim is portrayed as a quiet, distant, detached man, who is unable to display a warm, genuine, positive emotion. His cold demeanour and untrusting behaviour are often criticised by Michelle, who tries to break his icy shell to understand what is wrong. Coupled with his enigmatic and complex mathematical formula, Jim appears as a mystery, a closed box, which is a complete contrast to Wayne and Diane, who openly express their grief and loss.

Making the storyline this dense and multifaceted appears as Connolly's deliberate allusion to the chaos theory, or rather complex dynamic systems. However, it is not that difficult to understand the deterministic aspects of Jim's narrative arc. Traumatised by his father's suicide as a child, the only impetus behind his survival, the only restorative emotion to balance this feeling of loss seems to be revenge. This longing for vengeance and anarchy in him is so deep that it is impossible to pigeonhole it into a simple phase or stage in grief theory. However, it might be possible to name it. Linden and Maercker (2011) call it *embitterment* and argue that this psychological state is an explosive combination of frequent recollection of painful memories, despair, aggression, and deeply satisfying thoughts/plans of revenge.

Znoj (2011) goes a step further and develops a circumplex model of embitterment, which defines four outcomes of a major life experience. These are: 'depression'; 'aggression'; 'growth'; and 'embitterment'. He notes that individually perceived injustice can trigger embitterment, and this complex frame of mind is different to depression. While depressed people focus on their own perceived failures, embittered people are preoccupied with other individuals or events that caused their feelings of injustice. Therefore, retribution emerges as the only satisfying solution.

While embitterment is clearly a trigger for destruction, it is important to note that in Znoj's circumplex model he puts aggression, revolution, and violence in the 'optimism/hope for change' half of his circle. This suggests that embittered people can resort to violence or revolutionary acts when they think this act has the potential to generate a result for the better. Lynch (1965) defines hope as a basic understanding and feeling that there is a way out of difficulty and that there are solutions. Moreover, Lazarus (1999) defines hope as a belief that something positive, which is currently not present in one's life, could still materialise. Gäbler and Maercker (2011), on the other hand, describe revenge as a coping mechanism after a severe trauma, especially if it involves injustice and victimisation. They argue that vengeful feelings and thoughts can be considered as helpful and constructive because they reinstate hope, self-worth, and a sense of satisfaction in the individual.

In this sense, under Jim's cold, detached, misanthropic, mysterious, and revolutionary mathematician persona, which he constructed piece by piece over the years, lies a severely traumatised child seeking his own perfect, individual justice. In order to achieve this state of complete fairness, he is not even afraid to sacrifice his own career and future. Connolly makes an interesting juxtaposition here. His two characters, scarred and motivated by grief, make two different choices. As Wayne realises what he can lose and how he can make his life more difficult by killing Simon, he stops and lets go. Jim, on the other hand, embraces destruction as a way to restore his missing and timeless inner equilibrium. As the bank goes under within a few seconds, Jim is at the epicentre like a conduit between heaven and earth, delivering cosmic justice that is beyond time and space to a system, to an institution, and to a group of people that ruined many lives, both in the past and in the present. Just like in the infinity symbol he keeps drawing, two different worlds overlap and interact. Jim puts his own inner chaos into the mix in order to give the perfect adjustment to a system that is designed to steal from people.

The symbolic content regarding the infinity symbol, x–y axis, numbers, and their connections in mysticism, therefore, is not random but a methodical underlying narrative throughout the film, which gives *The Bank* a rather mythical, larger-than-life feeling. They are the same symbols that hold further clues into the dynamics of Jim's story from trauma to liberation. The next section will focus on this journey and its strong ties with psychological relief, completion, and healing from a Jungian perspective.

6.3 Healthy innate variability

Jim's complex mathematical formula is never fully explained in the film, partly because it is fictitious. However, its roots in chaos theory are repeatedly mentioned either in conversations in several scenes or visually in fractal imagery. A fractal is a shape that is recursively constructed or self-similar. In other words, its patterns recur at progressively smaller scales and is therefore often described as infinitely complex. Mandelbrot spotted a common thread in complex shapes such as clouds, coastlines, and Romanesco broccoli. By showing how visual complexity can be created from simple rules, he proposed his theory that things typically considered to be chaotic actually have an inherent order. In Jim's case, in order to heal his grief and avenge his father, he creates his very own and both individually and socially satisfying order, in other words justice, out of a seemingly complex and chaotic system of numbers.

Pythagoreans believed that numbers were the basis of the harmonic laws of the universe. In that sense, they were the building blocks and the symbols of divine order. Biedermann (1996) argues that our lives are governed by numbers, from the simple notes of music to the laws of the universe. This mathematical basis rules every form, therefore our experiences in life, no matter how complex, can be analysed through numbers and their harmonic interaction with each other.

The belief that numbers not only represent quantities but also notions is replicated in several religions and thought systems throughout the centuries, which contributed to the idea that numerology was mystical. The Greek pantheon of twelve gods, the Chinese concepts of Yin and Yang and I Ching, the sacred notion of the Holy Trinity and the Ten Commandments in Christianity, and the Jewish spiritual system Kabbalah are all examples of the recurring and inherent mysticism and symbolism associated with numbers. Similarly, with the discovery of cosmic cycles through astronomy, the numerical patterns of the heavens have contributed to the belief that numbers are actually the earthly manifestations of cosmic forces beyond human control summarised in the aphorism 'as above so below'.[7]

The references to numerical mysticism and symbolism in *The Bank* are multi-layered. The main visual references appear in the following scenes: after the opening credits where Jim is doing calculations (04:36); the first restaurant scene where Jim describes his formula to Simon via a drawing on the table-cloth (11:29); the second restaurant scene where Jim is about to perfect his formula on his own, again by drawing on the tablecloth (34:57); and the scene when Centabank goes under. In these scenes, two specific symbols keep reappearing: the mathematical symbol of infinity (∞); and the x-y axis which appears as a cross (+).

Representing spatial orientation in two dimensions, a cross represents much more than its powerful symbolism in Christianity, which links punishment, execution, and the Resurrection of the Christ with eternal life and victory over death. According to Champeaux and Sterckx (1966), the cross is also one of the four basic symbols[8] and it acts as a link between Heaven and Earth, time and space, universe and man.

Furthermore, the infinity symbol (lemniscate), is a number eight on its side, and the rich symbolism of number eight casts a light on Jim's hidden intentions and anarchic intervention at the bank.[9] Chevalier and Gheerbrant (1996a) summarise the symbolism of this number as cosmic balance. Composed of two overlapping circles, it represents the perfect harmony of Heaven and Earth. Across several cultural contexts, the number eight also appears: in the I Ching, as the trigram *Tui*, which it gives the attributes of pleased satisfaction (Van Over, 1971); in Dogon culture, as the last primal ancestor who represented the word, speech, and the Genius who sacrificed himself in order to guarantee the regeneration of the human race (Griaule, 1965); and in Christianity, as the Resurrection of the Christ and the rise of a heavenly state out of the horrors and tragedies of Calvary. In the traditional Marseilles Tarot deck, the eighth card appears as Justice[10] and is traditionally represented with scales, symbolising the upcoming or necessarily required balance of the material and mental worlds of the querent. Hopking (2001), while looking at Lurianic Kabbalah and the ten stages of the consciousness of Adam Kadmon, ties the archetypal eight with one of the Ten Commandments: *thou shalt not steal.*

In addition to all these symbols in the film, there is also a symbolic death: the death of Jim Doyle's persona and the emergence of the real identity behind it, Paul Jackson. This is a good example of a key component of Jung's thinking. This component is called sacrifice. Samuels, Shorter, and Plaut (2005, p.132) refer to Jung's writings and argue that sacrifice is an important factor in the development and healing of the human psyche. All individuals, at some point in their lives, are required to part with something, anything, in order to move forward and to heal:

> Sacrifice, literal or symbolic, bodily or financial, is necessary for healing – nothing is gained unless something is given up.
>
> (Ibid., p.65)

In order to understand the connection between sacrifice and healing, losing and gaining, it is important to remember Jim Doyle's storyline here. Twenty-four years ago, he lost his father to suicide. Sometime within this period he changed his name and studied mathematics, earned his doctorate, and built a life and a career around this assumed name and social position. However, he builds this life and persona as a smokescreen, to hide his real intention, which is to destroy Centabank. Straight after achieving this, he leaves the country using his soon-to-be-expired passport, which bears his real identity as Paul Jackson. In other words, he resumes his real self, which was put on hold and was hidden for 24 years. He sacrifices his persona (and everything related to it) to avenge his father, but gains satisfaction from this revenge and the freedom to be his authentic self once more.

James Hollis describes this as the 'Middle Passage', the period of one's life when the provisional personality formed during childhood is discarded in order to achieve individuation, the process of one's personality becoming a coherent and distinct whole. Hollis notes that, based on the bonds with parents, children assume that the world will relate to them in the same way and this assumption forms the basis of a core concept, namely trust. Furthermore, the way the parents deal with life's challenges is internalised by children as fixed perspectives in the perception of life and the world. Feelings of abandonment or traumatic experiences lead the way to a distorted view of the world, which forms the basis of neurotic behaviour. This Middle Passage, therefore, is where people let go of their acquired but limited standpoint in life and move to a more open and fuller version of themselves:

> The conscious experience of the Middle Passage requires separating who we are from the sum of the experiences we have internalised. Our thinking then moves from magical to heroic to human.[1]
>
> (Hollis, 1993, p.116)

As a child bereaved by suicide, Jim has internalised one unshakable perspective: the world is an unfair place marred with pain and destruction. Coupled with feelings of deep abandonment, his mistrust of other people who try to befriend him like Michelle fuels his reclusive and detached behavior, as depicted throughout the film. In addition to this, conscientization and embitterment solidify his persona. Such profound and chaotic resentments harboured in one's psyche for so many years would demand an equally powerful release: a chaos unleashed unto the financial institution that is the main source of all this. Van Eenwyk (1997) argues that the emerging chaos theory has identified self-regulatory patterns in what seems like entropic chaos, and these patterns are reminiscent of Karma. In other words, given enough time, stability and order emerge out of chaos, and this new order seems to belong in a bigger, self-organising dynamic system, which cannot be fully understood by limited

---

1 *The Middle Passage: From Misery to Meaning in Midlife,* James Hollis, published by Inner City Books.

human thinking. Fate, Karma, or chance may not be that random and they might simply be deterministic chaos.

Jim's grief, revenge and yearning for a relief is the deterministic chaos which not only destroys but builds a new order and brings stability to him. While it does not make much sense to Michelle when it is revealed to her during the airport scene where Jim is about to board a plane and leave Australia, it is the pattern which Jim has been seeing in numbers, formulas, and equations.

This pattern is condensed in three symbols that are repeatedly shown in the film: the infinity symbol/number eight, the cross/x-y axis, and Mandelbrot fractals. Jung argues that symbols are ultimately images but their meanings hugely transcend their contents. In *Symbols of Transformation* (CW 5), he describes how a symbol can make one's ego roam from consciousness to the unconscious and back to the consciousness. In other words, symbols have the power to transform perspectives (CW 5, para.344).

In Jim's case, these three symbols hold the key to his healing as all of them converge in one singular point of meaning: order. Jim's longing and search for meaning (and order) does not only include order in numbers, formulas, or patterns in the universe, but also transcends space and time to reach his traumatised self, waiting for a sense of justice, an adjustment to right a wrong. Fitting within the description of Hollis's Middle Passage, Paul's magical thinking as a child develops into a heroic act in the future, which paves the way for his individuation as a human with the sacrifice of his fake identity as Jim Doyle. There are two levels of symbolic travel here. On one level, young Paul travels to the future[11], his future, and disrupts the present. On the other level, these symbols help Paul's ego to cross from consciousness to the unconscious and back to the consciousness. After transforming his perspective that the world can include a sense of healing and completion, and after sacrificing his persona, he gains his personal justice and freedom to be himself once more.

The allegory of cosmic balance within the image of the infinity symbol (overlapping of two circles) is also an allegory of the separation and union that happens within one's psyche. Edinger's (1992) theory on ego-Self axis looks closely at this fundamental psychological development. Based on Jung's view that the Self is the archetypal wholeness, Edinger defined ego as the *subjective identity* (centre of conscious personality) and the Self as *objective identity* (centre of total psyche). He argued that throughout life people go through cycles of separation and union between these two identities, and produced four diagrams to illustrate his point. In these diagrams Edinger shows that the subjective identities go through a journey, starting with being one with the Self (meaning a merging of ego and the Self), and ending with a complete separation from the Self (meaning a full awareness of the ego-Self axis). His last diagram not only visually suggests the numerical symbol of eight, but also symbolises an ideal place between separation and union where these two identities form a harmonic balance.

Jim's storyline in the film never deviates from Edinger's last diagram until the persona/ego is sacrificed. He is not only aware of his own self as Paul Jackson but also aware of his subjective identity as Jim because it is his conscious creation. It is only at the end of the film, as he returns to his authentic identity, he also returns to his original archetypal wholeness. Similar to the theory of deterministic chaos, his ego–Self dynamic becomes unsustainable and unstable. However, out of disorder, chaos and destruction, a new order, the order he needs emerges. His individuation and healing mean the merging of ego and the Self, taking Paul back to his childhood where his psychological development was interrupted by his father's suicide.

Hopcke (1999), quoting Jung, argues that the merging of ego and the Self would trigger inflation in one's psyche, namely the emergence of exhibitionist grandiosity and the egomaniac. However, there is also an absence of an egoist, selfish behaviour in the film, and it is depicted in the very last scene. Connolly reveals that Jim, as an act of kindness, generosity, and apology, has redistributed some of Centabank's cash and put nearly a million dollars in Wayne and Diane Davis's account so that they can start a new life again. This act can also be read as the kindness and compassion Jim did not receive following his father's death. As Jim assumes the role of wounded healer for the couple, he also does something very unique: he symbolically re-writes his feelings of helplessness by helping another person, and therefore unlocks another part of self-healing.

Van Eenwyk (1997, p.166) calls these whole paradoxical and conflicting states of being as *the archetypal chaos of survival*[2], named after Jung's idea that the disorderly psychodynamics of symbols could lead to healthy growth. Quoting research into the healthy rhythms of the human body, he argues that chaotic health readings of patients might actually suggest that the body is more adaptable to shocks. He calls this inner chaos 'healthy innate variability':

> Research into EKG and EEG patterns suggests that chaotic patterns provide 'a healthy variability that allows the organ to respond quickly to a variety of stimuli'. Systems lose their capacity to respond to new situations when they are limited to regular patterns that never vary. The greater the diversity of available responses to changes, the greater the potential to survive the unexpected. Thus, 'a healthy psychological system has a certain amount of innate variability.[3]
>
> (Ibid., p.166)

It is this interesting take on grief, chaos, and healing that makes *The Bank* an engrossing film. Even though Connolly's main motivation is to make a political statement with his story, his converging storylines reveal an uncalculated, unplanned, and surprising insight into the notion of grief and the places people can go to in order to find healing and completion. His poetic justice delivered on the big screen might be satisfying for some as he destroys with one hand

---

2 *Archetypes and Strange Attractors: The Chaotic World of Symbols*, John R. Van Eenwyk, published by Inner City Books.

3 *Archetypes and Strange Attractors: The Chaotic World of Symbols*, John R. Van Eenwyk, published by Inner City Books.

what he believes as to be 'Public Enemy No: 1'.[12] However, he also restores order for people like Jim and Wayne, where corporate greed and the predictability of stock markets are beaten by the unpredictability of individuals, and where, even though in an alternate fictitious universe, David beats Goliath.

6.4 From destruction to reconstruction

The Bank depicts a thought-provoking example of an intrapsychic tomb. Similar to Chris Kelvin and Erica Bain, Jim Doyle neither allows himself to mourn nor fully accepts love and compassion (which Michelle tries to show him). Trapped in his crypt, he only operates within the limits of his fake persona, which is basically a modern-day trojan horse created to destroy Centabank from within. However, just like Chris and Erica, Jim is aware of what he is doing and what the consequences are. It is not a blind, unconscious choice.

Traumatic loss changes people completely. The unverbalised, unexpressed suffering and longing may lead them to choices and actions they never thought they were capable of doing. Suicide, murder, or anarchic behaviour are all shocking to other people, but not for these sufferers, as these people have crossed a line internally due to their trauma. Their choices, no matter how destructive, are always connected to the person they have loved and lost.

The next chapter explores this connection under a new light. I now – slightly – move away from the dark aspects of the psyche towards choices that not only let bereaved people walk out of their crypts, but also help them to repair the emotional damage they have suffered. The first choice explores letting someone into the crypt unintentionally. My query now is this: can the pain of a traumatic loss be soothed by connecting to another human being?

Discography

The Bank – Original Motion Picture Soundtrack (2001) Composed by A. John [Audio CD]. Australian Broadcasting Corporation Classics.

Filmography

The Bad Sleep Well (*Warui yatsu hodo yoku nemuru*) (1960) Directed by A. Kurosawa [film]. Japan
The Bank (2001) Directed by R. Connolly [film]. Australia
The Big Short (2015) Directed by A. McKay [film]. USA
Enron: The Smartest Guys in the Room (2005) Directed by A. Gibney [film]. USA
The Laundromat (2019) Directed by S. Soderbergh [film]. USA | Netflix
Margin Call (2011) Directed by J.C. Chandor [film]. USA
Pi: Faith in Chaos (1998) Directed by D. Aranofsky [film]. USA
Solaris (2002) Directed by S. Soderbergh [film]. USA
Trading Places (1983) Directed by J. Landis [film]. USA
Wall Street (1987) Directed by O. Stone [film]. USA
The Wolf of Wall Street (2013) Directed by M. Scorsese [film]. USA

Notes

1 The idea of using numbers and higher mathematics to predict patterns in life, like smaller ones of the stock market or the bigger patterns of creation within the universe, is also used in the film *Pi: Faith in Chaos* (1998).

2 A recent example would be *The Laundromat* (2019), which looks at the Panama Papers leak, and the corrupt links between law firms and wealthy individuals. Interestingly, the film portrays a grieving widow discovering this corruption while trying to find justice for her dead husband. The film's promotional poster also exhibits a piggy bank.

3 Saul argues that when people conform to corporatism, they eventually give up their rights as citizens in democratic societies. Giving up results in the abandonment of the public good in the pursuit of self-serving actions.

4 Apart from the reality of high legal fees, there are new hurdles in the way. For example, the frequent use of compulsory arbitration (Sternlight, 2005) and how the right to a jury trial is derailed by new legal processes before the case can come to court (Kaufman and Wunderlich, 2012) is a growing research topic.

5 There is an additional contrast between how Diane and Wayne are depicted in terms of their stages of grief (Depression and Anger). While Diane acts rationally and calmly, chooses to pursue legal action, and tries to find closure within the justice system at the beginning, Wayne is portrayed mainly as silent and despondent, following Diane's lead. When the court case is lost, their roles are reversed dramatically as Wayne turns into a homicidal man pouring out his anger, while Diane stays at home crying helplessly. The way female and male characters respond differently to death and loss is also another angle of the film which requires further analysis, but not within the scope of this one.

6 The film does not dwell on the nature of suicidal ideation, but actually hints that Roger may have killed himself in order to protect his parents. The hint is buried in the soundtrack. Alan John, the composer of the soundtrack, uses the same music (Lacrimosa) in two different scenes. The first scene is where Roger's dead body is found in the river. The second scene is where young Jim finds his father's dead body hanging in the barn. Even though Connolly does not directly say or show that Roger killed himself, suicidal ideation in children is not uncommon in real life. Mishara (1999) found out that children aged between 6 and 12 can have a perfect understanding of what suicide is. Sheftall et al. (2016) also did an interesting research on children (ages 5 to 11) and young adolescents (ages 12 to 14) who killed themselves.

7 This phrase can also be found in the New Testament, specifically in the tenth verse of the sixth chapter of the Gospel of Matthew, and appears in the King James version of the Bible: 'Thy kingdom come, thy will be done in earth, as it is in heaven'.

8 The other three are: the centre; the circle; and the square.

9 Connolly has used the symbolism of eight in another layer of the film as well: its soundtrack. Alan John, the composer, has specifically written an eight-note motif for the opening credits, which plays at four different tempos all at the same time, as a nod to the infinitely recursive nature of Mandelbrot fractals (*The Bank – Original Motion Picture Soundtrack*, 2001).

10 In the deck of Aleister Crowley, the word justice is replaced with adjustment. The Adjustment card features the Egyptian goddess Maat, the goddess of Law, Truth and Justice. Maat played a vital part in the judgement of the dead (Arrien, 1987).

11   This symbolic time travel's direction can be interpreted in a different way as well. It can be argued that the adult Paul goes back in time to heal his childhood self. This type of quantum level meetings with one's own self in different time periods is used in other films as well. A different one happens in *Solaris* (2002) where Chris Kelvin arrives at a junction in time where he understands his past, present, and future timelines in a singular moment.

12   This explosively political tagline was used, maybe in an unashamed and humorous way, in the promotional posters and TV spots of the film when it was released.

Bibliography

Abraham, N. and Torok, M. (1994) *The Shell and the Kernel: Renewals of Psychoanalysis. Volume I*. Chicago: University of Chicago Press.

Arrien, A. (1987) *The Tarot Handbook: Practical Applications of Ancient Visual Symbols*. London: The Aquarian Press.

Biedermann, H. (1996) 'Numbers' in *The Wordsworth Dictionary of Symbolism*. Hertfordshire: Wordsworth Editions.

Champeaux, G. de and Sterckx, D. (1966) *Introduction au monde des symboles*. Paris: Zodiaque.

Chevalier, J. and Gheerbrant, A. (1996a) 'Eight' in *The Penguin Dictionary of Symbols*. London: Penguin.

Chevalier, J. and Gheerbrant, A. (1996b) 'Pig' in *The Penguin Dictionary of Symbols*. London: Penguin.

Connolly, R. (2001) Interview with Robert Connolly, *Writer/Director of* The Bank. The Movie Show Episode 24 2001. Available at: www.sbs.com.au/nitv/video/1167 9299903/The-Bank-Robert-Connolly-interview

Cordaiy, H. (2001) Big Guys Versus the People: An Interview with Robert Connolly. Available at: https://theeducationshop.com.au/downloads/metro-and-screen-education-articles/metro-articles/big-guys-versus-the-people-an-interview-with-robert-connolly

Edinger, E.F. (1992) *Ego and Archetype: Individuation and the Religious Function of the Psyche*. Boston: Shambhala.

Freire, P. (1970) *Pedagogy of the Oppressed*. New York: Continuum.

Gäbler, I. and Maercker, A. (2011) 'Revenge after trauma: Theoretical outline' in Linden, M. and Maercker, A. (eds.) *Embitterment: Societal, Psychological, and Clinical Perspectives*. Vienna: Springer, pp. 42–69.

Goulart, R. (1970) *The Assault on Childhood*. London: Victor Gollancz.

Griaule, M. (1965) *Conversations with Ogotommeli*. London: Oxford University Press.

Hollis, J. (1993) *The Middle Passage: From Misery to Meaning in Midlife*. Toronto: Inner City Books.

Hopcke, R.H. (1999) *A Guided Tour of the Collected Works of C. G. Jung*. Boston: Shambala.

Hopking, C.J.M. (2001) *The Practical Kabbalah Guidebook*. Devon: Godsfield Press.

Jung, C.G. (1967) *The Collected Works of C.G. Jung, Volume 5: Symbols of Transformation*. Princeton: Princeton University Press.

Jung, C.G. (1971) *The Collected Works of C.G. Jung, Volume 6: Psychological Types*. Princeton: Princeton University Press.

Jung, C.G. (1966) *The Collected Works of C.G. Jung, Volume 16: Practice of Psychotherapy*. Princeton: Princeton University Press.

Jung, C.G. (1969) *The Collected Works of C.G. Jung, Volume 9, Part 1: Archetypes and the Collective Unconscious*. Princeton: Princeton University Press.

Kaufman, M.J. and Wunderlich, J.M. (2012) 'Access to justice: Investor suits in the era of the Roberts court', *Law and Contemporary Problems*, 75(1), pp.55–91.

Klein, N. (1999) *No Logo*. London: Picador.

Lawrence, D.H. (2000) 'The Ladybird' in *The Complete Short Novels*. London: Penguin.

Lazarus R.S. (1999) 'Hope: An emotion and a vital coping resource against despair', *Social Research*, 66(2), pp.653–678.

Linden, M. and Maercker, A. (eds.) (2011) *Embitterment: Societal, Psychological, and Clinical Perspectives*. Vienna: Springer.

Lynch W.F. (1965) *Images of Hope: Imagination as Healer of the Hopeless*. Baltimore: Helicon.

Mishara, B.L. (1999) 'Conceptions of death and suicide in children ages 6–12 and their implications for suicide prevention', *Suicide and Life-Threatening Behavior*, 29, pp.105–118.

Parkes, C.M. and Prigerson, H.G. (2010) *Bereavement: Studies of Grief in Adult Life*. 4th ed. London: Penguin.

Proudhon, P.J. (1876) *What Is Property? First Memoir: An Inquiry into the Principle of Right and of Government*. Princeton, MA: Ben J.R. Tucker.

Samuels, A., Shorter, B., and Plaut, F. (2005) *A Critical Dictionary of Jungian Analysis*. London: Routledge.

Saul, J.R. (1997) *The Unconscious Civilization*. New York: The Free Press.

Sheftall, A.H., Asti L, Horowitz L.M., Felts, A., Fontanella, C.A., Campo, J.V., and Bridge, J.A. (2016) 'Suicide in elementary school-aged children and early adolescents', *Pediatrics*, 138(4): e20160436.

Stepakoff, S. (2009) 'From destruction to creation, from silence to speech: Poetry therapy principles and practices for working with suicide grief', *The Arts in Psychotherapy*, 36, pp.105–113.

Sternlight, J.R. (2005) 'Creeping mandatory arbitration: Is it just?', *Stanford Law Review*, 57(5), pp.1631–1675.

Trifonas, P.P. (2018) '*Pedagogy of the Oppressed*: 50 years in review of education', *Pedagogy, and Cultural Studies*, 40(5), pp.367–370.

Van Eenwyk, J.R. (1997) *Archetypes and Strange Attractors: The Chaotic World of Symbols*. Toronto: Inner City Books.

Van Over, R. (1971) *I Ching*. New York: Mentor.

Wickie, S.K. and Marwit, S.J. (2000) 'Assumptive world views and the grief reactions of parents of murdered children', *OMEGA – Journal of Death and Dying*, 42(2), pp.101–113.

Znoj, H. (2011) 'Embitterment – a larger perspective on a forgotten emotion', in Linden, M. and Maercker, A. (eds.) *Embitterment: Societal, Psychological, and Clinical Perspectives*. Vienna: Springer, pp.5–16.

7 Human connection and
A Single Man

Christopher Isherwood's well-known 1964 novel *A Single Man* is an interesting meditation on traumatic loss, the difficulties of being and staying alive after loss, and the unexpected beauty which life can bring into the lives of trauma survivors. The novel had a reprint in 2010 (Isherwood, 2010). In this edition there is a short introduction by Tom Ford, who directed the film adaptation *A Single Man* (2009) and co-wrote the screenplay with David Scearce. In this introduction, Ford describes the gist of Isherwood's novel as human connection: a connection that defines every individual's life, a bond which can be painful, beautiful, and sometimes both. He speaks about his personal fascination with the author and how Isherwood's original description of a man who lost his way in life charmed him to tell the story in the cinematic medium.

Ford describes himself as a commercial fashion designer and he personally does not consider fashion an art (Feitelberg, 2012). However, seeking a new perfection in fashion, he created his luxury brand in an industry which is passionate about clothing, shoes, makeup, accessories, hairstyle, body, beauty, and youth. In the same introduction, he candidly speaks about his inner crisis during his late forties and how re-reading Isherwood's words convinced him to try his hand at a new artistic medium. In this sense, his unexpected dive into cinematography and motion picture storytelling seems to run parallel to the film's main character's feelings of disconnectedness and alienation within his environment.

Both the novel and the film depict a single day of an English professor called George Falconer (Colin Firth). George, having suddenly lost his partner Jim (Matthew Goode) due to a car accident, is traumatically bereaved and having difficulty finding a reason to carry on living as a – now – single man. During this particular day in the film, George, feeling dead inside and having planned his suicide meticulously, makes his final arrangements to end his life only to decide not to go ahead with it at the last minute due to an unexpected connection with another human being, which makes him feel alive again.

The melancholic crypt described by Abraham and Torok (1994) is visible here. Just like Chris Kelvin, Erica Bain, and Jim Doyle, George is unable to move beyond the traumatic loss and is on the brink of a destructive act. Society's hatred towards same-sex relationships in the 1960s also contributes

DOI: 10.4324/9781003292630-10

to this suicidal behaviour. He is not only silenced but also forced to live an invisible life, making his love and now grief impossible to be expressed and acknowledged openly.

In order to analyse this delicate grief narrative of the film, I will first present a detailed description of scenes; then a theoretical context of disenfranchised grief will follow; and finally, the Jungian elements of healing woven through the film will be discussed.

7.1 From pain to beauty – a breakdown of the story

Ford has made a few changes to the original story. Even though the past time-line is not very clear in the novel, the film states that Jim died eight months ago. Jim's irregular and prickly relationship with a woman, indicating his bisexuality, is not present in the film. George's suicide planning and the subtle hint of impending heart trouble are introduced. Four new but short narratives are incorporated: the bank scene; India the dog scene; Carlos the escort scene; and the opening and the final scenes of kisses. Apart from these changes, the film is faithful to its source material. It, however, makes the novel remarkably richer by turning it into a genuine, realistic, accessible, and visually stunning human drama.

A Single Man opens with sweeping music and an underwater dream scene, and shows George slowly and uncontrollably sinking, naked and without air, unable to reach the surface. This representation of drowning becomes a recurring one throughout the film and is used as a juxtaposition whenever George is shown helpless and feels cut off from the real world. The reason for the feeling of drowning is revealed in the next scene as George slowly walks towards a car crash site in his dream. He finds his dead partner Jim lying in the snow, kisses him, and lies beside him as he wakes up suddenly in his bed with a despondent face. The high angle shot here highlights his vulnerability and weakness.

In the following scene, George narrates how it hurts to wake up, his cold realisation of his return to the real world and his grief as he slowly walks past the suicide letters addressed to different people and laid on the floor. As he dresses up for his last day at the university, he describes the process as 'Becoming George', which highlights the striking difference between his persona in society and the real man inside. This is strikingly similar to how Chris Kelvin in *Solaris* (2002) is depicted in his reaction to loss. These two kindred spirits share the same difficulty in adjusting to a seemingly empty and meaningless world after their significant losses. Their lives and existence, which used to be centred around a love they have lost forever, are now just faded, insignificant copies of their pasts.

This fading, or rather the diminishing of liveliness, is very much colour-coded throughout the film. Using filmstock and not a digital camera, Ford deliberately uses a filter to make the colours look washed-out, tired, and low-key. This method makes every object, clothing, make-up, and accessory look faded and tired. The result of this colour-coding is that it matches George's psyche[1] in terms of his dull, slow, and hopeless existence. He never wears a lively coloured item. His wardrobe as a character is composed of blacks, greys, and whites, denoting a lack of vivacity through the colour chart.

The colours, however, come back in a few scenes. Utilising his skills in fashion, Ford makes the colours pop or get warmer every time George notices something beautiful or is able to make a genuine human connection: first, at the university when he notices the beauty/attractiveness of the tennis players against a backdrop of a boring conversation about the Cuban missile crisis; second, when he realises (and openly acknowledges) briefly how one of his female assistants looks beautiful; third, when he catches one of his young students, namely Kenny Potter's (Nicholas Hault) gaze during the classroom scene, becomes aware of his allure, and later on talks to him on their way to the bookstore; fourth, when he briefly talks to his neighbour Susan (Ginnifer Goodwin) and her daughter Jennifer (Ryan Simpkins) at the bank; fifth, when he bumps into Carlos (Jon Kortajarena) and appreciates his brief companionship; sixth, when he kisses the fox terrier called India as she reminds him of Jim; seventh, when he is with Charley (Julianne Moore); and finally in the last half hour of the film when he is in Kenny's company.

The persistent absence of strong colours mirrors the invisibility of his trauma. Ironically, George is living in a house mainly made of glass both in the novel and in the film. His presence in and around the house is visible to neighbours, but his bereavement is completely hidden from them. After the Second World War, and at a time when the Cuban crisis is brewing, American society is far from ready to accept a love between two men. George, therefore, continues to mimic his old self in order to function, even though it is now pointless to imagine a new life without Jim.

The hidden antagonism towards homosexuality in this society is established at the beginning of the film while George is getting ready for work in the morning and slipping into his stoic George persona. The telephone rings and he is instantly thrown back in time when he remembers the call he received from Jim's cousin, Harold Ackerley (Jon Hamm – voice), eight months ago. Even though the conversation is civilised, Mr. Ackerley makes it very clear that George is not wanted at the funeral as the service is planned for the family only. Marginalised by society and forced to hide his love, George becomes trapped and unable to find a socially valid and acceptable channel to mourn. In other words, he becomes a textbook example of disenfranchised grief.

George's predicament is twofold. On the one hand, he has to deal with his socially invisible and unspeakable loss. On the other hand, and this is revealed through the dinner scene with Charley later on in the film, he is also struggling with the fact that his relationship with Jim had always been socially negated. Even his lifelong close friend is unable to see it as a real relationship, despite the fact she witnessed it daily. His anger and frustration about his love for Jim not being accepted even by his friend, coupled with his inability to mourn and show his grief in public, puts him in an impossible position, which he cannot escape. His suicide planning, therefore, becomes the only escape hatch to break through his miserable existence. He describes his situation in a tragic statement. He says he is no longer able to imagine his future in any way.

George's interaction with others and the outside world is also portrayed as problematic. His morning routine, and constant reminiscing, is frequently interrupted. His neighbours crowd his privacy and annoy him with their incessant chatter and noises coming across the garden. The insistent phone calls from Charley visibly overwhelm him and contribute to him feeling detached. His suicidal ideation is hinted at as he packs his bag for work, putting Aldous Huxley's novel *After Many a Summer*[2] and a gun in. He also thanks his maid Alva (Paulette Lamori) as a way of saying goodbye, leaving her surprised.

In the next scene, he drives to the campus in a slow-motion shot highlighting how slow and unbearable his existence has become. His life between the tick-tocks of the clock is not flowing at its original pace anymore. His walk through a stream of students coming his way also shows how there is almost no sensitivity left in him for others. He does not move or give way to anyone as he walks in a sharp straight line while people move and split.

The classroom scene highlights his conflicting emotions. While the students are making random and uninspired comments about Huxley's novel, the scene intercuts with him struggling under water, indicating his world-weariness and the sensation of drowning. Then comes his monologue about minorities and fear. He specifically steers away from speaking about homosexuals as a minority but clearly alludes to them in his description when he talks about how some minorities can go unnoticed, and how this invisibility can stoke greater fear in society. His speech about fear ends with an indirect confession about his own reality. Out of patience, and now tired and drowning in grief, he gives a list of his own fears: old age, loneliness, being inadequate and inept, and being ignored by everyone else.

George is so engrossed in his own thoughts and plans for his suicide attempt that he does not realise that Kenny is actually following him around the campus, somehow aware that something is off with his tutor. George then cleans his office, and later on empties his safety deposit box at the bank, continuing with his suicide preparations. The two key scenes where he holds the black-and-white photo of Jim and remembers how he confessed his love for him, and then the scene with India, the smooth fox terrier[3] of a random woman, which reminds him of Jim's dog that got lost after the accident, show how he is still clinging on to memories. These memories are important because they connect him to distant moments of love and happiness which do not exist anymore in his life. The bank scene also displays the hidden animosity towards gay people in the society, which is revealed through the conversation with Jennifer where she mentions how her father wants to destroy him (39:42).

The next scene with Carlos further highlights George's feelings of being trapped and isolated. Even though Carlos is portrayed as a handsome escort on the prowl for lucrative clients, his short but rather philosophical comments make George feel a bit shaken because they mean a lot more to him than they actually sound. He likens lovers to buses and he says it does not matter if one misses one bus, meaning there is always another one round the corner. He then says how some terrible things can be inherently beautiful too in their own way. When Carlos points out how George seems to need somebody to be fond of him, George looks unable to respond. He gets in his car and drives off.

The suicide attempts scene (51:11), which directly follows the interaction with Carlos, indicates that George's tolerance towards both the outside world and his internal anguish has diminished. Ford, however, unexpectedly delivers a rather comical portrayal of a suicidal failure, which lowers the tension of the film building up to that scene. It is unclear at this stage of the film whether George gives a break to his attempts to see his old friend Charley for the last time before he shoots his brains out or gives up on the idea of suicide completely. The answer is revealed towards the end of the dinner scene where George discloses his new year resolution: to let go of the past, entirely and forever.

The music for the suicide attempts scene, selected by George, gives more insight into his turbulent mind. Sung by Miriam Gauci, the aria 'Ebben? Ne andrò lontana' (Well, then? I'll go far away) is from the first act of the famous opera *La Wally* by Alfredo Catalani. The opera tells the story of Wally, a non-conformist young woman who falls in love with the son of her father's enemy. However, this love is doomed, and at the end she throws herself into an avalanche high in the Alps. Even though Wally's suicide comes at the end of the opera, this aria foreshadows her destiny as she refuses to marry the guy her father asks her to and admits she would rather face the snow in the Alps than get married.

Mirroring Wally, George refuses to live in constant mourning and dying seems much easier than his currently empty and purposeless existence. He does not have to pretend that he is a functioning member of society, he does not have to tolerate disengaged students and colleagues at the university, and he does not have to endure needy friends like Charley who openly discount his bond with Jim and see it as a substitute for a real love/relationship, which, according to her, could only happen between a man and a woman.

George's last stop in his plan before dying is to go back to the place where everything started with Jim. With a complete and full-blown colour flashback sequence, it is finally shown how the two met at a beach bar, which navy officers frequented right after the Second World War. Being discreet but making their reciprocal interest noticeable to each other, the two men make the most important and valuable human connection of their lives in public. George's visit is another sign that he is saying goodbye to the memories, things, and places of his past. This time, however, there awaits an unexpected turn of events for him. Even though the camera shifts to present time, Kenny's appearance at the bar does not make the colours fade. George's (inner) world maintains its lively connection to Kenny.

The conversation with Kenny reveals the predicament of George and the core of his depressed state. He candidly discloses his relationship with time: his past is a source of heartache; his present is full of struggle; and his future will certainly bring ruin. He is completely trapped in his current existence and no direction in time offers sweet relief. His survival in the present is plagued by the necessity of being invisible and not being appreciated by the people close to him. His past, marred by Jim's loss, is agonising to revisit. His future is ruled by impending death, either by natural causes or his suicide. There is absolutely nowhere to go.

George's recurrent feeling of drowning finds its real-life equivalent when he and Kenny go for a sudden skinny dip in the ocean (79:01). Both literally and symbolically, Kenny saves George from drowning/dying, first by dragging him out of the sea, and then by hiding the gun at George's house (89:44). Even though the film ends with George dying after a heart attack, it is clearly established that he had found his way out of his trapped state of hopelessness, which makes the finale bittersweet but optimistic.

A Single Man depicts a soul battling with traumatic loss delicately, with an exquisite attention to detail. In the next section of this chapter, I will explore the deep roots of George's unhappiness through the theory of disenfranchised grief that makes him socially invisible.

7.2 Social invisibility – disenfranchised grief of a single man

Coined by Doka (1989; 2002a) and later developed by Attig (2004), the term 'disenfranchised grief' generally refers to feelings of loss that are not socially accepted. Worden (2010) notes that society's rejection of the bond between two people (for example, if they have a secret affair) complicates the process for the bereaved. Folta and Deck (1976) argue that grief theories in general have a main supposition that a close relationship is only to be found between spouses or next of kin. With the expansion of research, however, the concept of disenfranchised grief has become an umbrella term for losses that are either difficult to detect or socially invisible. These losses appear on the periphery of social life and include: bereavement after a pet's death (Baydak, 2000); the grief of family members of inmates who are on death row (Jones and Beck, 2007); the mourning of nursing assistants (Anderson and Gaugler, 2006); and the loss of cultural identity of immigrants (Robinson, 2007).

In George's case, his internal struggle in coming to terms with Jim's death is also hampered by a pervasive social disapproval and devaluation, which contribute to his feelings of helplessness, mental and emotional anguish, and suicidal behaviour. The exogenous depression of Chris Kelvin in *Solaris* (2002) is not only mirrored but also become more severe in a multidimensional way. In Freudian terms, George has lost his *Eros* (Laplanche and Pontalis, 1988), his life instinct as a principle of cohesion and preservation. His current state bears no resemblance to his previous life with Jim. It is devoid of meaning, full of meaningless effort, and he has no reason left to hold things together. His day-to-day life only compares to a silent, invisible, and inescapable drowning.

Even though the phone conversation demonstrates Mr. Ackerley's concern towards George, his call with bad news only shows the extent of this good-will. His voice is flat, almost emotionless, and he utters no words of genuine sympathy. The reason behind the call is that he thought George should know, and that is where his concern ends. The exclusion of George from the family funeral is clearly stated and shows the antagonism of Jim's family towards his relationship with George. As their bond is socially unacceptable, there can be no need (or room) for George to visibly display what Jim meant to him.

Social exclusion and isolation upset what might have been a natural reaction to loss and can transform it into a pathological or 'complicated grief', which is included as a diagnosis in the DSM-5 (Shear et al., 2011). In order to create a clear description of disenfranchised grief, Doka (1989) named three key sources of origin. These are: the deprivation of social recognition of the grieved relationship; the lack of acknowledgement of the personal bereavement experience; and the absence of appreciating the mourning individual. In other words, disenfranchised grief is not only the simple result of a lack of recognition, but a multi-faceted response towards an intricate array of stressors.

The film and the novel add another source to Doka's list: the discounting of the grieved relationship by a loved one. Charley is shown as the only close friend and confidant available to George. It is also revealed that the pair had a romantic and sexual affair in the past, but it did not last, and they chose to stay as friends. Charley became the sole witness of George's outpouring of grief, especially after Mr. Ackerley's call. Therefore, she is the only person alive who both witnessed George and Jim's relationship and the aftermath of Jim's death.

The dinner scene is the only scene where George is shown to be himself and relaxed. Thinking he is emotionally safe and accepted, he enjoys the evening with dancing and laughter, as if trying to enjoy the last few hours of his life fully. His suppressed grief is triggered when Charley carelessly devalues George and Jim's relationship. Verbalising the norms prevalent in society, her claim that a real relationship can only happen between a man and a woman throws George off balance completely. His visibly angry defence becomes a clear sign of his disbelief and disillusionment, which adds to his complicated grief process. He is lonely, unable to be himself and express his loss openly in society, and his lost bond is unappreciated by his only close friend.

For people suffering with disenfranchised grief, talking therapies and counselling interventions might be helpful. These interventions can lead to the empowerment of the individual as they would be able to restore meaning-making processes, work through any negative feelings like anger, guilt, shame, or simply the sense of unfinished business, alleviate PTSD symptoms (if there are any), and help the bereaved to give voice not only to their silent suffering but also their ability to recover and heal.

Jordan and Neimeyer (2003) argue that the core problem of disenfranchised grief is ultimately a failure of empathy. The absence, shortage, or simply the incompetence of emphatic support around a bereaved person hinders the meaning-making process, and therefore makes the grief journey chaotic. Doka (2002a) states that grief is ultimately a collective act of meaning making, and if this collective act is hampered the individual would feel isolated. This isolation would then further complicate the grief process.

While Kuhn (2002) identifies the effect of faith/spiritual communities on the bereaved as an alternative way out, Pesek (2002) mentions the importance of support groups, and Doka (2002b) indicates the value of rituals and mentions other techniques such as writing a journal and bibliotherapy. It is also important to note that while the research into and the interventions offered for disenfranchised grief include sexual minorities, especially gay men who lost their friends and partners to AIDS, the extent of the studies falls short when it comes to exploring the grief of 'other sexual minority clients, such as those who have lost a partner other than to AIDS' (Curtin and Garrison, 2018).

Within this context, George Falconer's suffering is the result of a sudden traumatic loss that is neither acknowledged nor empathically supported by society or close friends. The alienation and emotional isolation destabilise the possibility of a more straightforward grieving process. Plus, the absence of professional support or clinical intervention makes his life completely unbearable as there is no outlet for his internal anguish. This trapped and painful existence is the reason behind his inability to find an exit in all directions in time when he describes past, present, and future to Kenny in such a bleak manner.

The only suitable solution for his misery appears to be suicide. This is why his new year's resolution indicates his intent of completely eliminating his past. For a living person, however, it is impossible to let go of the past in its entirety because of how the human mind and memory work. The preservation of information over time in human memory is what enables one to learn, develop, function, form connections, relationships, and, most importantly, personal identity. Giving up on the past, or the deleting the past, also means a letting go of one's own unique and complex web of memories, which makes one who they are. George's very specific intention of purging his past indicates his determination to carry on with his suicide plan as it is the only way of achieving that level of purification. This cleansing, of course, includes getting rid of his current misery and grief as well.

The sweet relief of (sudden) death offered to George both by Isherwood and Ford is hardly poetic justice. They, however, both deviate from the conventional solutions suggested to grieving people by showing that an (unexpected) alternative is also possible: the pain of a (lost) human connection can also be relieved by the beauty of another.

7.3 Natural rhythm of the universe

The film uses recurring visual clues to indicate George's frame of mind. One of the most prominent and frequent is also the one that opens the film, where George is seen completely submerged and unable to break out of the water. This dream imagery, which is completely in George's mind, finds its real-life equivalent as a proper physical experience during the skinny-dipping scene.

Freud (1900) examined dreams as one of the main revealing mechanisms of the unconscious. The symbolism of drowning, in George's case, not only exposes his trapped mental and emotional position, but also his wish to die, which manifests itself by his carefully planned suicide attempt. The line that divides his two states of mind, namely his dreaming and waking states, is blurry because his feelings of helplessness are present in both.

Drowning is the inability to defeat the force of water invading the body. Mythologically speaking, water is the source of all life, the primeval element. However, it is also the liquid substance which dissolves matter and can be destructive. George's drowning illustrates a situation of being overwhelmed by difficult emotions when his fighting for survival becomes in vain. His struggle to survive as a person also applies to his identity, as his relationships with other people do not allow his real self to come to the surface.

Jung (1939), on the other hand, considers water as the key symbol for the unconscious. Water is the primary representation of all the energy contained in this realm. This energy can be dangerous if and when it overflows or cannot be contained properly. The drowning/dying imagery in George's mind manifests itself not only in his unconscious while he is dreaming but also spills over to his daily life. In other words, his ego does not have the strength anymore to determine what may pass into his consciousness. The psychic energy of his unconscious floods his conscious state where suicide becomes the seemingly rational solution to his unexpressed and unacknowledged grief, which is slowly drowning him.

Water acquires another layer of symbolism in Christianity as it becomes the cleansing element in baptism. Immersion becomes regenerative, wipes out sins, and establishes the individual as reborn. This purification is of course spiritual and symbolic, but still powerful. The unexpected inner rejuvenation of George in the film is also triggered when he goes under the powerful waves of the ocean. Chevalier and Gheerbrant (1996) point out the connection between salty water and joy, referring to an inner transformation. Quoting the theologian and mystic Richard of Saint-Victor, they argue that salty waters of the sea correspond to a bitterness in the heart of man. However, if man goes through this bitterness like a fearless explorer, the bitterness of the heart will transform into joy.

In darkness and underwater, George loses his sense of direction just like he has lost his way in life. He goes into the ocean with a bitter and wretched heart only to be literally rescued from drowning by Kenny, who brings the elusive solution to his dilemma: he can only be saved by the love, compassion, and responsiveness of another human being.

Kenny becomes a lifeline for George not only in the physical world. Fuelled by his youth, risk taking, and unpredictability, coupled with his seductive boyish charm, Kenny feels like a new breath of life to George. In Jungian terms, he displays the qualities of the *puer aeternus*, the archetype of eternal youth, daring, and over-optimism, whereas George personifies the *senex*, namely old age, wisdom, authority, melancholy, and a lack of imagination. These two archetypes, active in the human psyche, are a matched pair of opposites that eternally search for a union.

Jung states that it is impossible to eradicate or replace the opposites in the psyche because they are indeed the psyche's building blocks (CW 14, para.206).

This view finds more ground especially in the collision theory in chemistry, which states that in order to create a reaction one needs two disparate components. In human psyche, out of these colliding forces comes a new and a third possibility. This contradictory situation offers neither a rational yes or no for a psyche suffering in a dilemma but holds a potential that is far beyond the limited comprehension of the conscious mind, and which breaks the relentless swing between a binary choice.

In the film, George is stuck between a life he does not want to carry on living and a wish to end his suffering. His only two obvious choices are either a meaningless existence or the annihilation of self. This is why he finds his new breath of life when he discovers that Kenny has hidden his gun in a benevolent act. Kenny's naïve compassion and companionship, without being needy or judgemental like Charley, show George that he can connect to another human being, which seemed so impossible at the beginning of the day. Kenny's simple act, without knowing George's past, his choices, and, most of all, his grief, turns into a catalyst of healing for George.

Within the spiritual and archetypal world of Jungian psychology, Kenny also carries the alchemical and the mercurial aspect of the Trickster. Saving George from himself, he introduces transformational qualities to his psyche and initiates the process of diminishing his sense of meaninglessness. Samuels, Shorter, and Plaut (2005, p.152) argue that 'the Trickster is both a mythical figure and an inner psychic experience. [...] Hence, he symbolises the propensity for enantiodromia'. In other words, this mercurial process facilitates the ego to switch from the temptations of a subjective state which keeps one in darkness. This new and profound awakening is the result of an adaptation to life, balancing the dual pressure of internal energies and external stimuli. George describes his new-found healing towards the end of the film (90:54) in a touching monologue. In this scene, as he looks into the night, he reveals how he experienced moments of coherence, simplicity, and precision in his life. During those moments, he says, he reaches a Zen state unwittingly, and the calmness in him shuts the chaos of the world out. He starts experiencing life through his feelings rather than his thoughts, which makes the universe look bright and brand new. Through this enriching experience, he realises, no matter how short or fleetingly, that there is a beautiful and meaningful order to things which he is a part of.

The key phrase George uses when he describes himself is this: he experiences life through his feelings. This indicates a major shift in his psyche where the trapped state of his mind gives way to an un-thinking state of peace. The experience of traumatic loss, which sucked the life out of him, and the impossibility of finding a rational solution dissolve in a transmutational process. George, so out of sync with life, time, and people until now, becomes synchronised again with the natural rhythm of the universe, of separation and union. His absolute clarity is synonymous to turning lead into gold.

While the attraction between George and Kenny is slightly sexualised and the tension between the two is visible in the film, the connection they form is more than skin-deep. This is revealed especially during the bar scene (76:23) where Kenny admits how lonely he feels. He says he has always felt alone and stuck in his body, coming into contact with life only through his one-sided and rather distorted perspective because of this.

Mirroring the perceptive insight of Carlos about the human condition, Kenny gently addresses the egocentric predicament George is in. Describing how George feels alone, constrained and boxed in, without knowing George's real situation, Kenny also suggests the idea of one being limited to their own perceptual world. The reply that comes from George is hardly true. He says he is authentic in his appearance to people. Although he is in fact, on the surface, how he appears to people, underneath his exterior shell, which he wears every morning before leaving his house, there is also a wounded man who only perceives the world through his grief. The feeling that he might also have imprisoned himself emotionally paves the way to the skinny-dipping scene where he symbolically takes off his shell and walks into the water, feeling free and weightless for the first time in eight months.

The connection of George and Kenny also evokes the Jungian concepts of *Eros* and *Logos*. Eros is the son of Aphrodite and the Greek god Love, whereas Logos means speech, word, or reason in Greek (Wilmer, 1991). These two appear as opposites in both sexes, and they are the ruling principles behind the conscious personalities of men and women (Eros, for love, tenderness, and empathy; Logos, for thinking, judgment, and logic). The dominance of one of these principles can eclipse its opposite which, in turn, creates an imbalance between thinking and feeling in one's psyche.

Wilmer (Ibid.) also states that the conscious personality of men is predominantly Logos but the unconscious is Eros. When George 'becomes George' every morning, his consciousness shifts to a realistic, detached, and logical state where his 'professor of English persona' operates. There is almost no room left to feel anything. Even when there is, it is mostly a pervasive sadness. This adds to his social exclusion and isolation where he is not allowed to display his real feelings. But the fact is, he is also unable to be in touch with them because they are unbearable.

Kenny, on the other hand, brings a new variable into the equation: the connecting and relating qualities of a feeling mind. Through his gentle but persistent sympathy towards his tutor, he is able to break through George's exterior shell and create a spark of new life and a flurry of emotions in George's psyche. Kenny's simple but compassionate act of hiding the gun makes George realise that the life he finds so meaningless, the life he is so ready to throw away is actually more precious than he thinks. Kenny, through an unspoken display of empathy, shows how important and irreplaceable George's life and presence are for him.

This short scene of surprise and quiet realisation is where George's faith and trust in connecting to another human being is restored in the film. His severed relationship with Jim, his minimal, dull, and monotonous link with society, and his upsetting friendship with Charley is replaced with an authentic human connection, which he did not expect. He is now aware that the beauty of one connection has the potential of soothing the pain of another. This awareness and the shift in his psyche are verified in the next scene where he puts the gun in the drawer (90:28) and locks it, then takes all of his suicide letters and throws them in the fire (91:31). This burning act is symbolic, because he not only destroys what used to be his old way of thinking but also lets his feelings take over and regenerate himself from within.

The symbolism of fire in this scene can be read in many ways. As one of the main four elements, which was stolen from the gods, fire is fundamentally sacred, and it has the power to purify in Greek mythology (Biedermann, 1996). According to the Chinese divination system I Ching, fire is called *Li* (brightness) and it also corresponds to heart and liberation (Huang, 2010). Fire not only warms and illuminates but is also the necessary component in the changes between different phases of matter (such as solid to liquid, and liquid to gas). Séjourné (1957) sees it as the crucial force in the eternal cycle of transformation and renewal.

Within this context, when George burns his suicide letters, he purifies his mind and gets rid of his suicidal ideation. In Jungian and alchemical terms, he reaches his *putrefactio* stage where he casts off his old neurotic ways. As he starts feeling again, his heart/Eros are liberated, and not blocked by thinking/Logos anymore. His frozen state of grief finally receives the warmth of true compassion which, in turn, alters his perception and ultimately supports him in appreciating the present without a shadow from the past or a fear of the future.

It is also possible to read his newfound, albeit momentary, relief from Jim's death as the perfect marriage, or a sublime harmony of thinking and feeling. Through a fusion of knowledge, spiritual perceptiveness, ability to endure the evils of the world, and phronesis, he achieves a transcendent wisdom where everything in life, even Jim's death, finds its place and meaning in an infinitely complex and connected world.

This is probably why Ford chooses to show an owl as a symbol of this wisdom as George gazes into the night (90:30). Primarily a solitary and nocturnal creature, the owl is the sacred bird of the Greek goddess of wisdom, Athena. Symbolically, owls represent the quality of foresight, using experience and knowledge to make sensible decisions. Just like an owl, which can see in the dark, it is clear that George has now the gift of second sight, a wiser outlook that makes everything more visible and meaningful to him.

The scene that concludes the film is also a transposed version of the scene that opens it. In a closing circle, Tom Ford chooses to start his film with a kiss and finish with another one. As a symbol and act of love and affection, kissing makes two people come together and connect. Even though these scenes do not appear in the novel, Ford links George's kisses with death: the first one when he kisses the dead body of Jim and lies next to it, and the second one when Jim appears as a vision to assist George cross over.

George's death in the novel comes out of the blue and ends the story rather abruptly, making the main character's journey almost meaningless and a bit absurd. Ford, on the other hand, ties this loose ending with the skill of a cou-turier. At the beginning of the film, he hints at impending heart trouble by showing George briefly holding his chest with a grimace. This short scene gets retold in a full-blown heart attack sequence where George slowly drifts away towards the gentle kiss of Jim just before the credits.

As he wrote in the introduction for the novel's 2010 reprint, Ford focuses on what really matters in the end for people: a genuine connection with another human being. This becomes the main focus of the film and George's grief journey. Even though his connection with Jim brings him unbearable pain, he departs the physical plane with a rejuvenated spirit and the appreciation of all the beauty in the world. As a result, the film (as a direct opposite to its source material) wraps up on a poignant, optimistic, and progressive note, suggesting an alternative healing and a way out of the crypt for people who are lost in disenfranchised grief.

7.4 From connecting to letting go

George Falconer's story arc includes the destructive tendencies of a psyche trapped in a crypt. Similar to Chris Kelvin in *Solaris* (2002), he thinks suicide is the only choice as a way out. However, unlike Chris, George finds not only the strength but also the wisdom to acknowledge the experience as an inevitable separation from a loved one, which awaits every human being. This bittersweet understanding only comes after he is truly acknowledged by another person, with all his flaws, fears, and pain. A human connection that he cherished but eventually caused him to get trapped in a crypt is replaced with another one that opens this inner tomb and invites him out.

The poignant ending of his storyline also presents a challenge. It is difficult to predict how his life would have changed and continued. Kenny's modest and gentle watchfulness certainly helped him build the courage to step out of his shell and enjoy life again, no matter how short. But the questions remain: what might happen after such a life-changing inner realisation? What might be the next constructive step for traumatised people?

In order to explore the answers to these questions, I will now present another film analysis: *Saving Mr. Banks* (2013). This film's storyline shares some qualities with *The Bank* (2001) in terms of its portrayal of a traumatised child who, as an adult, carries the loss (and the crypt) everywhere she goes. Unlike Jim Doyle, this adult is not destructive. Yet, the unhappiness and the grief permeate every living moment.

In a nutshell, this analysis builds on the human connection aspect of *A Single Man* (2009). In this film, the traumatised protagonist meets another traumatised individual without the need to hide. Out of this remarkable meeting of wounded souls comes a new insight: holding on to a memory relentlessly locks one in a crypt. Therefore, my query now focuses on a reconstructive choice: how can one dispel the influence of the past voluntarily?

Discography

La Wally (1999) Composed by A. Catalani [Audio CD]. London: Decca.

Filmography

The Bank (2001) Directed by R. Connolly [film]. Australia
Nocturnal Animals (2016) Directed by T. Ford [film]. USA
Saving Mr. Banks (2013) Directed by J.L. Hancock [film]. USA
A Single Man (2009) Directed by T. Ford [film]. USA
Solaris (2002) Directed by S. Soderbergh [film]. USA

Notes

1 Ford's preoccupation with colour (or lack of) actually turns out to be his directorial trademark. He takes his unique technique of colour coding characters and their psyche much further in his second film *Nocturnal Animals* (2016) and creates an alternative, more symbolic narrative underneath the main storyline.
2 The novel's American edition is titled *After Many a Summer Dies the Swan*, and it coincidentally explores the philosophical concepts around mortality, slowing down the aging process, fear of death, happiness, and enlightenment.
3 Both India and Angus, Ford's dogs in real life, appear in the film.

Bibliography

Abraham, N. and Torok, M. (1994) *The Shell and the Kernel: Renewals of Psychoanalysis. Volume I.* Chicago: University of Chicago Press.

Anderson, K.A. and Gaugler, J.A. (2006) The Grief Experiences of Certified Nursing Assistants: Personal Growth and Complicated Grief. Available at: http://citeseerx.ist.psu.edu/viewdoc/download?doi=10.1.1.834.6661&rep=rep1&type=pdf

Attig, T. (2004) 'Disenfranchised grief revisited: Discounting hope and love', *Omega*, 49, pp.197–215.

Baydak, M.A. (2000) Human Grief on the Death of a Pet. Available at: www.collectionscanada.gc.ca/obj/s4/f2/dsk2/ftp01/MQ53087.pdf

Biedermann, H. (1996) 'Fire' in *The Wordsworth Dictionary of Symbolism*. Hertfordshire: Wordsworth Editions.

Chevalier J. and Gheerbrant, A. (1996) 'Water' in *The Penguin Dictionary of Symbols*. London: Penguin.

Curtin, N. and Garrison, M., (2018) '"She was more than a friend": Clinical intervention strategies for effectively addressing disenfranchised grief issues for same-sex couples', *Journal of Gay & Lesbian Social Services*, 30(3), pp.261–281.

Doka, K.J. (ed.) (1989) *Disenfranchised Grief: Recognizing Hidden Sorrow.* Lexington, MA: Lexington Books.

Doka, K.J. (2002a) *Disenfranchised Grief: New Directions, Challenges, and Strategies for Practice.* Champaign, IL: Research Press.

Doka, K.J. (2002b) 'The role of ritual in the treatment of disenfranchised grief', in Doka, K.J. (ed.) *Disenfranchised Grief: New Directions, Challenges, and Strategies for Practice.* Champaign, IL: Research Press, pp.135–148.

Feitelberg, R. (2012) 'Tom Ford on family, fashion and film' in *Women's Wear Daily*. Available at: www.wwd.com/fashion-news/designer-luxury/tom-ford-calls-the-shots-at-92y-5902064/

Folta, J., and Deck, E. (1976) 'Grief, the funeral, and the friend', in Pine, V., Kutscher A.H., Peretz, D., and Slater, R. (eds) *Acute Grief and the Funeral*. Springfield, IL: Thomas, pp.123–132.

Freud, S. (1900) 'The interpretation of dreams', in *The Standard Edition of the Psychological Works of*, Vol. 4–5, London: Hogarth Press.

Huang, A. (2010) *The Complete I-Ching*. Rochester, VT: Inner Traditions.

Isherwood, C. (2010) *A Single Man*. London: Vintage.

Jones, S. and Beck, E. (2007) 'Disenfranchised grief and nonfinite loss as experienced by the families of death row inmates', *Omega*, 54(4), pp.281–299.

Jordan, J. and Neimeyer, R.A. (2003) 'Does grief counselling work?', *Death Studies*, 27, pp.765–786.

Jung, C.G. (1939) *The Integration of Personality*. New York: Farrar & Rinehart.

Jung, C.G. (1970) *The Collected Works of C.G. Jung, Volume 14: Mysterium Coniunctionis*. Princeton: Princeton University Press.

Kuhn, D.R. (2002) 'A pastoral counselor looks at silence as a factor in disenfranchised grief', in Doka, K.J. (ed.) *Disenfranchised Grief: New Directions, Challenges, and Strategies for Practice*. Champaign, IL: Research Press, pp.99–126.

Laplanche, J. and Pontalis, J-B. (1988) *The Language of Psychoanalysis*. London: Karnac Books.

Pesek, E.M. (2002) 'The role of support groups in disenfranchised grief', in Doka, K.J. (ed.) *Disenfranchised Grief: New Directions, Challenges, and Strategies for Practice*. Champaign, IL: Research Press, pp.127–134.

Robinson, E. (2007) 'Long term outcomes of losing a child through adoption: The impact of disenfranchised grief', *Grief Matters: The Australian Journal of Grief and Bereavement*, 10(1), pp.8–11.

Samuels, A., Shorter, B., and Plaut, F. (2005) *A Critical Dictionary of Jungian Analysis*. London: Routledge.

Séjourné, L. (1957) *Burning Water: Thought and Religion in Ancient Mexico*. New York: The Vanguard Press.

Shear, M.K., Simon, N., Wall, M., Zisook, S., Neimeyer, R., Duan, N., Reynolds, C., Lebowitz, B., Sung, S., Ghesquiere, A., Gorscak, B., Clayton, P., Ito, M., Nakajima, S., Konishi, T., Melhem, N., Meert, K., Schiff, M., O'Connor, M-F., First, M., Sareen, J., Bolton, J., Skritskaya, N., Mancini, A.D., and Keshaviah, A. (2011) 'Complicated grief and related bereavement issues for DSM-5', *Depress Anxiety*, 28(2), pp.103–117.

Wilmer, H.A. (1991) *Practical Jung: Nuts and Bolts of Jungian Psychotherapy*. Wilmette, IL: Chiron Publications.

Worden, W.J. (2010) *Grief Counselling and Grief Therapy*. Hove: Routledge.

8 Letting go and *Saving Mr. Banks*

Choosing to live when feeling hopeless and helpless after a traumatic loss requires an extraordinary amount of inner strength. However, surviving a loss can also turn into a life sentence that harms the psyche and diminishes the chance of a constructive recovery. As shown in the case of Jim Doyle, this is particularly true with people when they suffer a bereavement early in their lives.

Nevertheless, not every traumatised child becomes destructive. They can forge a new life and even have a successful adult life as someone famous. But this does not mean that the bereavement is forgotten or does not cause distress anymore. What can be an even more complex problem is that the crypt might become tangible through art, an escape hatch into a fantasy world that was built to cover up a painful memory.

This chapter deals with this type of intrapsychic tomb where the trauma is translated into a reparative fantasy. The only semi-biographical case study of this book which includes real people, *Saving Mr. Banks* (2013) looks at the inner workings of rather harmful attachments to both the memory of the trauma and the romanticised version of that trauma. As another example of Abraham and Torok's (1994) blameless sufferers, it highlights the impact of personal choices when it comes to dealing with loss.

The film's script follows the real-life story of P.L. Travers, who not only wrote the series of *Mary Poppins* novels but also interacted with Walt Disney for a film adaptation. Throughout the film, she is addressed in several different ways: Ginty; Helen; P.L. Travers; Mrs. Travers; or simply Pamela. The same applies to Walt Disney. He is addressed as Mr. Disney, Walter, or Walt. I have preserved this approach in this chapter in order to stay faithful to the source material.

8.1 Disneyfying reality

Ian McEwan (2007) concludes his famous metafictional novel *Atonement* in a bittersweet paragraph. The guilt- and grief-ridden secret life of his main character, Briony Tallis, comes to a poignant end where she finally confesses and expresses her main motivation behind changing the factual past of her autobiographical novel: that she had been a coward and unable to put things right before the death of her sister and her sister's boyfriend. Therefore, instead of

DOI: 10.4324/9781003292630-11

telling everything as it happened, she decided to change the ending of their story to serve a better purpose. According to her, there was no sense in providing the facts in their historical accuracy. That is because they were so painful, they would have put the readers off. There was no room for delight or hope for the future after reading the characters' misery. Instead, as a good example of poetic justice, she rewrote the entire ending to give her sister and her boyfriend the happiness they deserved.

Alteration of facts and events is also prevalent in *Saving Mr. Banks*. The film is based on the events that took place before and during the making of the famous Disney film *Mary Poppins* (1964) which is based on the book of the same name which is in turn inspired by the life of its author, P.L. Travers. This multi-layered storytelling gets its own further reimagining of events in the hands of the director John Lee Hancock and Walt Disney Studios, but similar to *Atonement*, the film achieves a rare quality in terms of displaying how an art form can be a facilitator of healing and closure.

Even though *Saving Mr. Banks* rewrites and reinvents several historical facts, it sticks to telling the little-known backstory of how the film *Mary Poppins* was produced and explores the inner mechanisms of a troubled and wounded soul with poignant perceptiveness. The main storyline is quite straightforward. Completely committed to fulfilling his promise to his daughters, Walt Disney (Tom Hanks) has tried to obtain the rights of P.L. Travers's (Emma Thompson) book so that he could turn it into a film, only to be rejected by Travers every time he attempted to do so due to her fear of an unnecessarily frivolous Disney adaptation. Now in 1961, as Travers is struggling financially, she agrees to meet Disney and supervise the adaptation. During the course of two weeks and through several flashbacks, the film portrays not only how the novel was transferred to the big screen but also how deeply rooted it was in Travers's childhood trauma. While the abrasive, ice-cold, and condescending Travers as an adult is juxtaposed with a sensitive but helpless Travers as a little girl who was forced to watch her father slowly kill himself through alcohol, it is also revealed that the Mr. Banks character, whom Mary Poppins actually saves from becoming a cold, detached father, was created based on Travers's own father, Travers Robert Goff (Colin Farrell), whom Travers could not save as a little girl. It is only after Disney reveals his own difficult childhood that Travers is convinced that he will do the novel justice and grants him the rights. During the film's world premiere in 1964, Travers finally experiences her much needed catharsis as she watches her symbolic father enjoying good times with his children as the film becomes both a healing antithesis to her own unhappy childhood and an act of letting go, concluding the story of a story of a story, a true mise en abyme.

In its own re-imagined universe, the film wraps up the thorny relationship between Travers and Disney neatly and satisfactorily. However, that is largely fictitious. Most of the events that are depicted during the production of *Mary Poppins* never took place. Disney studios had already secured the rights, and according to Gillan (2014), Walt Disney was not at the studio when P.L. Travers visited L.A.

In real life, on the other hand, the meetings of Travers with the screen-writer and the songwriters were audiotaped at Traver's request and are part of the historical record. However, Walt Disney certainly did not travel to London to talk to Travers. Moreover, even though Travers did cry during the premiere, it was allegedly due to her anger and frustration of seeing how her personal vision of Mary Poppins was butchered by an American. Her dislike of the film adaptation was so deep that she not only took it to the grave but also beyond. In her will, according to Lawson (2006), she forbade selling the film rights of any of her remaining books to any American studio/director ever again.

In the BBC documentary (Thompson, 2013) about the film and its characters, Jenny Koralek describes Travers as a complex, extraordinary woman who lost her parents very early and kept these parts of her life confidential. Moreover, Brian Sibley describes Walt Disney, who, as an adult, idealised a happy family in his films due to his difficult relationship with his own stern father. While Travers, as an author, had complete control over her books and creativity, Disney pursued a different type of creativity over his theme parks, films, and animation. However, they shared one quality: neither of them liked handing over control. In other words, these two people had considerable sensitivities, which defined their difficult interaction with each other.

Pamela Lyndon Travers was certainly a complicated person. As a single woman, she adopted a child[1] in 1939 when she was in her forties, determined to create herself a new family different to the current social values of the time (including the nuclear family she described in *Mary Poppins*). She was born Helen Lyndon Goff in Australia and her father's death when she was seven left the family dependent on wealthy (and strict) Great-Aunt Ellie, who became the source material and inspiration for the character of Mary Poppins (Lawson, 2006). This bereavement may have contributed to her search for a loving, supportive, and enduring male figure in her life, such as Æ (George William Russell), George Gurdjieff (whose book can be briefly seen at the beginning of the film), and Jiddu Krishnamurti. Her turbulent relationship with her adopted son and many other facts of her life are never mentioned and kept hidden in *Saving Mr. Banks*.

The film does not go into the details of Walter Elias Disney's life either. According to Gabler (2007), a combination of a troubled relationship with a deeply religious father, childhood poverty, and frequent change of home within the USA and Canada seems to have triggered a drive in Disney not only to escape a harsh reality but also to create a controlled fantasy world. While Disney's little-known past as a hard-working and responsible boy who lost his childhood and became a child labourer, delivering papers in support of his family, finds a brief sequence in the film, his chain smoking, drinking, and shy personality hidden behind the successful public image (Schickel, 1986) are barely mentioned in the screenplay. His remarkably high expectations regarding staff performance but unusually limited praise for good work (Norman, 2013) are also not highlighted.

This deliberate act of selective and controlled storytelling finds its definition in the rather unflattering word 'Disneyfication'.[2] Used to describe a substantial makeover of content (for example, turning something complex and gloomy into fun and bright in order to suit the taste and expectation of family audiences), this term has been used by several scholars (Archer, 2014; Bryman, 2004; Choi, 2012; Kapferer, 2003; Kehoe, 1991; Mortensen, 2008; Zukin, 1995) to describe the sociological results/ripple effects of Disney's approach and choices, both as a businessman and as a company/studio. From a sociological point of view, the term 'Disneyfication' becomes a label that highlights the sanitisation of reality and facts while promoting consumerism and a Westernised lifestyle in a fantasy land.

While *Saving Mr. Banks* does exclude or sugar-coat some of the darker sides of both Travers and Disney, it certainly does not shy away from depicting their complex personalities and what they bring from their childhoods into their adult selves. In doing so, the film becomes a multi-layered and original exploration of grief and healing. In order to examine these layers of storytelling, I will explore the storyline in the next three sections: the first section looks at the multiplicity of symbols used in the film; the second section explores the connections to grief theory and Jungian analysis; the final section looks at how Pamela chooses to come out of her crypt due to a fateful encounter with another traumatised adult.

8.2 Recurring in eternity – symbols in *Saving Mr. Banks*

Even though the film was advertised as based on a real-life story, *Saving Mr. Banks* edits, omits, and enhances certain parts of the story it was based on. While doing so, it also uses specific images and concepts to convey its message and to strengthen its narrative structure. This symbolic language embedded in the storyline is condensed in a few images, words, and actions in the film that keep reappearing. These are: wind-mist; east-west; house; Buddha; journey; white horse; and the Sun.

The film starts with an aerial shot. The camera floats through big clouds and blue sky with a voiceover. It is the voice of Travers's father, slowly and calmly reading a poem. The poem is about a wind, blowing from the east, bringing mist, change and new unknowns. However, the poem is quite mystical as well, because it refers to cyclical events, happening again and again through eternity.

This poem, even though it opens the film, gets repeated at the very end during the closing sequence, making the story come full circle. It not only introduces the idea that something is about to change but also highlights that there is a timeless quality to this change as it happened before and will happen again. Because the film is about the cinematic adaptation of *Mary Poppins*, the sky, wind, and flying symbolism is natural here as Mary Poppins, the new nanny of the Banks children, is carried by the wind into their home. In terms of P.L. Travers's storyline in the film, however, these symbols represent something more, especially when combined with the poem.

Wind is basically air in motion, caused by the temperature and pressure differences in the atmosphere. As the Earth spins, so does the air. It carries rain across continents, and it scatters snow and hail. But it also disperses flower seeds, causing fertilisation on land. It follows the seasons, and it helps things transform and grow. Ronnberg and Martin (2010c) also point out the unpredictable factor of wind, that it sometimes determines the course or forces people to change course, just like ships on the sea.

In the poem, the wind is blowing from the east and bringing mist in. Often associated with spirituality, wisdom, and the metaphysical (Chevalier and Gheerbrant, 1996a), the east is also the source of light due to the symbolism of sunrise. In Sufi mysticism, a journey to the west is required for deep alchemical changes in the psyche before embracing the eastern wisdom. Of course, the opposites between the two are highlighted: the West is the centre of materialistic world whereas the East is the centre of spirituality. Mist, as a symbol used in the poem, is also a mixture of three elements: air, water, and fire. Like a soft white blindfold over the eyes, it represents the vanishing of figures and contours as well as a possible psychological uncertainty that can cloud the mind and judgement.

Even though *Saving Mr. Banks* is about the making of *Mary Poppins*, Pamela Travers's emotional journey as the protagonist is the main story on two different timelines. As flashbacks from 1906 intercut the current course of events in the 1960s, Pamela's separation from her father (both physically and emotionally) is fleshed out. At the beginning of the film, Pamela is portrayed as an economically trapped woman who is about to lose her house in London. She cannot afford to pay her maid anymore, her income from her books has dried up, and the only lifeline in this situation appears to be the contract she has been offered by Disney. Her refusal to sign it for the last 20 years shows how obstinate and resistant to change she normally is. However, the culmination of events and the results of her choices so far have driven her to a critical junction in her life where she is required to alter her direction. Like a force of nature, there is a change that awaits her in Los Angeles. Its seeds were sown a long time ago, and they are now slowly coming to shape. Her trip from London to L.A. is similar to a mystical western exile, an exile to a decadent, materialistic Hollywood studio. This is where she has to cast off some of her qualities in her character in a purification process and separate from her old ways and attachments in order to be spiritually (or rather psychologically) rejuvenated.

This transformation of the psyche is especially hinted at by two symbols that appear in the film: house and the Buddha statue. Throughout the film, Pamela makes three small houses out of twigs and leaves: the first one appears at the opening of the film as a flashback where she sits in the park as a little girl (01:13); the second one appears by the Goffs' new house in the Australian outback, again as a flashback; and the third one is the one she makes while sitting on the grass at Disney studios while talking to her designated driver Ralph (Paul Giamatti). The small Buddha statue, on the other hand, first appears at the beginning in Pamela's house (01:37), then reappears in the hotel room in L.A.

According to Bachelard (1948), house is a feminine symbol of sanctuary, protection, womb, and the mother. However, house is also a place where conflicts and opposites dwell (Ronnberg and Martin, 2010b). A house can make someone feel free to be themselves within its boundaries or feel completely trapped. A grey area between domestic happiness and misery, house is a universal symbol of inner transformation.

Furthermore, the Śākyamuni Buddha statue carries another transformation symbolism in its sitting pose. Apart from its visual nod to Travers's interest in mysticism, it displays a specific *mudrā* called *bhūmisparśamudrā*. As he sits in lotus position (*padmāsana*), his right hand points towards the earth, gently reaching out to touch it (*bhūmisparśamudrā*). His left hand gesture means he is meditating. This is a symbolic representation of Śākyamuni's conquering of his demons and achieving his true enlightenment. In other words, it is the symbol of attaining his Buddhahood.

P.L. Travers appears as a troubled soul in real life who is uprooted to go and live in a new place several times. In the film, she lives in three different houses in three different places: Maryborough; Allora; and London. She is shown to have a yearning for a stable home, additionally indicated in her attempt to keep her house in London. However, home is both where she is deeply wounded and the ideal place she is trying to escape to in her Mary Poppins books. This complex psychological quest is further enhanced by her unspoken wish to make peace with her troubled past, subdue her demons and reach a form of inner serenity, symbolised by the Buddha statue she carries with her.

Pamela's inner journey from a rigid and unwavering psychological position to a more accepting and calmer one is mirrored by the physical journeys in the film. Not only does she travel between L.A. and London, but she is also driven by Ralph between her hotel and the Disney studios several times. During these journeys, she repeatedly remembers moments from her past in which her father's white horse, the unrelenting heat, and the sunshine of Australian outback are highlighted.

Journeys, either those an individual undertakes physically or within themselves, are rich in symbolism. They highlight a pursuit of truth, peace, immortality, treasures, or simply the realisation of a spiritual, mental, or moral centre, an equilibrium after an escape from one's self. Chevalier and Gheerbrant (1996b) also note that a journey can be a symbol of a significant internal need, either due to dissatisfaction or enthusiasm for new discoveries.

Horse, on the other hand, is a more complex symbol. As Biedermann (1996) points out, historically speaking, people's viewpoints on horse symbology fluctuated between dark and light, life and death, and from the depths of the Earth to the heavens. For example, Woden (as the Germanic version of Odin, the Norse god) had a troop of riders in the sky who were basically dead warriors' ghosts. Helios, the Ancient Greek deity of the Sun, also harnessed his horses to drive his chariot across the sky and bring sunlight everywhere he went.

Horse, as a dual-natured divine animal, ultimately represents man's authority over nature, and his mastery over his instincts. Its specific connection to the Sun and light symbolises the annihilation of darkness, resurrection, and the rejuvenation of life force. Ronnberg and Martin (2010a) also point out this symbol's links in alchemy and draw connections between the golden rays of the Sun, the illumination of the mind, and the attainment of truth.

All of these recurring symbols throughout the film help to clarify the way P.L. Travers changes internally and finally gains control over the troubling memories that ruled her life as an adult. Travelling to L.A. and being exposed to lots of sunshine (contrary to the rainy London weather and similar to the Australian outback) brings her traumas back into her consciousness. During this journey, however, her interaction with Walt Disney (who himself is a symbol of a loving, compassionate father) and the cathartic experience of watching *Mary Poppins* help Pamela part with the memory of a self-destructive father. Her rejuvenated character at the end of the film shows how profoundly this positive separation affected her psyche. Like Buddha, she has been through her exile in the West, subdued her demons, and attained her enlightenment.

Although *Saving Mr. Banks* looks as if it is a film about the making of a film, it is actually dealing with the much more profound and altogether darker subjects of separation, alcoholism, loss, early psychological maturity, and their effects on character and adult life. The next section will look at the depiction of unresolved and complicated grief in the film.

8.3 Attack from the deep – complicated grief

Roughly midway through the film, P.L. Travers speaks to her literary agent on the phone and complains about how emotionally difficult her trip to L.A. has been (52:00). She describes this difficulty as an 'attack of her subconscious'. While this description and her personal perception are open to debate, the film does depict her remembering several moments of her past that contain strong emotional and psychological activity.

The storyline opens with the memory of a sunny and peaceful day in Pamela's childhood where she is sitting under the sun, smiling and relaxed. This nostalgic moment is suddenly interrupted by the arrival of her agent making her cross. Her facial expressions (and the conversation with the agent) reveal how much she is annoyed by the intrusion of this reality. This scene indicates how much she wants to escape her current situation. In a way, she uses her happy memories as means of escapism, shielding herself from frustration and pain.

This personal method of escaping reality completely breaks down during her journey to L.A. Despite being surrounded by unfamiliar people and objects, random events start to trigger painful memories from her past, which overwhelm her psychologically. In other words, it becomes clear that it is not her subconscious that attacks her; it is her inability to make peace with her past and move on. This is almost identical to the problem explored in the chapter for *Solaris* (2002). Memories trigger inner disturbances in the present and alienate a person from reality. Moreover, those memories can be activated (directly or indirectly) by events, people, or objects.

It is important to remember here what Schaer (1951) said: physical reality ultimately liberates the contents of the psyche. Pamela's exposure to L.A.'s bright sunlight brings back the haunting memories of an alcoholic father and a suicidal mother on a corporeal level. Additionally, her obsessive rejection of pears (she throws them out of the hotel room as soon as she walks in) and the colour red (she insists that there should not be anything red in the film *Mary Poppins*) are explained quite clearly in the film: the former was brought to her as a gift by her father, and the latter is the symbol of haemoptysis her father was suffering from just before he died. In short, just like Chris Kelvin in *Solaris*, Pamela is forced to face her grief even though both characters choose different routes to deal with a similar problem.

Pamela also displays several traits that are common in prolonged grief disorder (Horowitz, 1993; Prigerson et al., 1999). These are: avoidance of the reminders of the loss; inability to trust others; bitterness; difficulty in making new friends; and social withdrawal. In the film, until Walt Disney shows up in London and talks about his own childhood scars, Pamela is portrayed as either rude and condescending or socially inept and awkward. For example, even when she builds up the courage to engage in small talk with the bartender at the hotel (41:23), she starts the conversation by talking about the benefits of drinking tea, an opening gambit that is swiftly ignored by him. Pamela sees most individuals, including her literary agent, as people trying to get something from her that she is not prepared to give or part with. This perspective also feeds her mistrust in forming relationships.

Interestingly, she only lets one person, her designated driver Ralph, call her by her first name and get close to her emotionally. The scene where Ralph sits with her on the grass and builds another house with her patiently (70:17) is where she finally reveals how lonely she is by saying that she does not have a family who would notice or care where she is. Ralph, in return, talks about how sorry he is due to his daughter's disability, but also how much he likes the sunshine of L.A. because his daughter can sit in the garden freely. Without being judgemental, and free of any demands, Ralph simply stays present with her.

This scene is preceded and followed with crucial flashbacks from Pamela's childhood in 1906. Her father is on his death bed. When he asks the doctor for more painkillers, the doctor refuses, knowing he might try to overdose. He then asks Pamela to bring him a bottle of alcohol, but she says her mother removed it. He gets annoyed and belittles her poem because she seems to resist the idea of giving him more alcohol. In return, she goes and finds the bottle, and slips it into her father's hand, who's now sleeping, effectively contributing to his death.

This scene evokes euthanasia and, coupled with Pamela's important flashback scene where she stops her mother in the river before she drowns herself, it explains how both parents failed her. In a way, the parents who are supposed to be responsible, loving, and caring, are portrayed exactly the opposite in the film. With a melancholic father who is slowly killing himself with alcohol, and a shy, highly emotional mother who sees no harm in telling her little daughter to take care of her siblings before she tries to kill herself[3], Pamela is severely let down by both her parents and forced to be self-sufficient. It can also be argued that the way she was reduced to being a contributing factor in her father's death has truly broken her. She, as an adult, now thinks any request will lead to more loss and pain, and that is why she tries to hold on to everything she has, including the rights to her book, which is the epitome of her imagination, escapism, and a safe house.

Moreover, as Hecht (1973) notes, children of alcoholics quickly learn that communication is not only what is said, but also what is not said. These children lose the ability of trusting verbal communication very early on and they start to rely on visible and verifiable actions which only, in turn, make them even more sceptical towards people in the long run.

Pamela, until the emotional climax of the film, never ceases to express her mistrust and displeasure. She, without a trace of kindness or care, treats Walt Disney, his staff, the songwriters, and even the passenger with a baby on her flight to L.A. with an aggressive disdain. The reasons for this icy, detached, and ill-mannered behaviour can be explained by the object relations school of depth psychology, as Hollis (1996, p.60) points out in his book:

> The infant child's experience of the 'primal objects', namely the parents, creates a profoundly phenomenological identification of self and Other, from whose influence we never escape. The experience of such attachments, be it smothering or abandoning or some range in between, constitutes a recurrent message about relationship. And the message of the literal dependence of that terribly vulnerable child on its relationships is profoundly overlearned, overconditioned.[1]

Abandoned both physically and emotionally by her parents, but especially by her father, Pamela now suffers in a perpetual prison of unresolved grief. Her only escape (and relief) is her imagination, the fantasy family of the Banks where the children's needs are met, the parents are present, and the father is saved by Mary Poppins. Therefore, it is no surprise that she desperately clings on to her only breathing space and gives Walter Disney a hard time.

In Jungian terms, her almost one-sided psychological and emotional state suggests an *animus possession*. Possession is a term that illustrates the taking over of ego and personality by a complex or other archetypal content (Samuels, Shorter, and Plaut, 2005). This jeopardises one's psychic equilibrium, and their ability to think and act autonomously:

> Possession by either anima or animus transforms the personality in such a way as to give prominence to those traits which are seen as *psychologically* characteristic of the opposite sex. Either way, a person loses individuality, first of all, and then in either case, both charm and values. In a man, he

---

1 *Swamplands of the Soul: New Life in Dismal Places*, James Hollis, published by Inner City Books.

becomes dominated by anima and by the Eros principle with connotations of restlessness, promiscuity, moodiness, sentimentality [...] A woman subject to the authority of animus and Logos is managerial, obstinate, ruthless, domineering.

(Ibid., p.24)

Furthermore, Pamela's one-sidedness and unresolved grief are put to the ultimate test by her trip to L.A. It is important to remember her own description here: she thinks she is attacked by her subconscious. She feels overwhelmed by her memories, which flood her consciousness. This is similar to *solutio*, one of the stages of transformation in alchemy. It means the dissolution and melting stage that matter must go through to transform. In psychological terms, it corresponds to a purification of feelings and the breaking down of the structures in the psyche. Pamela's psyche, in this sense, is in the process of transformation during this journey. It is trying to dissolve her animus possession/established structures not only by remembering but also by letting go.

The force that triggers this transformation is embodied in the character of Walter Disney, as Travers calls him. He is depicted as the jovial, good-natured, patient and caring powerful man who wants to keep his promise to his daughters. He also appears quite different to Pamela's own father, Travers Goff, who could not love and support his family consistently. The film does not explore how much of this difference contributes to Pamela's explicit antipathy towards Disney[4] but, owing to her well-established mistrust in people, Pamela considers Walter shallow and money-oriented, and calls him a 'trickster' (91:22) because he hides his animation sequence from her.

The Trickster, as a Jungian term, fits in well in terms of describing Walter Disney, but not in the way Pamela uses it. Jung sees the Trickster as a harbinger of freedom and relief (CW 9i, para.472). An archetype that disrupts the order but also brings liberty and a fresh breath of creativity, the Trickster does not always imply duplicitous and dishonest people/behaviour. As mentioned in the previous chapter, the Trickster figure can appear as a trigger for deep psychic change in an individual. It can create a revolution in the psyche, transform meaninglessness into significance and value. It can deliver enantiodromia.

Up until the last 30 minutes of the film, Pamela is shown as a lonely, grumpy woman whose imagination and creative abilities have dried up. She seems to be eternally trapped in prolonged grief disorder with a deliberate avoidance of her past traumas. In other words, her mind is focused on evasion, and she has strong internal defences against her loss. However, this one-sidedness is also the reason behind the powerful counter-position of her psyche which floods her consciousness during her trip to L.A. In the scene where Walter Disney visits Pamela in her house in London, he (as the Trickster) becomes the initiator of this transformation in her by gently inviting her to free herself from a painful, meaningless existence through conscious letting go. Through the creation of the Mary Poppins film, he triggers an enantiodromic change in Pamela. Her inability to embrace her inner child, her bitterness, loneliness, and grief gradually turn to their opposite: she starts smiling, dancing, forming a friendship with Ralph, and makes peace with her loss.

Even though *Saving Mr. Banks* tells the story of the making of a film, it actually focuses on how individuals lose their way in life due to traumas. In the case of P.L. Travers, her grief and how she navigates through her loss become the main ingredients in a multi-layered film. The next section will look at another layer which is closely tied to her healing: choosing to let go.

8.4 Liberation through images

Creative activities such as writing, drawing, painting, and sculpture are considered therapeutic for people who are dealing with loss. Generally grouped under the umbrella term art therapy, expressing feelings of loss in tangible formats sometimes helps the bereaved see their losses from a different perspective and come to terms with their separation (Irwin, 1991; Lattanzi and Hale, 1984; Simon, 1982; Schut et al., 1996; Turetksy and Hays, 2003). *Saving Mr. Banks* establishes the idea that P.L. Travers created her fictional character Mr. Banks based on her perception and experience of her father. Therefore, her novel can be seen not only as escapism but also as her personal attempt (or atonement) to make peace with her loss and troubled past where her father gets saved eventually and learns to be more affectionate towards his children. While the book is Pamela's own expression in writing, it does not help much in terms of completing her grief process because she does not fully express her true feelings and loss.

This is where *Saving Mr. Banks* gets interesting. The film deliberately uses flashbacks from 1906, intercutting the current flow of events taking place in the 1960s, in order to display how and why Pamela is in her obstinate and angry state. The images/events from Pamela's past are shown overlapping the images/events that are in her present so that the viewers would see the connections and understand not only the film's narrative but also Pamela's personal story. This interwoven build-up reaches its peak during the *Mary Poppins* première scene in the film where Pamela watches the screen adaptation. In this scene, Pamela's memories, her climactic responses to the film, and the scenes from the adaptation merge. This powerful synthesis contributes to Pamela's exit from her inner crypt.

This key scene brings all the narrative threads explored in the film to a fitting climax. Here, the images and the music of the film *Mary Poppins*, fused with Pamela's own memories of her father create the perfect catharsis for her. While she is watching Disney's new film on the big screen, her uncontrollable sobbing becomes the final and the most powerful emotional cleansing she desperately needed. Her journey to L.A., which started the whole traumatic process of remembering the past, also takes her to a much-needed destination: a release from a self-created mental and emotional prison, her intrapsychic tomb.

In Pamela's case, it is important to reiterate Jung's concept of enantiodromia here. The idea that everything eventually turns into its opposite finds a clear cinematic representation in the film. Pamela's trauma, her fear of loss turns into release and a source of wisdom for her. This therapeutic freedom also has an abreactive quality. Jung describes *abreaction* as a recurrence or repetition which decreases the effect of a trauma and eliminates its distressing hold over the psyche (CW 16, para.262). Meaning, the discharge of emotions is a way for people to gain insight, to have a better understanding of their own psyches as dynamic wholes, and to grasp the meaning (or the results) of repressed experiences. While Pamela does not re-live the death of her father in reality, she certainly re-lives the separation on a symbolic level, and what she has been repressing comes back to the surface.

This is where her separation that she experienced as a helpless child turns into learning how to let go as an adult. *Saving Mr. Banks* clearly depicts two interwoven steps of letting go: mental and emotional. Her mental letting go, which is a deliberate, conscious choice, takes place when Walter Disney flies to London and talks to Pamela about his own difficult childhood. His genuine and caring speech (104:18) becomes the critical turning point for Pamela to sign off the rights to her book. As Disney reveals his own sad memories and childhood wounds in front of Pamela, he also acknowledges Pamela's difficult bond with her father Travers Goff. He points out how storytellers, like himself, create order out of chaos, right every wrong, and produce hope even when despair rules the world. Then he promises that he would deliver what Travers Goff missed out in real life: a loving, happy family now immortalised on the big screen.

In this touching scene, two opposing forces meet: Pamela's *Logos* and Walter's *Eros*. Pamela as the judgemental, discriminatory, and intolerant woman subject to the authority of animus and *Logos*, finds her match in the loving, intimate, and affectionate Walter as he calmly and gently invites her to liberate herself from her past, which is defined by grief. This invitation to come out of her crypt is not turned down this time, as in the next scene Pamela signs the studio's contract as she says 'enough' to herself, letting her creation go free while making a choice to put a stop to the way her past determines her present. The result of her choice is shown in the next scene. A smiling and friendly Pamela, her creativity unblocked and now writing, is planning a series of books with her literary agent.

However, her letting go is not yet fully complete until her emotional dependence on her father melts away during the première. This is where her fear of separation turns into a bittersweet freedom. Even though she starts watching *Mary Poppins* in a disapproving way, she starts crying when the Banks children say they think their father does not love them. The three-layered intercut of images is the key to understand what is going on in Pamela's psyche: the scenes from *Mary Poppins*; her physical response to these scenes; and her childhood memories, which are the roots of her response. The film she so desperately tried to avoid/derail becomes the film that actually saves not only her father in an imaginary way but also saves her in reality.

This scene is also where the symbolism of the wind, east-west, the Buddha, white horse, and the Sun reach their full potential in Pamela's psyche: they are united. As she is sobbing through the 'Let's go fly a kite' scene in *Mary Poppins*,

Saving Mr. Banks shows her remembering a ride with her father on their white horse on a sunny day. Her self-rejuvenation, triggered by the journey, is now complete. Her lost life force is now re-claimed as her psyche reaches an equilibrium, an enlightenment where her demons are subdued. Her desire to control, dominate, or to hold on is no more. By choosing to let go, she earns her way out of her crypt. James Hollis (1996) explains this state of harmony as being in tune with the fleeting and temporary state of things, just like the enlightened Buddha. He argues that Gautama reached his enlightenment and became the Buddha only after realising the core of human suffering: the never-ending desire to control and hold on to transitory objects, people, even life. Voluntarily giving up on this desire brings liberation, tranquillity, and wisdom.

Saving Mr. Banks ends with a repeat of the opening scene and follows a circular, in fact a very Jungian, ouroboric pattern, indicating a completion of a cycle in Pamela's psyche. There is, however, one difference: Travers Goff holds his daughter affectionately in the park. This tiny change further suggests that the sense of separation in Pamela's psyche is now healed and replaced with an eternal parental embrace. Walter Disney, with his film adaptation, transforms the needless inner anguish of Pamela into a meaningful separation, which contributes to Pamela's healing.

However, there is a big problem. The events that are depicted in *Saving Mr. Banks* either did not take place at all or took place in completely different ways, even though the film was marketed as the untold true story. As mentioned earlier, Walt Disney did not visit Pamela in London. Even though Pamela did cry during the premiére, it was (allegedly) not due to a therapeutic release but due to anger and frustration. There was no friendship with Ralph the driver because he did not exist in real life. This makes *Saving Mr. Banks* almost completely fictitious, and the film is actually selling a polished fantasy. In other words, the untold true story is Disneyfied.

Nevertheless, this is where the term and the act of Disneyfication is redeemed as well. It is important to remember the painful statement of Briony Tallis from *Atonement* here: she could not find any purpose in telling her sad story as it happened in real life. Because, she thought, it would not deliver the necessary optimism, happiness, and fulfilment to her readers. Therefore, the question remains: what purpose would be served if Disney studios told everything as it happened? What sense of hope would a viewer derive from such a bleak, unsatisfying ending where Walt and Pamela parted ways as two strangers and Pamela stayed unimpressed (probably unhealed) and annoyed by the film adaptation for the rest of her life?

The discussion of these questions is beyond the scope of this analysis. Plus, they do not change the fact that *Saving Mr. Banks* is a unique film that exemplifies the Latin maxim, *fortis imaginatio generat causum* – a strong imagination causes the event itself. In its fictitious universe, a woman's imagination to save her father leads not only to his symbolic saving but also to her own. Just like Walt Disney's perceptiveness about storytellers restoring order and instilling hope, the film becomes a stylish portrayal where letting go turns into an inspiring art form.

8.5 From letting go to learning to forgive

In Pamela's case, the choice to let go, the willingness not to hold on to a traumatic separation, helps her find the way out of her crypt. Jung calls the act of letting go as the most essential requirement for psychological maturity (CW 9i, para.562). Meaning, in order to expand the boundaries of consciousness one must relinquish their attachment to ego and its mechanisms, just like the Buddha. This would eventually and undoubtedly bring about the much-needed equilibrium in the psyche, which, in this case, is the result of Pamela's choice.

By describing letting go in this way, Jung refers to the Taoist concept of *wu wei*, the idea of action through non-action. In *Alchemical Studies*, he describes this concept as an art, and makes a point about the deliberate and constant interference of consciousness. Jung argues that our conscious mind is always critical, questioning, and intrusive, which hinders the processes in the psyche (CW 13, para.20). In order to master this art, one must step back, quieten the mind, and stop its unnecessary involvement in the deep psychic processes.

Before the kind intervention of Walter Disney, Pamela was unable to come out of her trapped state of anguish. But by choosing to let go, choosing to relinquish her control over the Disney adaptation, she actively gives her psychic processes a chance to unfold. She gives them the room to operate, and she lets the power of change in. Only after allowing herself to go with the natural flow of her life does she gain the chance to leave her crypt behind. This is similar to George Falconer's case in *A Single Man* (2009). Both George and Pamela become wiser, aware and in tune with the rhythm of the universe: a rhythm of connection and separation.

In the next chapter, I will focus on a different choice and a different type of connection and separation. This time I will be looking at the group dynamics of a bereavement where three people are affected by the same death. Because of this common trauma, these three people are trapped in their crypts in different ways and unable to find their way out. However, by choosing to forgive (themselves, each other, and other people) they gradually move forward. Therefore, my question reflects this choice and is simple: is forgiveness a way out of a crypt?

Filmography

Mary Poppins (1964) Directed by R. Stevenson [film]. USA
Saving Mr. Banks (2013) Directed by J.L. Hancock [film]. USA
A Single Man (2009) Directed by T. Ford [film]. USA
Solaris (2002) Directed by S. Soderbergh [film]. USA

Notes

1 According to the same BBC documentary (Thompson, 2013) John Camillus Hone (who became Camillus Travers) was chosen by P.L. Travers specifically after she consulted her astrologer to decide whether the baby would be suitable for her. He found out he had been adopted by pure luck after bumping into his twin.

2 This term also appears as 'Disneyisation' or 'Disneyization', but the meaning is still the same.
3 Even though this attempt is true, it did not happen in the way it is depicted in the film. One day, out of desperation, Pamela's mother left all her children at home, announced she was going to kill herself and took off. Pamela spent the whole day telling her siblings stories to calm them down. Her mother returned in the evening, drenched and looking distressed, probably after an unsuccessful suicide attempt (Lawson, 2006).
4 *Saving Mr. Banks* makes it clear that Travers Goff is idealised (and immortalised in her books) by Pamela. Therefore, it is natural for her to dismiss any man who does not match this model father. Walt Disney, with his stable and affectionate behaviour, appears to be the antithesis of Pamela's mercurial father, a father she never had and had no experience of.

Bibliography

Abraham, N. and Torok, M. (1994) *The Shell and the Kernel: Renewals of Psychoanalysis. Volume I.* Chicago: University of Chicago Press.

Archer, K. (2014) 'Central Florida, Disneyfication of' in Pillsbury, R. (ed.) *The New Encyclopedia of Southern Culture: Volume 2: Geography.* North Carolina: University of North Carolina Press, p.45.

Bachelard, G. (1948) *La terre et les rêveries de la volonté.* Paris: Librairie Jose Corti.

Biedermann, H. (1996) 'Horse' in *The Wordsworth Dictionary of Symbolism.* Hertfordshire: Wordsworth Editions.

Bryman, A. (2004) *The Disneyization of Society.* London: Sage Publications.

Chevalier, J. and Gheerbrant, A. (1996a) 'East–West' in *The Penguin Dictionary of Symbols.* London: Penguin.

Chevalier, J. and Gheerbrant, A. (1996b) 'Journey' in *The Penguin Dictionary of Symbols.* London: Penguin.

Choi, K. (2012) 'Disneyfication and localisation: The cultural globalisation process of Hong Kong Disneyland', *Urban Studies*, 49(2), pp.383–397.

Gabler, N. (2007) *Walt Disney: The Biography.* London: Aurum Press.

Gillan, J. (2014) '*Saving Mr. Banks* by John Lee Hancock, Alison Owen, Ian Collie and Philip Steuer', *The Journal of American History*, 101(1), pp.362–364.

Hecht, M. (1973) 'Children of alcoholics are children at risk', *The American Journal of Nursing*, 73(10), pp.1764–1767.

Hollis, J. (1996) *Swamplands of the Soul: New Life in Dismal Places.* Toronto: Inner City Books.

Horowitz, M.J., Bonanno, G.A., and Holen, A. (1993) 'Pathological grief: Diagnosis and explanation', *Psychosomatic Medicine*, 55, pp.260–273.

Irwin, H.J. (1991) 'The depiction of loss: Uses of clients' drawings in bereavement counselling', in *Death Studies*, 15, pp.481–497.

Jung, C.G. (1966) *The Collected Works of C.G. Jung, Volume 16: Practice of Psychotherapy.* Princeton: Princeton University Press.

Jung, C.G. (1968) *The Collected Works of C.G. Jung, Volume 13: Alchemical Studies.* Princeton: Princeton University Press.

Jung, C.G. (1969) *The Collected Works of C.G. Jung, Volume 9, Part 1: Archetypes and the Collective Unconscious.* Princeton: Princeton University Press.

Kapferer, R. (2003) 'It's a small world after all, or, consultancy and the Disneyfication of thought', *Social Analysis: The International Journal of Social and Cultural Practice*, 47(1), pp. 145–151.

Kehoe, A. (1991) *Christian Contradictions and the World Revolution: Letters to My Son*. Dublin: Glendale Publishing.

Lattanzi, M. and Hale, M.E. (1984) 'Giving grief words: Writing during bereavement', *Omega*, 15, pp.45–52.

Lawson, V. (2006) *Mary Poppins, She Wrote: The Life of P.L. Travers*. New York: Simon & Schuster.

McEwan, I. (2007) *Atonement*. London: Vintage Books.

Mortensen, F. (2008) '*The Little Mermaid*: Icon and Disneyfication', *Scandinavian Studies*, 80(4), pp.437–454.

Norman, F. (2013) *Animated Life: A Lifetime of Tips, Tricks, Techniques and Stories from a Disney Legend*. Burlington, MA: Focal Press.

Prigerson, H.G., Shear, M.K., Jacobs, S.C., Reynolds, C.F., Maciejewski, P.K., Davidson, J.R.T., Rosenheck, R., Pilkonis, P.A., Wortman, C.B., Williams, J.B.W., Widiger, T.A., Frank, E., Kupfer, D.J., and Zisook, S. (1999) 'Consensus criteria for traumatic grief: A preliminary empirical test', *British Journal of Psychiatry*, 174(1), pp.67–73.

Ronnberg, A. and Martin, K. (eds) (2010a) 'Horse' in *The Book of Symbols: Reflections on Archetypal Images*. Cologne: Taschen.

Ronnberg, A. and Martin, K. (eds) (2010b) 'House/Home' in *The Book of Symbols: Reflections on Archetypal Images*. Cologne: Taschen.

Ronnberg, A. and Martin, K. (eds) (2010c) 'Wind' in *The Book of Symbols: Reflections on Archetypal Images*. Cologne: Taschen.

Samuels, A., Shorter, B., and Plaut, F. (2005) *A Critical Dictionary of Jungian Analysis*. London: Routledge.

Schaer, H. (1951) *Religion and the Cure of Souls in Jung's Psychology*. London: Routledge.

Schickel, R. (1986) *The Disney Version: The Life, Times, Art and Commerce of Walt Disney*. London: Pavilion Books.

Schut, H., de Keijser, J., van den Bout, J., and Stroebe, M.S. (1996) 'Cross-modality group therapy: Description and assessment of a new program', *Journal of Clinical Psychology*, 52, pp.357–365.

Simon, R. (1982) 'Bereavement art', *American Journal of Art Therapy*, 20, pp.135–143.

Thompson, A. (2013) The Secret Life of Mary Poppins: A Culture Show Special. Available at: www.bbc.co.uk/programmes/b03kk4yv

Turetsky, C.J. and Hays, R. (2003) 'Development of an art psychotherapy model for the prevention and treatment of unresolved grief during midlife', *Art Therapy*, 20, pp.148–156.

Zukin, S. (1995) *The Cultures of Citie* alden, MA: Blackwell Publishers.

9   Forgiveness and *Rabbit Hole*

Adapted from David Lindsay-Abaire's play of the same name, which won the 2007 Pulitzer Prize Drama Award, *Rabbit Hole* (2010) tells the story of a mother, a father, and a teenager whose lives have suddenly changed after a tragedy that affected them in different ways. Both the play and the film revolve around this joint traumatic loss, how this bereavement traps three people in grief, and how these people find their own way out of this shared intrapsychic tomb.

Similar to the unexpected loss explored in *A Single Man* (2009), the reason for this trauma is a traffic accident. One fateful day, Jason (Miles Teller) is driving his car in a posh and leafy neighbourhood in New York, enjoying his life as a 17-year-old boy. Danny (Phoenix List), the four-year-old son of Becca (Nicole Kidman) and Howie (Aaron Eckhart), runs after their dog Taz into the street. Jason is unable to stop the car and hits Danny, killing him in front of Becca. Eight months later, these three characters are still mourning in their unique ways and unable to find relief or closure. Becca appears stoic, but she is angry, volatile, and brutally honest, hurting everyone around her in different ways (including physically attacking a stranger at a supermarket). Howie appears more in touch with his feelings of loss, but he is extremely attached to every single artefact and memory of Danny, unable to part with him. Jason appears quiet and shy, but he is forever transformed by the experience of accidentally killing someone, making him a rather joyless teenager.

The film explores the ins and outs of this shared traumatic experience and the three-way interaction of these people bound by grief. Additional characters bring new perspectives into the complex array of emotions and choices in regard to the question of what happens after a traumatic loss. These characters include: Becca's free-spirited (or sometimes irresponsible) sister Izzy (Tammy Blanchard); Becca's rather religious mother Nat (Dianne Wiest), who lost her son and Becca's and Izzy's brother Arthur to suicide (which is a contentious subject between her and Becca); and Gabby (Sandra Oh), who not only is a regular participant of the child bereavement support group that Becca and Howie occasionally attend but also is the extramarital romantic interest of Howie.

In the case of *Rabbit Hole*, and as its title suggests, Becca, Howie, and Jason dwell in a deep burrow of loss. In other words, this experience becomes the

DOI: 10.4324/9781003292630-12

intrapsychic tomb in which they are trapped in and unable find a way out. Even so, each character tries to lessen their pain in different ways: Becca tries to get rid of everything that belonged to Danny, attempting to delete his physical memory and her loss; Howie gets emotionally closer to Gabby because he finds Becca cold and unfeeling; Jason writes and draws a science-fiction comic book about parallel universes where a boy attempts to rescue his father from death.[1] This, of course, not only echoes Pamela's creative attempts of psychological recovery in *Saving Mr. Banks* (2013), but also underlines his need to escape to an imaginary world away from the horror of the real world.

Unfortunately, these attempts do not bring the intended relief for these characters. During the course of the film, however, they learn to forgive each other and themselves. Additionally, they extend this forgiveness to other people which gradually paves the way out of their shared *crypt* (Abraham and Torok, 1994). In order to explain this shift from suffering to relief in detail, I will explore the film in three parts: the first part will look at the contextual background and the visual symbols of the film; the second part will examine the shared trauma; and the last part will discuss the act of forgiving in Jungian terms.

9.1 Convergence and separations – symbols in *Rabbit Hole*

In the Blu-ray extras of the film's German edition, there are short interviews with the director, producers, and cast. Each interviewee briefly explains what the film is about from start to finish. The director, John Cameron Mitchell, sees the film as a guidebook on how to move on in the face of forces that can buffet people throughout their lives. This very idea of moving forward following a tragedy, no matter how difficult or painful, becomes the overall theme of the film. The producer Leslie Urdang also argues that by depicting the possibility of enduring the unendurable the film becomes cathartic.

In describing how to endure, how to come out the other end, the film does not push a prescriptive agenda. It combines sadness and grief with dark humour and sharp, witty sarcasm. By doing this it stays faithful to Lindsay-Abaire's original intention, which he states clearly in the play's author notes:

> Yes, *Rabbit Hole* is a play about a bereaved family, but that does not mean they go through the day glazed-over, on the verge of tears, morose or inconsolable. That would be a torturous and very uninteresting play to sit through. The characters are, instead, highly functional, unsentimental, spirited and, often, funny people who are trying to manoeuvre their way through grief and around each other. [...] It's a sad play. Don't make it any sadder than it needs to be. Avoid sentimentality and histrionics at all costs.
> (*Rabbit Hole* by David Lindsay-Abaire, 2006, p.159)

Mitchell certainly sticks to this vision in his film. Even the new scenes and dialogues written for the film carry the same dramedy edge. The script follows a narrative where the timeline of events is almost absent, apart from the information that it has been eight months since Danny's death. This timeless quality adds to the overall universal appeal of the story.

Rabbit Hole starts in medias res. Set in Larchmont, New York, Becca and Howie Corbett were living the life of a happy and wealthy suburban couple when the tragedy struck eight months ago. Now, Becca is stuck as a home-maker who cannot go back to her job at Sotheby's and is almost imprisoned emotionally in a big house full of memories of Danny. She also feels isolated, alienated, and angry because her best friend Debbie did not even call her after the incident. Even though Howie finds some distraction through his work as a broker and at occasional squash matches with his close friend and Debbie's husband Rick (Jon Tenney), the way Becca shifts between being irritable and aloof makes things extra hard for him. They try to attend the meetings of a family bereavement support group, but Becca is unable to stand the religious character of some of the participants and publicly rebukes them. Her thorny mood gradually pushes Howie towards Gabby, another mother in the group who feels as ignored at home as Howie. Izzy's unexpected pregnancy, Nat's regular references to religious comfort in the face of adversities, Becca's unsuc-cessful attempt to go back to work, and her dislike of the family dog Taz (which stays with Nat and Izzy) make the couple's relationship even more fraught. These emotional entanglements are further tested when Becca runs into Jason at a public library out of the blue and decides to follow him. Out of this rather stalky behaviour grows an interesting new type of relationship: not a friendship due to age difference, not an alternative mother–son bond, but a meeting of minds marred by a trauma. This relationship paves the way for them to verbalise their inner anguish and forgiveness. As Jason tells more of his science-fiction story of parallel universes, both he and Becca find some unexpected comfort in the possibility that their current lives might simply be the saddest version of their existences in a multiverse. Through the simple and sincere act of being together without pointing blame, Becca's inner turmoil slowly eases. As Howie realises that he loves Becca and cannot be unfaithful, Becca extends her forgive-ness towards her friend Debbie, and becomes more tolerant towards Nat and Izzy. The film ends with a big garden party where Becca and Howie are smiling and genuinely making an effort to enjoy the company of other people. As the guests leave, they are left behind sitting in the garden, holding hands, clearly determined to support each other to face another day.

Lindsay-Abaire, who also wrote the script for the film, has specifically expanded one storyline, and changed another one entirely. In the play, Howie's strictly romantic affair is only discussed between Izzy and Howie in a conver-sation, and Gabby is not even a character. In the film, however, she is portrayed as the female version of Howie, suffering both the loss of her child as well as criticism and neglect from her husband. Because of their failing marriages and traumas, Gabby and Howie find solace and a brief breathing space in each other's company. Also in the play, Jason is portrayed as a teenager who is surpris-ingly wise beyond his years. He contacts the Corbett family and actively seeks an opportunity to talk to them both in person to tell his version of events and feelings. In the film, this rather confident, enthusiastic, and maybe a bit unrealistic portrayal of a teenager is changed with the depiction of a shy and pensive young man who communicates his self-reproach only after being stalked by Becca.

There are a few more short scene additions which do not appear in the play: Becca's gardening scene at the beginning; her unsuccessful visit to Sotheby's to fish for a new job; Izzy's birthday party at a bowling alley; Jason and Becca's secret meetings at a park; Howie's dog-walking scene with Taz; and his scenes with Gabby. These scene additions, however, do not change the overall story arc, and the film follows the play's main narrative focus from start to finish.

Throughout the film, several visual symbols are repeatedly shown. As with previous films analysed, these symbols and their rich meanings contribute to the way the characters come out of their crypts. In *Rabbit Hole*, there are five recurring universal symbols. These are: garden; house; kitchen; car; and dog.

The film starts with a garden scene (01:23) and ends with another one (84:36) which makes the storyline come full circle. However, there are striking differences between the two. In the first garden scene, the director shows images around the house and the neighbourhood as the film begins: the big city in the distance; a familiar tree down the road with cat-eye reflectors on; and a slightly ajar gate to the garden. These are the first clues to understanding the suburban life and the traffic accident that will be revealed later. Becca is seen in the garden pulling a big sack of compost. According to the director, this is a great metaphor for her grief, which she drags around and which she is trying to create a new life out of. This is symbolised in her attempt to garden and to grow new plants. She is visibly trying to be busy to distract her mind. It also is a nod to her nurturing character as a mother, a wife, a sister, and a daughter. She plants the flowers, smiles at them, and starts to water them when her neighbour Peg (Patricia Kalember) walks into the garden and invites her and Howie to a party that evening. Peg accidentally but carelessly steps on one of the plants Becca has just planted. Becca kindly turns down the invite, saying they had plans, but looks sad because of the now crushed plant, another nod to the accident where her son was taken away from her due to what she perceives as the carelessness of a stranger. In this scene Becca is on her own, looking isolated, and the fact that she turns down her neighbour's invite indicates that she is not fond of socialising at that moment in time.

The final garden scene of the film shows all the characters mentioned or seen in the film together, except Danny, Jason, and Gabby. In this scene, the social isolation or the desire to be away from people is no more. Becca is surrounded by friends and family, smiling, and making a conscious effort to enjoy life's more positive moments. The film ends with her and Howie in the garden after the party is over, holding hands, and looking into the distance. This time Becca is not on her own. She and Howie are physically and emotionally supporting each other when nobody is around, indicating that not only they have forgiven themselves and each other but also their love for each other is strong enough to survive the loss of Danny.

Jung refers to garden symbology quite a few times in his *Collected Works*. For example, he mentions the pre-Homeric idea of *hieros gamos* in relation to the rebirth myth and the garden of the gods, the eternal union of the sun and the sea (CW 5, para.364). When listing psychological typologies, he describes introverted people as individuals living in a secluded garden, away from inquisitive people (CW 6, para.977). He also refers to the Garden of Eden (CW 9i, para.73) as a symbol of both paradise and individuation, mentioning the Tree of Life and the Tree of Knowledge.

Biedermann (1996) refers to the Garden of Eden from an alchemical perspective. He argues that, as a symbol, the Garden of Eden represents a destination that requires considerable struggle to reach. Chevalier and Gheerbrant (1996a), however, point out another meaning of garden symbolism. They refer to the dreamwork of Ernest Aeppli and describe gardens as places where fundamental psychological growth transpires. Ronnberg and Martin (2010c), on the other hand, argue that neither a garden nor the human soul can be entirely domesticated.

These alternative perspectives of garden symbolism point out a figurative, extra narrative. Becca's first appearance in the film as a traumatised, isolated, and a slightly introverted woman is highlighted by her presence in a carefully tended garden, which she tries to create new life out of. This garden, which came before Danny, appears as the first creation of her marriage to Howie. Even though they built this small patch as a loving and nurturing space for themselves, they were not only unable to protect Danny from a stranger outside the garden boundary, but now cannot protect the plants from careless neighbours inside the garden. In other words, the protection and the domestication attempts fail.

Garden symbolism continues in another context when Becca and Jason start meeting at a big public park. They sit under a tree and gently talk about the incident that changed them forever. As Jason admits his possible errors on the day of the accident and as Becca forgives him, they symbolically enter a new realm of compassion for each other (and themselves), which flourishes out of a traumatic loss. They find their inner peace, which fits in with Biedermann's description of the (alchemical) Garden of Eden.

Another symbol that ties in with this nurturing idea of a garden is the house. Becca and Howie live in an exquisitely decorated and well-kept house with many floors and rooms. Mitchell's camera shows several parts of the house all throughout the film: the living room; attic; exercise room; utility room; basement; Becca and Howie's bedroom; and Danny's old room. It is easy to guess that their original intention was to live happily ever after in this blissful state as a family. However, after Danny's death, their home is now joyless and feels like a prison that they cannot escape. Filled with Danny's memories, being in the house is a daily torture for them. Ronnberg and Martin (2010d) also point out these contrasting meanings of house symbology in a similar way. From domestic bliss to domestic violence, from a yearning to be home to a fear of going back home, house essentially represents both the light and the dark side of the psyche, which develops and ultimately transforms.

Jung wrote about house symbolism too. In fact, his famous house dream in 1909 eventually led to his break-up with Freudian psychology and the emergence of his collective unconscious theory (Jones, 2007). In *Experimental Researches* (CW 2) and *Symbols of Transformation* (CW 5), there are numerous references to word associations and dreams of houses/homes. But he also argued that home/house, as one of the most universal symbols of man, is also at the epicentre of changes in his consciousness (CW 8, para.428).

This perspective is helpful for explaining the situation in *Rabbit Hole*. Becca and Howie's sense of a perfect and happy home gets tarnished by Danny's untimely death, and they are pushed in opposite directions, which strains their relationship. Becca wants to sell the house because it is unbearable for her to spend her days at home reminiscing about Danny and the trauma. Howie, on the other hand, wants to hold on to the house as it is still full of good and happy memories which he is strongly attached to even though they hurt him. The friction of these conflicting wishes creates a challenge that Becca and Howie are not emotionally ready to handle. Becca thinks Howie is too soft and attached to the past, and Howie thinks Becca is too logical and insensitive as she wants to get rid of literally everything that reminds them of their little son (including his clothes, toys, videos, and ultimately the house itself). In other words, they are emotionally undermined by the approach and avoidance conflicts in them.

However, their house, which brought them together and now pulls them apart, also triggers a change of consciousness. This change is further suggested by one specific part of their house: the kitchen. Historically speaking, fireplaces and stoves were commonly placed at the centre of rustic houses (Snodgrass, 2004). As a source of both heat and nourishment, a kitchen is an indispensable part of a house, where different ingredients are chopped, seasoned, boiled, roasted, combined, and transformed by heat to become more appetising. In other words, a kitchen is a domestic science lab.

Kitchen symbology builds on these actual physical and chemical changes that foods go through. Chevalier and Gheerbrant (1996b) argue that kitchens appear at the core of alchemical and psychological changes. This is of course due to food processing and its effect on our senses and tastebuds. Ronnberg and Martin (2010d) share the same view and point out the consequences of these transformations deeply embedded in all cultures. Kitchen, generally regarded as 'the heart of the house', is where people gather, talk, and create meals by bringing different ingredients together. Like bringing order out of chaos, kitchen is the dynamic centre of homes where the necessary nourishment for the body and mind comes from.

Mitchell included seven different kitchen scenes in *Rabbit Hole*: first, Becca and Howie are preparing their dinner straight after the opening scene of the film; second, Becca offers Izzy crème brûlée and Izzy announces her pregnancy; third, Becca stands alone in the kitchen, looking sad and lost, then removes the drawings and breakfast items of Danny; fourth, the beginning of the open house day when Becca is baking a cake for potential buyers who will visit their house; fifth, when Jason unexpectedly walks into the kitchen at the end of the open house day and surprises Becca, Howie, Izzy, and Nat; sixth, the evening of that same day when Becca is baking again when she asks Howie about his secret pot smoking and Howie asks Becca about her secret meetings with Jason; and seventh, the morning conversation of Becca and Howie in the kitchen after they spent the night separately for the first time.

In four of these scenes, Becca is either busy with cooking or offering food to other people. Therefore, the kitchen setting not only indicates her nurturing nature but also her repeated attempts in finding a useful/tasty distraction from the horror of the trauma, symbolically navigating between the chaos of raw ingredients and the order of a well-cooked meal. Becca and Howie's kitchen is also used as a centre where important talks and arguments take place. This is especially evident in the fifth scene, when Jason walks in unannounced to drop his finished comic book and triggers an argument. Seeing the teenager who killed his son, Howie reacts furiously, but Becca, having already forgiven Jason, is torn between protecting Jason and Howie, and tries to avoid a physical confrontation between the two. In the last kitchen scene, which ties into the peaceful and bittersweet flashforward scene in the garden that ends the film, Becca and Howie decide to keep the house, face the future storms together as a couple, and forgive each other and themselves for the death of Danny. In this sense, kitchen symbolism plays a heavy part in the film, constantly mirroring the pressures, fluctuations, convergences, and separations, and of course the inner transformations these characters undergo throughout the story.

Another symbol that keeps appearing in the film that ties in not only with the transformation but also with the emotional journey of the characters is car/automobile. Clearly the car symbol is central to the story, since Danny was killed in a traffic accident. In other words, the trauma that trapped Becca, Howie, and Jason in their shared crypt is caused by a car. Mitchell shows Becca, Howie, and Jason in a car (either as a driver or a passenger) several times throughout the film. It is, however, unknown whether this directorial choice is alluding to the accident consciously or unconsciously.

Jung examined several symbols in his studies into dreams and alchemy. He surveyed cars, airplanes, and trams under one general category: vehicles. According to him, vehicles, whether old or contemporary, are linked to the ego. They echo different aspects of one's inner life in relation to its journey in time, always moving forward either alone or with other people (CW 12, para.153). Building on Jung's dream work, Ronnberg and Martin (2010a) point out that car is also a symbol of power, social status, individuality, speed, our direct interaction with other people/drivers on the road, and, therefore, our capability to abide by the law.

In *Rabbit Hole*, the car that killed Danny was driven by Jason. Therefore, his development towards becoming a responsible, independent adult is now disrupted by an unfortunate accident. As a result of this misfortune, he does not drive in the film and is reduced to being a passive passenger in other vehicles. Becca and Howie, on the other hand, continue to drive, and their relationships with their cars are different. Howie not only uses his car to go to work and to the child bereavement support group meetings but also enjoys moments of feeling carefree and adolescent as he shares a spliff with Gabby in her car. This common and forward inner journey symbolism is further emphasised in the way Becca uses her car. She drives around to get rid of Danny's belongings and also deliberately follows Jason's school bus twice while stalking him, before she gets caught.

The last car scene of the film highlights the difference between the individual life paths of Becca and Jason. Becca drives to Jason's house to see him. As soon as she arrives, she sees that Jason is getting ready to leave for his prom night with his friends. As the classic cabriolet drives by with cheerful teenagers, Becca starts sobbing (74:23) and wailing uncontrollably in her car, lost in conflicting emotions: feeling happy for Jason, seeing him move on but also thinking how her boy would never see a prom night and how her happy future with Danny is no more. This heart-breaking scene encapsulates two opposite and separate life paths and journeys. Jason will not continue to hang out with Becca because she is neither a friend nor a mother substitute. He will build another life for himself. It is also here that Becca realises she will have to choose to live despite the loss of Danny, and his absence will not be filled by Jason.

This duality is also reflected in one other symbol as well: dog. The symbolism of dogs is explored in Chapter 5. The gist of them is depicted again in *Rabbit Hole*. Becca and Howie's dog Taz, just like Erica's dog Curtis at the end of *The Brave One* (2007), plays a part in steering the protagonists to situations, choices, and worlds between life and death.

Taz first appears as an unwanted pet, now staying with Nat and Izzy. This is probably due to two reasons: firstly, his presence constantly reminds Becca and Howie of the accident and Danny's death – because if Danny had not run after Taz, he would have still been alive; and secondly, their feelings of anger and helplessness have been projected onto Taz and therefore he is banished from his loving home. Becca is so adamant about Taz being away that this leads to a heated argument with Howie which ends up with him accusing Becca of being uncaring.

After this argument, Taz comes back home, but there is considerable tension between the couple. This tension leads to a bigger argument between Jason and Howie when Jason unexpectedly visits during the open house day. Howie, feeling betrayed by Becca due to her secret meetings with the person who killed his son, takes Taz for a walk in a fury. Under the pressure of conflicting emotions and possibly with a bit of resentment towards the dog, he yanks his lead violently to hurt him. Az Taz whimpers in pain, Howie instantly regrets his action and hugs Taz in tears, apologising and finally forgiving the dog for doing something he does naturally: running and playing.

Therefore Taz, just like Curtis is for Erica in *The Brave One*, becomes the motivator of an inner shift in Howie. Howie, progressing from the point of being a simple owner, to having a resentful attachment, and finally to feeling unconditional love towards Taz, learns not only how to forgive but also how to love another even when wounded by them. Ronnberg and Martin (2010b) describe this inner growth as a gift, a rewarding result of a profoundly emotional relationship with an animal. By mirroring the treatment they receive from humans (good or bad), dogs ultimately appear as a symbol of opposites that reflect human nature.

While all these recurring symbols contribute to the overall psychological transformation of Becca, Howie, and Jason, the main problem of the film stays fixed: the sudden death of Danny. This trauma is the reason why the relationships are so strained, the conversations are so prickly, and the emotions are running so high. In other words, it is this trauma that has trapped these three characters in a shared crypt. The memory of the accident is the ghost that haunts them wherever they go and whatever they do. In the next section, I will explore the inner workings of this three-way trauma and its grief-theory perspectives.

9.2 Trauma-related ruminations and forgiveness

As explored in *The Brave One* (2007), post-traumatic stress disorder (PTSD) is a condition that manifests itself after a traumatic event like accident, rape, murder, natural disaster, war, etc. Moreover, as explored in *A Single Man* (2009), a sudden loss following a lethal traffic accident can burden the bereaved with a state of anguish, which can be diagnosed as complicated mourning. In *Rabbit Hole*, these two conditions are present and affect the daily lives of Becca, Howie, and Jason visibly. However, in contrast with both *The Brave One* and *A Single Man*, the protagonists are neither homicidal nor suicidal.

According to two different studies (European Child Safety Alliance, 2007; Peden et al., 2004), traffic accidents in developed countries are the top cause of death among children and adolescents. In Europe, roughly 9,000 individuals younger than the age of 19 perish and 355,000 are injured annually on the road. Therefore, Danny's death unfortunately reflects a common sociological problem that affects many parents and survivors. Plus, Becca, Howie, and Jason do not display destructive behaviours even though they are directly affected by the accident. They, however, display a common symptom, which is described as trauma-related rumination.

Trauma-related rumination is a cyclic harmful mode of thinking that follows a distressing experience. Survivors of these experiences are caught up in a repetitive but unhelpful questioning of the specific event that traumatised them. These questions focus on the causes and the consequences of the event and generally include other associations related to the trauma (Ehlers and Clark, 2000; Elwood et al., 2009). The 'why did this happen to me?' question and the 'could I have done something else to prevent it?' question are the two most common questions that follow such an experience (Birrer and Michael, 2011; Michael et al., 2007). Because the survivors' minds focus on the causes and the consequences of a past event, trauma-related rumination is thought to be different than other forms of unhelpful and repetitive thinking (for example, the thinking of depressed people) (Elwood et al, 2009). Ehlers and Clark (2000) also argue that this rumination is a type of cognitive avoidance, and it unfortunately assists people in avoiding the necessary emotional engagement with (and therefore the constructive processing of) the traumatic event itself.

There are several distinctive features that are observed in survivors of sudden death (Worden, 2010). These survivors sometimes look and feel confused as if their loss is not real. Due to the abruptness and the unexpectedness of their traumatic separation, they can have complex feelings of regret, guilt, powerlessness, and a strong urge to blame third-parties. Especially difficult cases, like murder or accidents, and their legal proceedings can frustrate what might have been a natural mourning process. Recurring nightmares and/or depression can also deeply trouble the survivors. Furthermore, sudden death derails the meaning-making process and survivors are left with a simple but unanswerable question of 'why'. Parkes and Prigerson (2010) also mention that especially if the untimely death is witnessed by the bereaved, the memories related to this event may become intrusive and bury other pleasing memories so deep that the grief might become overpowering.

In the film, Becca, Howie, and Jason are not only caught up in trauma-related rumination but also display a combination of some of the features mentioned above. As revealed towards the end of the film in a short flashback scene, Becca witnessed the accident as she ran out of the house after Danny. Throughout the film, she is depicted as snappy, snarky, brutally honest, and, on one occasion, physically violent to a stranger at the supermarket. The reason for this behaviour is revealed in the scene where Howie accuses Becca of deliberately deleting videos of Danny that he kept on his phone: she tries to contain her emotions even though she feels guilty and helpless.

In this crucial scene, Howie realises that Danny's videos are gone and starts shouting at Becca. Becca tries to explain that she did not delete them intentionally but might have done so by mistake when she was trying to find the roofer's phone number. The conversation turns into a painful and heated argument where they express their misplaced and untrue guilt about the accident. Becca thinks if she had not answered the phone on the day she would not have been distracted and could have run out to prevent Danny from stepping into the road. Howie thinks if he had not brought home the dog, then Danny would not have chased after him anyway. Howie also accuses Becca of trying to get rid of anything that has some connection to Danny, his drawings, clothes, their house, implying that the deletion of the videos looks suspicious. Becca then accuses Howie of not seeing and understanding how difficult it is for her to bear this pain and still look as normal as possible. Howie says he is unable to continue like this and says he wants the dog back because he misses him a lot.

What this scene reveals is the fact that Becca and Howie are still mourning, but in different ways. They both feel guilty, helpless, and blame themselves for different reasons. While Becca is trying to block the traumatic memory by either donating Danny's clothes and toys or putting them in the basement, where she cannot see them as painful reminders, Howie is going to the other extreme of being constantly attached to any digital or physical artefact that belonged to or reminds him of Danny. It is clear from the argument that none of these actions really work, and their feelings of helplessness are intensified by their inability to stop the pain.

Jason, on the other hand, is depicted as a silent, shy teenager absorbed in his thoughts. When he first appears in the film, he is on his school bus going home. He is not speaking to anyone, and he gazes out of the window with a sad face and in a completely disengaged state. When he appears again in the film, he is in a public library returning a book called *Parallel Universes* by Fred Alan Wolf (1990). This is where he bumps into Becca, unaware of being followed by her. It is inferred by the shocked look on Jason's face that he has not seen Becca since the accident. In his third scene, where he confronts Becca and asks if she was following him, he is still cautious and anxious about talking to her because he does not know how she may react.

While these three key scenes indicate that Jason is as much traumatized as Becca and Howie, his self-blame, grief, and rumination are revealed in the next scene where he accepts Becca's offer to talk at the park. They sit in the shade, under a tree, facing a big wide open green space fully bathed in sunlight (40:49). In the distance, a mother and her son are playing frisbee in the sunshine. The composition of light and dark in this scene is quite significant in terms of Becca and Jason's position in life compared to the mother and son in front of them, playing games and enjoying life. Becca and Jason's short, unpretentious, and tender conversation echoes a dialogue between a grieving mother and a surrogate son.

In their first scene together in the park, both look apprehensive but compassionate. It starts with Becca asking Jason about whether this situation feels weird for him. When Jason says no, the conversation starts with small talk about his education to break the ice. After a brief moment of silence, Jason says he is sorry and how he wished he had driven somewhere else on that day. This makes Becca tearful immediately, not only because of her loss but also because she now sees how Jason owns the damage he caused. She briefly says his apology is helpful and continues to sit on the bench alone after Jason is gone, completely in shock and awe of what happened.

Jason's confession of self-guilt comes in his second meeting with Becca at the same park bench (49:48). This time the camera faces them directly, not showing the shadows, but the light is reflected on their faces. Meaning, there is something changing, there is some new lightness in all this heavy drama. During this poignant confession and forgiveness scene, Jason slowly reveals the fact that he might have been going slightly over the speed limit when the accident happened. He says he is not sure, but at least he acknowledges the possibility. This confession makes them both tearful. Becca simply says it is ok. Jason simply thanks her.

The link between wrongdoing and forgiveness is always a curious one, and it has been one of the recurrent themes in art especially since Greek drama. The *Oxford Dictionary of Philosophy* (2016) defines forgiveness as a paradox because the act of forgiving fundamentally treats people who have done something wrong better than they deserve. The same article refers to the advice of St.

Augustine of Hippo that people hate the sin rather than the sinner because the character of the sinner may only be accidentally connected to the action itself (Ibid., p.182).

In *Rabbit Hole*, forgiveness is achieved on many levels. Becca's act of forgiving Jason slowly changes her to become more tolerant towards her religious mother Nat and extends towards her friend Debbie, who finally appears at the end of the film in a scene of a happy extended family get-together. Howie not only forgives his dog Taz but also realises he cannot have an extra-marital affair with Gabby just because Becca is emotionally distraught and unavailable. Jason's act of owning up to his momentary distraction behind the wheel brings a compassionate understanding from Becca which ultimately helps him to forgive himself and move on.

While all of this complex human drama is fictional in the film, it surprisingly can happen in real life as well. In an episode of the *Morning Edition* programme on National Public Radio (NPR, 2015), three people who were affected by an unfortunate traffic accident found a new connection and forgiveness. Titled as 'Out of tragedy, an unexpected connection is made' (Ibid.), the episode told the inspiring story of Megiddeh Goldston who formed a bond with the Hameed family in Colorado Springs after her sister accidentally killed Raphael Hameed's five-year-old son Ish. Two days after the tragedy, Megiddeh's sister asked for forgiveness, which helped everyone move forward and eased their suffering.

The consequence of choosing to forgive appears to alleviate the symptoms of PTSD and trauma-induced rumination in real life. For example, Strelan and Covic (2006) argue that forgiveness can be a constructive coping strategy for people who face the aftermath of a traumatic event. Forgiveness of others, especially when the offender is at fault, might trigger a decrease in PTSD symptoms (Weinberg, 2013; Weinberg, Gil, and Gilbar, 2014; Worthington, Witvliet, and Lerner, 2005). It is discovered that some of the negative emotions, such as anger and hatred against the offender decreased in victims if they showed mercy. The earlier studies of Worthington (2001) also indicate a link between the act of forgiveness and a general sense of improvement in PTSD sufferers.

It is important to note that grief theorists such as Parkes, Bowlby, Worden, and Kübler-Ross do not elaborate on how forgiveness can be an important component in dealing with loss. However, the philosophical analyses of Hannah Arendt (1959) point out that the act of forgiving breaks the causal relationship between wrongdoing and retaliation. Research into the psychology of forgiveness (Bergin, 1988; Cunningham, 1985; Droll, 1984; Smith, 1981) also shows that when/if the forgiver sees the offender under a new light (for example, their sorrow, regret, or simple humanity masked by the offence itself) it fosters feelings of empathy, which help both sides move beyond the vicious circle of pain and hurt.

Rabbit Hole clearly shows that all three characters finally break out of this cycle in two key scenes, which follow each other at the end of the film. The first scene is Jason and Becca's last scene at the park, straight after Jason's school prom. In this poignant scene, and for the first time, they walk together in the sunshine (78:31). This simple and ordinary physical act is a perfect symbol of the shift in their psyches, moving from the darkness to the light. Even though they briefly talk about the myth of *Orpheus and Eurydice*[2], their conversation is about Jason's comic book on parallel universes. Jason believes that because space is infinite then everything is possible, there are tons of different possibilities for everyone. Becca then acknowledges that this version of them is a sad version and that somewhere out there, in another universe, she and Jason are happy, and everything works out for them. She finds this thought comforting, thinking that she is having a good time somewhere else.

The second scene, which is also the very last scene of the film, is the complete reversal of the opening scene and it is a visual proof of Becca and Howie's ongoing healing process. As I explored earlier, the garden where Becca was on her own and isolated at the beginning of the film turns into a haven where her friends and family come together, celebrating the love they feel for each other and the joy of being alive. This touching finale depicts how the act of forgiving themselves and each other helps Becca and Howie come out of their trapped states of anguish and grief. It contributes to a collective (or even universal) insight that one is not alone, that there is a new life after death and loss.

These complex layers of storytelling make *Rabbit Hole* a captivating but hopeful human drama. As the producer Gigi Pritzker says in her interview, the film charts a journey from a devastating beginning to an optimistic ending, signifying the possibility of recovery after a traumatic loss. In the next section, I will explore this journey of moving forward and how trauma can be transformed.

9.3 Fine, actually – transforming trauma

Unlike the previous films I have analysed so far, *Rabbit Hole* comes across more like a documentary and less like fiction to me. It is this confident realism that keeps the narrative relatable to many trauma sufferers. For example, there are no science-fiction elements of the kind in *Solaris* (2002); no one-dimensional bad characters of the type in *The Brave One* (2007); no exaggerated and weaponised impossible mathematical formula such as that in *The Bank* (2001); no sudden death of the protagonist, such as the one in *A Single Man* (2009); and no manipulation of facts of the kind in *Saving Mr. Banks* (2013). Instead, there is a multidimensional, lifelike and searingly honest portrayal of people who are genuinely trying to find a solution to their emotional suffering. In other words, *Rabbit Hole*, even though it is fiction, has a lot of soul and candid humanity put into it.

This candidness is very much reflected in the dialogues. For example, during the first family bereavement support group scene (12:35), Becca cannot contain her annoyance when one of the mothers attending the meeting expresses the comfort she found in religion. She says she believes that God needed another angel, so He took her daughter. Hearing this, Becca snaps and asks everyone in the room why God, being so powerful and all, did not just create another angel instead of taking their son Danny. The question is logical, cold, maybe inappropriate, but utterly honest and human given the delicate and painful situation.

Jung referred to honesty mainly within the contextual framework of confession. Based on the Catholic rite called the sacrament of penance, he wrote about the human need to confess and the need to be forgiven. He sees confession as a method to relieve the tension of guilt, shame, or remorse, and also as a way to end social estrangement (CW 4, para.432). Once the burden of a personal and hidden wrongdoing is shared with another person, the loneliness that comes with hiding it is reduced.

In the three-way trauma of Becca, Howie, and Jason, the deeply personal, individually felt and differently shaded guilt obstructs their paths to recovery. As a result, they become estranged, bitter, or simply lost in grief. Becca feels guilty because she thinks that she did not pay enough attention to Danny on the day of the accident. Howie feels guilty because he thinks that his idea of getting a dog for Danny paved the way to his death. Jason feels guilty because he thinks that he was doing the wrong thing at the wrong place at the wrong time. However, they each confess their guilt to each other in absolute honesty, no matter how painful or unspeakable it might seem to them. In return, their grief eases off as they forgive each other and themselves, and their moral isolation ceases.

Jung inevitably (and perhaps predictably) drew parallels between the Catholic practice of confession and the relationship between a therapist and a patient. In a psychotherapy setting, a therapist is the person who is officially/clinically permitted to listen to their client's factual or supposed wrongdoings, contain their mental and emotional turmoil, and offer guidance/support when necessary. Out of this close contact, a liberation, or in Jung's words, a catharsis, emerges, which cleanses the consciousness of any incompatible or disturbing content. However, he also notes that this type of cathartic cleansing needs not just a logical, forensic retelling of facts but also owning and freeing up repressed feelings (CW 16, para.134).

It is important to note that there is neither a psychotherapist nor a therapy scene in *Rabbit Hole*. However, the catharsis is still achieved by Becca, Howie, and Jason. Their unwavering truthfulness, the way they are honest with themselves and each other, is what delivers their needed relief. According to Todd (1985), a sincere confession ultimately brings a sense of healing to people's wounded selves. She argues that the presence of another person who hears the confession, and acknowledges the pain and sorrow, is crucial. Because being perceived is the key to end the loneliness and estrangement.

Confession and forgiveness typically require the faculty of speech because the quickest way for human beings to express their thoughts and feelings is to talk. One of the alchemical stages that Jung lists and refers to in his *Collected Works* is called *fermentatio* (CW 12, para.340). Based on the chemical process where enzymes anaerobically break down an organic compound, convert its molecules into acids, gases, or alcohol, and create something new (such as vinegar, wine, beer, cheese, etc.), *fermentatio* refers to the transmutation of the elements in the psyche. The maturation, the renewal, the passage from a state of decay/death to a state of a new life are all connected with this alchemical stage. Physically, *fermentatio* is sometimes linked with the rousing of energy in the body, which then gets expressed via the throat as the energy is released in spoken words.

Ronnberg and Martin (2010e) also point out that any negative emotion can stiffen and constrict the throat, restricting vocal expressions and, therefore, blocking these energies in the psyche without a suitable outlet. In *Rabbit Hole*, the blockage in Becca, Howie, and Jason that was caused by the death of Danny is simply cleared by speaking about their inner truths openly. By expressing their thoughts and feelings sincerely, they not only heal but also transmute their anguish/state of decay into a new, hopeful state of living.

Of course, it is important to mention another alchemical process taking place specifically in the relationship between Becca and Jason: *coniunctio*. This is the symbolic union of opposites, which in return produces something new. At the beginning of *Mysterium Coniunctionis* (CW 14, para.1), Jung gives a detailed list of some of these (symbolic) opposites, which are explored throughout his *Collected Works* in different ways: good/evil; up/down; light/dark; hot/cold.

In *Rabbit Hole*, Becca and Jason not only come together as feminine and masculine opposites, but also as the injured and the injurer. The way they find harmony out of the chaos caused by the death of Danny, the way they see each other's sorrow and acknowledge the loss, is certainly an attraction forged in and shaped by compassionate love. It is crucial to remember Erica Bain's impasse explored in the finale of *The Brave One* (2007) here. As a victim, she was face to face with her attacker, who neither showed any compassion nor remorse. The opposites in that film confronted each other in enmity. There was no room for forgiveness to flourish. In *Rabbit Hole*, however, out of the sympathetic union between the injurer and the injured comes the birth of serenity, a renewed strength to face another day no matter how terrible the loss is.

This serenity, this calm wisdom after such a traumatic loss, is also beautifully encapsulated in the scene where Becca and her mother Nat are emptying Danny's room, clearing up the space, then taking his belongings to the basement. As mentioned earlier, home is at the centre of spiritual quests and psychic transformations. In this basement scene (68:59), Nat, as a mother who lost her son to suicide, passes on her wisdom to her daughter, who is suffering from a different traumatic loss. By answering her heart-breaking question about grief in a candid but caring way, she also helps Becca transform. Exquisitely written by David Lindsay-Abaire, I see this dialogue as an honest, realistic description of surviving trauma:

BECCA: Does it go away?
NAT: What.
BECCA: This feeling. Does it ever go away?
NAT: No. I don't think it does. Not for me it hasn't. And that's goin' on eleven years.
    It changes though.
BECCA: How?

NAT: I don't know. The weight of it, I guess. At some point it becomes bearable. It turns into something that you can crawl out from under. And carry around – like a brick in your pocket. And you forget it every once in a while, but then you reach in for whatever reason and there it is: 'Oh right. *That.*' Which could be awful. But not all the time. Sometimes it's kinda… . Not that you *like* it exactly, but it's what you have instead of your son, so don't wanna let go of it either. So you carry it around. And it doesn't go away, which is…

BECCA: Which is what?

NAT: Fine… actually.

(*Rabbit Hole* by David Lindsay-Abaire, 2006, pp.129–130)

9.4 From forgiveness to self-compassion

One of the things I find really interesting about this film (and the play) is that the author/scriptwriter David Lindsay-Abaire did not experience such a loss in his life. He based his play on the stories he had heard about couples losing their children and had the inspiration after he used his biggest fear to create the story: the fear of losing a child unexpectedly (Riley, 2006).

The reason I find it interesting is that the film, even though it is fictional, portrays a couple deep in mourning convincingly. Their battle to move forward, their anger, their boredom, their occasional light-heartedness, and their tense and strained relationship with the rest of the world appear authentic. This authenticity is further reinforced by the real-life example I have mentioned earlier: some couples, even in their darkest moment, have the power to listen and offer their forgiveness to a stranger who, completely by mistake, wounded them for life. Only through compassionate honesty are they able to find their way out of their shared crypt and traumatised state.

Their way out is also reflected in the film's tagline: the only way out is through. This expression, probably first used by Robert Frost in his 1915 poem 'A Servant to Servants' (Frost, 1979), summarises their journey. By truly acknowledging each other's fears, regrets, sorrow, and good intentions, they are able to move forward. By moving forward, they finally come out of their intrapsychic tomb.

This interesting blend of imagination and real-life experience continues in the next and last film analysis. In this chapter, I will be looking at another choice and another way out of a crypt. My last inquiry brings together several of the previous storylines and Jungian concepts I have discussed earlier and explores the importance of self-compassion. Hence, my question is simple but provocative: can healing be a choice?

Filmography

The Bank (2001) Directed by R. Connolly [film]. Australia
The Brave One (2007) Directed by N. Jordan [film]. USA

Rabbit Hole (2010) Directed by J.C. Mitchell [film]. USA
Saving Mr. Banks (2013) Directed by J.L. Hancock [film]. USA
A Single Man (2009) Directed by T. Ford [film]. USA
Solaris (2002) Directed by S. Soderbergh [film]. USA

Notes

1 Even though it is never mentioned in the film (or play), it is implied that Jason's father is dead and that his comic-book is an extension of his wish fulfilment. Of course, Becca reads the entire thing differently and from her own perspective, imagining Danny is well and alive in a parallel universe.
2 In this famous Greek myth (Guirand, 1996), Orpheus, the famous hero of Thrace, falls in love with and marries a nymph, Eurydice. However, she dies after she is bitten by a snake. Orpheus, now inconsolable, travels to the Underworld and implores Hades to let Eurydice walk back to life with him. Hades agrees, with one condition: Orpheus should not turn and look back at his wife during the journey. Impatient and filled with excitement, Orpheus turns and looks at Eurydice just before reaching the gates of the Underworld, which results in her being forever claimed by Hades. Orpheus dies from grief. While this short story can be another example for the crypt theory, it is also possible to read it as a cautionary tale where the hero refuses to move on after his loss and faces his tragic end.

Bibliography

Abraham, N. and Torok, M. (1994) *The Shell and the Kernel: Renewals of Psychoanalysis. Volume I.* Chicago: University of Chicago Press.
Arendt, H. (1959) *The Human Condition: A Study of the Central Dilemmas Facing Modern Man.* New York: Doubleday Anchor.
Bergin, A.E. (1988) 'Three contributions of a spiritual perspective to counseling, psychotherapy, and behavioral change', *Counseling and Values*, 33, pp.21–31.
Biedermann, H. (1996) 'Garden' in *The Wordsworth Dictionary of Symbolism.* Hertfordshire: Wordsworth Editions.
Birrer, E. and Michael, T. (2011) 'Rumination in PTSD as well as in traumatized and non-traumatized depressed patients: A cross-sectional clinical study', *Behavioural and Cognitive Psychotherapy*, 39(4), pp.381–397.
Chevalier, J. and Gheerbrant, A. (1996a) 'Garden' in *The Penguin Dictionary of Symbols.* London: Penguin.
Chevalier, J. and Gheerbrant, A. (1996b) 'House' in *The Penguin Dictionary of Symbols.* London: Penguin.
Cunningham, B.B. (1985) 'The will to forgive: A pastoral theological view of forgiving', *The Journal of Pastoral Care*, 39, pp.141–149.
Droll, D.M. (1984) *Forgiveness: Theory and Research.* PhD Thesis. University of Nevada, Reno.
Ehlers, A. and Clark, D.M. (2000) 'A cognitive model of posttraumatic stress disorder', *Behaviour Research and Therapy*, 38, pp.319–345.
Elwood, L.S., Hahn, K.S., Olatunji, B.O., and Williams, N.L. (2009) 'Cognitive vulnerabilities to the development of PTSD: A review of four vulnerabilities and the proposal of an integrative vulnerability model', *Clinical Psychology Review*, 29, pp.87–100.

European Child Safety Alliance (2007) *Childhood Road Safety: Facts.* Amsterdam, The Netherlands: EuroSafe.

Frost, R. (1979) *The Poetry of Robert Frost: The Collected Poems.* New York: Henry Holt and Company.

Guirand, F. (ed.) (1996) 'Orpheus and the heroes of Thrace' in *The Larousse Encyclopedia of Mythology.* London: Chancellor Press.

Jones, R.A. (2007) 'A Discovery of meaning: The case of C.G. Jung's house dream', *Culture & Psychology*, 13(2), pp.203–230.

Jung, C.G. (1961) *The Collected Works of C.G. Jung, Volume 4: Freud and Psychoanalysis.* Princeton: Princeton University Press.

Jung, C.G. (1966) *The Collected Works of C.G. Jung, Volume 16: Practice of Psychotherapy.* Princeton: Princeton University Press.

Jung, C.G. (1967) *The Collected Works of C.G. Jung, Volume 5: Symbols of Transformation.* Princeton: Princeton University Press.

Jung, C.G. (1968) *The Collected Works of C.G. Jung, Volume 12: Psychology and Alchemy.* Princeton: Princeton University Press.

Jung, C.G. (1969) *The Collected Works of C.G. Jung, Volume 8: The Structure and Dynamics of the Psyche.* Princeton: Princeton University Press.

Jung, C.G. (1969) *The Collected Works of C.G. Jung, Volume 9, Part 1: Archetypes and the Collective Unconscious.* Princeton: Princeton University Press.

Jung, C.G. (1970) *The Collected Works of C.G. Jung, Volume 14: Mysterium Coniunctionis.* Princeton: Princeton University Press.

Jung, C.G. (1971) *The Collected Works of C.G. Jung, Volume 6: Psychological Types.* Princeton: Princeton University Press.

Jung, C.G. (1973) *The Collected Works of C.G. Jung, Volume 2: Experimental Researches.* Princeton: Princeton University Press.

Lindsay-Abaire, D. (2006) *Rabbit Hole.* New York: Theatre Communications Group.

Michael, T., Halligan, S.L., Clark, D.M., and Ehlers, A. (2007) 'Rumination in post-traumatic stress disorder', *Depression and Anxiety*, 24, pp.307–317.

NPR (2015) 'Out of tragedy, an unexpected connection is made', *Morning Edition*, 2 January.

Parkes, C.M. and Prigerson, H.G. (2010) *Bereavement: Studies of Grief in Adult Life.* 4th ed. London: Penguin.

Peden, M., Scurfield, R., Sleet, D., Mohan, D., Hyder, A.A., Jarawan, E., and Mathers, C. (2004) *World Report on Road Traffic Injury Prevention.* Geneva, Switzerland: World Health Organization.

Riley, J. (2006) 'Down the 'rabbit hole': David Lindsay-Abaire', *Back Stage West*, 13(40), p.11.

Ronnberg, A. and Martin, K. (eds) (2010a) 'Car' in *The Book of Symbols: Reflections on Archetypal Images.* Cologne: Taschen.

Ronnberg, A. and Martin, K. (eds) (2010b) 'Dog' in *The Book of Symbols: Reflections on Archetypal Images.* Cologne: Taschen.

Ronnberg, A. and Martin, K. (eds) (2010c) 'Garden' in *The Book of Symbols: Reflections on Archetypal Images.* Cologne: Taschen.

Ronnberg, A. and Martin, K. (eds) (2010d) 'House/Home' in *The Book of Symbols: Reflections on Archetypal Images.* Cologne: Taschen.

Ronnberg, A. and Martin, K. (eds) (2010e) 'Neck/Throat' in *The Book of Symbols: Reflections on Archetypal Images.* Cologne: Taschen.

Smith, M. (1981) 'The psychology of forgiveness', *The Month*, 14, pp.301–307.

Snodgrass, M.E. (2004) *Encyclopedia of Kitchen History*. Oxon: Fitzroy Dearborn.

Strelan, P. and Covic, T. (2006) 'A review of forgiveness process models and a coping framework to guide future research' in *Journal of Social and Clinical Psychology*, 25, pp.1059–1085. The Oxford Dictionary of Philosophy (2016) 'Forgiveness' in *The Oxford Dictionary of Philosophy*. Oxford: Oxford University Press.

Todd, E. (1985) 'The value of confession and forgiveness according to Jung', *Journal of Religion and Health*, 24(1), pp.39–48.

Weinberg M. (2013) 'The bidirectional dyadic association between tendency to forgive, self-esteem, social support, and PTSD symptoms among terror-attack survivors and their spouses', *Journal of Traumatic Stress*, 26, pp.744–752.

Weinberg M., Gil S., and Gilbar O. (2014) 'Forgiveness, coping and terrorism: Do tendency to forgive and coping strategies associate with the level of posttraumatic symptoms of injured victims of terror attacks?', *Journal of Clinical Psychology*, 70, pp.693–703.

Wolf, F.A. (1990) *Parallel Universes: The Search for Other Worlds*. New York: Simon & Schuster.

Worden, W.J. (2010) *Grief Counselling and Grief Therapy*. Hove: Routledge.

Worthington E.L. (2001) *Five Steps to Forgiveness: The Art and Science of Forgiving*. New York: Crown Publishers.

Worthington E.L., Witvliet C.O., and Lerner A.L. (2005) 'Forgiveness in health research and medical practice', *Explore (NY)*, 1, pp.169–176.

10 Self-compassion and *Cake*

When Viktor Frankl's famous book *Man's Search for Meaning* (Frankl, 2004) was first translated into English it had a different title. It was called *From Death-Camp to Existentialism*. As a profound testament for hope when faced with an impossible situation, the book highlights the importance of the frequently forgotten human ability of choosing, and how making a choice can transform the experience of suffering into meaning.

The last film and case study of this book is *Cake* (2014). Its simple and short name denotes sweetness, layers, sustenance, and celebration. In many ways, *Cake* embodies several story threads explored previously: it depicts suicide attempts; it portrays physical violence towards another person; it includes a vengeful threat to bring down an organisation; it has a human connection; it muses on letting go; and it certainly has a kind-hearted statement on forgiveness.

This multi-layered storytelling certainly fits in well with the film's name. However, *Cake* also manages to say something very important about a traumatised state and a way out of an *intrapsychic tomb* (Abraham and Torok, 1994): the significance of self-compassion. In order to say this, it narrates the tale of Claire Bennett (Jennifer Aniston), and it depicts her journey from anguish to hope, from suffering to meaning.

After a terrible traffic accident, Claire not only loses her little son but also her physical, mental, and emotional wellbeing. Roughly a year later, former attorney Claire has changed completely: she has visible scars on her body; due to her chronic pain she now has a severe opioid addiction; she is suffering from amaxophobia as she refuses to sit upright in a car (and face the road in front of her), and therefore always travels lying down; due to her trauma, she has alienated everyone around her, including her husband Jason Bennett (Chris Messina), and she has become a social recluse. She is so crippled with physical pain and grief that her personality has transformed for the worse, and she has become an increasingly combative, irritable, selfish, and unlovable person. Her only lifeline is her Mexican carer, housekeeper, and driver Silvana (Adriana Barraza) who puts up with her rudeness on a daily basis partly because she needs the job and partly because she genuinely feels sorry for Claire and her loss. Claire's opioid abuse slowly spirals out of control as her dead friend Nina Collins (Anna Kendrick) from her chronic pain support group starts appearing

DOI: 10.4324/9781003292630-13

in Claire's opioid-fuelled nightmares and hallucinations, sometimes taunting Claire to kill herself. After Claire gets kicked out of her support group due to her bellicose behaviour, she threatens to sue them for their discrimination and blackmails the group's facilitator Annette (Felicity Huffman) in order to get Nina's home address. Then, she befriends Nina's husband Roy Collins (Sam Worthington), who is battling with his own grief after Nina's suicide. This eccentric bonding over anger, loss, and isolation helps Claire to see her situation differently. Following two half-hearted suicide attempts and a violent attack on Leonard (William H. Macy), who was responsible for the accident, Claire slowly faces the core of her grief: guilt. During her final suicide attempt, she manages to confess to herself that she was not responsible for her son's death. Her self-compassion and self-forgiveness ultimately steer Claire to her psychological recovery.

Cake depicts an interesting example of an intrapsychic tomb: Claire is lost in grief and slowly decaying with the memory of and the misplaced guilt for her son's death. Her psychological entrapment is complicated further as she is also trapped in her scarred and aching body which she cannot soothe. Therefore, her life is reduced to a state of pure anguish. Similar to Chris Kelvin in *Solaris* (2002), she has lost the hope for any meaningful recovery, and therefore she is easily attracted to the idea of suicide.

This final chapter not only investigates the inner workings of her three separate suicide attempts, but also explores the theories of mental, emotional, and physical pain with their ties to a traumatic loss. I specifically interpret Claire's final suicide attempt as a powerful self-release from her crypt, which is explicitly tied to the film's final shot. Therefore, Claire's way out of her intrapsychic tomb is determined by the acknowledgement of her own self-worth. Making the case studies in this book come full circle, I also revisit the research of Rosen (1975), who made the curious connection between close encounters with death and the healing of self-destructive urges. In this context, my final discussion will be on the act of choosing to heal.

10.1 Blending real and imaginary

Probably due to its serious and heavy subject matter, *Cake* was not a huge hit at the box office. Even though it runs a little over 90 minutes, its story covers quite a vast landscape of human suffering and the strangest of situations in which humans can find hope. During the film, Claire's unspoken trauma is slowly revealed and her grief journey reaches its poignant conclusion in a period of roughly ten days. The narrative focuses on the moments before the actual psychological transformation takes place, how she gets there, and what happens afterwards. Daniel Barnz, the director, depicts an abrasive, cantankerous, and sarcastic main character. However, as he slowly discloses the reasons behind her bitter attitude, he also alters the way she is perceived. In many ways, Claire Bennett shares the qualities of P.L. Travers portrayed in *Saving Mr. Banks* (2013): a traumatised woman who cannot function socially and is unable to show an ounce of kindness to people. Barnz's directorial style is also similar to the style of John Lee Hancock and John Cameron Mitchell. They all depict bereaved women with dark humour, which is conveyed through either unconventional situations or dialogues. This method certainly helps the subject matter become more tolerable for the viewer because it brings comic relief.

Cake shares another similar quality with *Saving Mr. Banks*: they are both inspired by real events. The film's script, written by Patrick Tobin, has a haunting real-life story behind it, linking anti-depressant medication with destructive tendencies. Tobin wrote the script as a result of his experience of looking after his brother Tim, who tragically lost his wife, nine-month-old daughter, mother-in-law and father-in-law. On February 14, 1998, Don Schell, Tim Tobin's father-in-law, who had never been violent before, shot his family dead and then killed himself. After an arduous court case, a U.S. District court jury found the anti-depressant which Don Schell was taking as the 'proximate cause' of killings (Parry and Boon, 2015).

Bringing grief, chronic pain management, depression, and prescription medication together, Tobin criticises the way Americans want a quick route to a pain-free life, and describes his motivation for writing the script in two steps: acknowledging pain without dulling or killing it; and discovering new ways to live with pain without being consumed by it.

Even though the film is purely fictional, the real-life difficulties of traumatic bereavement, opioid addiction of chronic pain sufferers, and how a combination of these two can drive sufferers to suicide are not. Barnz sustains this blend of real and imaginary in the film's narrative as well. In *Cake*'s fictitious universe, Claire frequently interacts with Nina, who appears in front of her even when Claire is sober and not high on opioids. In other words, the film's own reality merges with fantasy. Before going into further analysis of *Cake*, I will first describe Claire's three suicide attempts, and after that I will investigate the symbols embedded in the film to discuss how Claire's psyche changes throughout the story.

10.1.1 *Attempt 1*

Claire's first suicide attempt takes place at a public pool. This attempt is briefly foreshadowed by a dream sequence the night before she actually tries to drown herself. In this dream sequence, Claire is pushed into her pool by Nina's ghost[1] who blatantly argues that Claire does not believe in anything (including a higher power). Therefore, there is no reason for her not to kill herself because it looks as if it is the only logical solution to her painful, miserable existence. Nina throws Claire into the water and keeps her head down forcibly while Claire struggles to escape only to wake up screaming and in a cold sweat.

This nightmare scene (18:01) starts gently. The setting is Claire's own house, and it is sometime during the night. Claire suddenly wakes up with a loud knock on the window and realises that Nina is enjoying the pool on an inflatable lilo. Nina's casual and hilarious appearance is boosted by her asking for a drink. After a few seconds of disbelief, Claire decides to go with the flow, and the two women start having margaritas by the pool. Nina appears as nasty as Claire and their banter is darkly funny. However, this eccentric exchange abruptly turns lethal, and Claire wakes up gasping for air.

When the actual attempt takes place, Claire is on her own ruminating beside the public pool (20:56). She has already been kicked out of the chronic pain support group due to her being uncooperative and insensitive. Bonnie (Mamie Gummer), her physiotherapist, also rejected her after trying to help her for six months only to be treated with rudeness and contempt. Claire is in never-ending pain, inside and out. Her physical and emotional trauma defines her and poisons every relationship she has. She thinks maybe Nina had a point in her dream. Her gaze fixed on the water, she imagines how Nina jumped off the highway pass. After taking a few more opioids for courage, she picks up one of the swimming weights and gently sinks down to the bottom of the pool, eyes open and calmly sitting down as if she is doing yoga. Her deep and long scar all along her left leg, a visible confirmation of her physical pain, is seen. Claire stays at the bottom of the pool briefly. As she is in a cranky mood constantly, it is not clear if she got bored of the idea of dying/suicide or if she realised she could not kill herself. After a momentary evaluation, she decides to let go of the swimming weights that pulled her down and resurfaces gasping for air with moans of pain, just as she woke up from that nightmare with Nina.

10.1.2 Attempt 2

Claire's second suicide attempt takes place after the lunch scene where Silvana, Roy, and Roy's son Casey (Evan O'Toole) were present. This lunch is quite symbolic too. It is an attempt by Silvana to bring a bit of joy to Claire's gloomy life as she is aware that Claire enjoys Roy's company as a friend. In return, Claire makes an effort to look and behave nicely. She even does her hair and puts some make-up on which is a complete contrast to how she generally looks: weary, with puffy eyes and greasy hair, wearing the same clothes day in and day out. In short, her physical appearance for this lunch does not match her inner depressed state for the first time in the film. Following a different lighting setting compared to her first suicide attempt, Barnz specifically infuses the scene with lots of sunlight and a warm colour palette, visually indicating a small blossom of healing in Claire's psyche.

The build-up towards this second suicide attempt can be described as a domino effect. The first hint of an impending breakdown is when Claire offers Casey a swimming suit. Instead of waiting for Silvana's help to fish them out of her dead son's room, Claire walks in the room visibly fearful of a flood of emotions. Her inability to open the carefully sealed boxes which contain her son's items is an example of her inability to face the past, her trauma, and her grief. As everything is neatly packed and placed in this room, it is a further indication that Claire is not only locked in her intrapsychic tomb but also in her house with the belongings of her dead son.

The second hint comes when Roy reveals his plans to move away as it is difficult for him to live with his dead wife's memories in the house. This presents a problem for Claire as Roy has been the only authentic human connection she was able to form and sustain for some time. Her visibly shaken response to Roy's plans is an indication of her inability to go through another separation. She immediately goes to the bathroom to take some more opioids. However, she manages to stop herself before taking any.

Building on the previous two, the third and the last hint appears as the meal is served. In this very short and quick conversation, Roy notices the blank space on the wall and asks what was there. Claire's evasive answer is a lie[2] and it shows again how she is so unwilling to face and acknowledge her loss.

This sunny, friendly but emotionally challenging day gets completely derailed with the arrival of Leonard. Leonard visits Claire out of the blue, simply to repent: to confess how sorry he is for the accident that killed Claire's son, and how he was manipulated by his lawyers during the court case to deny any wrongdoing. He is there simply to ask for forgiveness because he cannot live with himself. Claire, now already being triggered emotionally by her dead son's clothes, Ray's departure plans, and her constant physical pain, suddenly erupts into violence. The things she tried to keep out from her memory and life are now invading her house and her consciousness. Seeing the person who caused all the misery, trauma, and the pain in front of her, Claire loses her control. She savagely hits and kicks Leonard on the floor while cursing and crying, until Roy and Silvana rush out to separate them.

This sudden burst of violence carries on into the next scene (69:41) where Claire aggressively scrubs off the make-up from her face and starts taking opioids one after the other while crying. The outward destructive urges in her psyche now turn inward. When Claire is shown in the next scene, she looks numb and sedated in front of the TV. It is unclear when and how she decides to stay alive, but a hand-held shaky camera shot following (and mirroring) her unstable walk to the bathroom seems to imply she is still hesitant about dying.[3] She sticks a finger down her throat, makes herself vomit to flush the excessive opioids out of her system, and then faints on the floor, completely and utterly exhausted after her fight through the day.

Just like the first suicide attempt, there is no music during this scene, and its absence heightens the raw anguish displayed on screen. The main sound effect is the electronic rewind/fast forward sound which indicates that Claire's mind is now completely incoherent. The fact that this second attempt takes place at Claire's house symbolises two more things: one, the physical and personal space she is trapped in; and two (in alchemical terms), the place where the dark night of her soul reigns, the cauldron of her *nigredo* stage.

10.1.3 Attempt 3

The final suicide attempt takes place straight after Claire is discharged from the hospital. During her stay at the hospital, she is portrayed as if she has actually hit her lowest point and from then onwards she will recover emotionally. This impression is specifically reinforced by the scene where she refuses to take any more medication intravenously and rips off the tubes attached to her arm. As she is discharged, she asks Silvana to drive them to the last drive-in cinema in Los Angeles, making Silvana think that she wants to have a nice time. However, Claire has other plans as the Riverside drive-in cinema was the place where she and Jason had their first date. Visiting such an iconic location can only mean one thing: she wants to say goodbye to the place where everything started for her, just like George Falconer does in *A Single Man* (2009). At some point during the film they are watching, she leaves Silvana in the car and walks towards the railway lines where she sees Nina's ghost waiting for her. She lays down beside Nina on the tracks and they have a poignant conversation on the edge of life (79:58).

The blend of the real and imaginary is once more visible when Nina's ghost suddenly reappears in this scene. At this point in the film, it is already established that Claire has no opioids in her system, so the imaginary conversation between Nina and Claire as they both lay down on the rail tracks is surprising. But it is safe to assume that Claire's internal turmoil and physical anguish are so extreme now that the difference between imaginary and real for her is completely lost.

What is especially significant in this attempt is that Claire, for the first time and with the encouragement of Nina, admits to herself and accepts the fact that she had been a good mother. The weight of her grief and loss, combined with the guilt that she failed to protect her son is released suddenly through that simple confession as she faces imminent death for the third and last time.

The mise-en-scène of this last attempt, in some ways, resembles the second one. It is dark at night, and the only source of light is a streetlamp barely illuminating the tracks. Claire looks as if she is back to square one and cannot hold off or fight the darkness inside of her. The appearance of Nina seems to act like a confirmation of her choice to die. However, Nina behaves kindly and soothingly. The mentioning of Saint Jude, as the Saint for the hopeless and the despaired, involves a double meaning. Claire claims that even Saint Jude would take his own life if he were in her shoes and indicates her wish to die. Saint Jude, on the other hand, is a powerful symbol of impossible causes in Christianity which indicates that nothing is impossible with God. As Saint Jude intervenes and brings hope to people in despair, Claire's last suicide attempt slowly evolves into a psychological miracle where her grief, physical pain, and mental anguish create a chain reaction to make her see that she does not have to feel guilty. Accepting that she had been a good mother to her dead son, her grief dissolves in self-compassion and she finally releases herself out of her intrapsychic tomb.

Saint Jude is not the only symbol that keeps appearing in the film. *Cake*, just like the previous films investigated in this book, depicts several symbols which enrich the metaphoric narrative. Some of them are already discussed in other chapters: for example, house represents both the nurturing and the violation of the self; car represents independence and aggression; water represents cleansing, rejuvenation, and being reborn. It is not possible here to examine every recurring symbol in *Cake*. However, I must mention the following ones because they contribute to the transformation and the healing of Claire. These are: crossroads; medicine; wound; suicide; and wind chimes. The next section will look at these symbols and their importance.

10.2 Symbols of *Cake*

The film starts with the chronic pain support group meeting scene. This scene shows different women sitting in a circle who come together to talk about their experiences at different stages of their pain management. This scene also provides a lot of information about where and how Nina died – thanks to Claire being extremely detailed and graphic. Even though she was a valued participant of the group, Nina one day decided she could not bear the pain any longer. She went to a specific and busy L.A. highway interchange, picked her spot, and jumped off an overpass. Later in the film, Claire specifically visits this spot to get information from a security guard who witnessed Nina's suicide. As she looks down to the complex grid of roads below her (24:53), she closes her eyes and imagines doing the same thing with an eerie sense of calmness and desire.

Jung talks about crossroads within the context of Greek goddess Hecate (CW 5, para.577) who was associated with magic, witchcraft, necromancy, ghosts, protection of the household, and childbirth. He also mentions Hecate's link to the Roman Trivia, the ruler and the protector of junctions and three ways where roads come together but also part. Crossroads are indeed the physical symbols of meeting and parting of ways, connections, destinations, journeys, and places of transition. Ronnberg and Martin (2010a) highlight this metaphorical association within the context of decisions and fate. At every crossroads, there is the inevitability of choice, which determines an individual's path in every step towards its intended finish line.

Crossroads, or simply the meeting point of different paths, reappear as railway lines near the end of the film. Inspired by Nina's choice of location to kill herself, Claire decides to end her life on rail tracks, which signify transport, journeys, and transitions. Plus, just like a crossroads herself, Claire lies on the railway line with two equally strong opposite wishes and destinations: she wants to die, but she also wants to heal and live. However, during her final suicide attempt, the proximity of death enables her to confront the necessity of making a choice. She understands she can no longer live in a limbo, without knowing which way to go, which path to choose. Hence, she confesses to herself that she was a good mother, forgives herself, and chooses to live.

On her journey towards self-compassion, Claire is depicted as an opioid addict. She deliberately and frequently abuses her prescribed painkillers. When she finishes bottles of it, she even travels to Tijuana to smuggle more of them back into L.A. without a proper prescription. In numerous scenes, she is shown to take two or more tablets in one go as if she is eating sweets. Therefore, her medicines are repeatedly shown in the film.

Jung argues that medicine, first and foremost, deals with human being as a physical being (CW 16, para.210). This means medicine is only interested in a fraction of the psyche underneath that physiology. In the film, Claire's pain management is not working because she is constantly trying to numb her pain, physical or otherwise. She not only avoids seeing her son's photo or belongings but is also evasive in her interaction with her husband as he is also a reminder of her son. Even when Roy learns about the accident and says he is sorry for her loss, Claire chides him for being sentimental. However, it is only when she stops taking her medication at the end of the film, she becomes able to face her pain and assess her trapped situation with a clear(er) mind.

The world mythology around Imhotep, Asclepius, Panacea, Dhanvantari, and Sukuna-biko include several stories of healing lotions, remedial herbs, and the usage of medicinal concoctions. However, medicine, just like crossroads, is a symbol of opposites coming together. For example, in chemotherapy, medicine is considered as both a remedy and a poison for the body. Bridging sickness and health, medicine is not only the necessary element between these two states but also the solution which can be harmful in high quantities.

Claire's painkiller usage follows a similar pattern in the film. Even though the tablets she uses are designed to be an antidote, to alleviate her pain and improve her quality of life, they act like a poison to her mind where she completely loses her grip on reality and starts seeing and talking to Nina even while she is awake. However, they also contribute to Claire's journey towards a total breakdown of the walls she built around her. In other words, without the drug induced delirium and hallucinations, Claire could not have seen how low a point she had reached in her life.

As mentioned earlier, Claire's depressive (and desperate) state is depicted through her rather unwashed, shabby look with no make-up. However, there is also another physical reminder: her wounds. Apart from the scar on her face, there is also a scar that runs along her leg which is specifically visible during her first suicide attempt. Claire is able to knock herself out with opioids to forget about the accident briefly, but every time she looks at her body there is physical proof looking back at her.

Trauma is the Greek word for wound. As a completely traumatised woman, Claire is not just wounded physically. She embodies trauma in her mind and heart as well. As a woman who experiences pain on many levels and with different connections at the same time, she leads a life defined by physical and psychic wounds. Jung argues that certain experiences can be so powerful that they can debilitate a person's own relationship with themselves (CW 8, para.594). These harrowing incidents can leave their mark on the psyche so deep they can be likened to a lasting wound, a wound that poisons the soul, or even obliterates some of its parts.

Ronnberg and Martin (2010b, p.734) also point to Jung's argument (CW 16, para.472) that psychic processes include both the causing and the healing of wounds, and they can ultimately expand one's self-knowledge. Based on Dennis Slattery's book called *The Wounded Body* (Slattery, 2000), they argue that as a gateway to a more enlightened mind, there is a seed of wisdom in being wounded which ultimately extends to human connections and transforms them, even in the darkest moments of suffering.

In the film, and through a surprising twist in the narrative, Claire definitely benefits from her pain, her traumatised state, and her grief to reach a compassionate relationship with her own self. During her final suicide attempt, and from the depths of her suffering, she is able to pull the self-acknowledgement and self-forgiveness she desperately needed to heal.

I have examined suicidal ideation and suicide in Chapter 4. Therefore, I will not repeat the psychological and the social aspects of self-destruction. However, as *Cake* heavily focuses on this taboo subject repeatedly, I will revisit it briefly, this time as a symbol, an approach which Jung also took. It is important, again, to note that Jung clearly sees suicide as an act that deviates from normal (CW 8, para.547). However, he also admits that within the self-regulatory structure of the psyche, it may play a part in compensation, meaning the psyche's aim for an equilibrium (CW 14, para.149). This is because self-destruction appears as an attempt to remove the unproductive and unpleasant aspects harboured in the psyche.

The trajectory of Claire's three separate suicide attempts can be re-read within this context. She is slipping into a self-destructive state because she is unable to see an alternative way to end her constant suffering. However, as depicted in her last attempt, out of this inner chaos her much-needed equilibrium emerges. During those brief moments where she faces death for the last time, she is able to (symbolically) destroy not herself but her misplaced guilt, which helps her accept her pain, her loss, and her love for life in a compassionate, self-embracing way.

The last symbol to be considered is a playful one: wind chimes. They rather curiously appear repeatedly in *Cake*: in Claire's house by the pool; by the entrance to Roy's house; during the scene where Roy hangs one over Nina's grave; and again, at the end of the film where Silvana and Claire hang one over her son's grave. Even though they do not contribute directly to the narrative in any way, their symbolic meaning enriches the story of Claire.

Wind chimes are mainly decorative ornaments which can also be used as percussive instruments in music. Also known as wind-bells, they can be constructed from suspended materials which strike each other with the natural movement of air. Due to their random sound-generating nature, they are sometimes used in making aleatoric music.

Wind chimes also play a significant role in the Chinese art of Feng Shui. This Chinese term refers to two main elements which repeatedly flow and change: air and water. As observed in China and other Asian countries, Feng Shui is the specific placement of objects, furniture, and other materials with the intention of changing one's luck, wealth, and health (Fareri and Stocker-McLane, 1999). Aiming to strike a positive balance between constructive and destructive energies, Feng Shui is the art of using life forces with good intentions.

Feng Shui uses several elements of decoration to create the necessary flow in a given space: colours; fabrics; plants; and of course, objects (Rossbach and

Lin Yun, 1994). Wind chimes are not only used in creating natural, gentle, and relaxing sounds, but also in attracting a positive life force. Furthermore, utilising wind chimes in designing calm and helpful spaces is a technique used in psychotherapy (La Torre, 2006). Using soothing sounds in a therapy room (as a part of Feng Shui) plays an important part in empowering clients and reducing their stress in therapeutic processes.

Even though Claire does not benefit from wind chimes in a therapy setting, their symbolic reference to her recovery and healing in the film becomes apparent, especially at the end of the film where she and Silvana hang a colourful wind chime over her son's grave. As a Feng Shui symbol of inviting desirable influences, she is now open to love and her destructive inner force which was stifling her has flowed away. Of course, it is possible to read this simple act from a Buddhist perspective as well. As Chevalier and Gheerbrant (1996) point out, bells are used as protection to keep sinister influences away and to purify environments with sound. In this context, Claire, by choosing to be compassionate to herself, has been released from her crypt and she is purified of her cryptic mourning. Her misplaced guilt for her son's death does not influence her anymore.

Cake is a multi-layered film of death, love, pain, and healing. With its eccentric situations, dialogues, and symbols, which blend real and imaginary, it depicts a woman suffering from a multi-layered trauma. In the next section of this analysis, I will be looking at three distinct clinical aspects of Claire's pain.

10.3 Bittersweet – pain in *Cake*

No matter how much sweetness its title suggests, *Cake* depicts a human being forced to re-define her life in and by pain. As described earlier, this pain is constant, pervasive, and debilitating. Claire's physical pain turns into an inescapable torture, and it is only amplified by the unbearable loss of her son. She is both trapped in a house with happy memories of the past which she wants to forget and in a scarred body she wants to dispose of. Therefore, it is no surprise that her mind turns in on itself and acts like an enemy to her wellbeing.

The film's unique representation of this three-layered torment provides an interesting terrain to explore clinical theories related to Claire's situation and understand her suffering multi-dimensionally. Focusing on how she is depicted throughout the film, I will briefly visit three theoretical perspectives: physical pain; emotional pain; and mental pain.

10.3.1 Physical pain

Since one of the earliest surveys in 1994 which found that 50 percent of chronic pain patients had significantly considered suicide due to their pain disorder (Hitchcock, Ferrell, and McCaffery, 1994), and the first literature review on this topic (Fishbain, 1999), there has been extensive research into the link between chronic pain and suicidal ideation. In her comprehensive review of chronic pain and suicide risk, Mélanie Racine (2018, p.269) argues that 'depressive symptoms, anger problems, opioid drugs, sleep problems, helplessness, lack of coping strategies related to hoping, mental defeat, perceived burdensomeness and thwarted belongingness' are all risk factors for suicidality in chronic pain. In the film, Nina leaves a wounded husband and a small child behind after her suicide due to physical pain. In Claire's case, there is the added loss of her son on top of her loss of physical wellbeing. However, it is her chronic pain that turns her life into a living nightmare as her opioid abuse leads to hallucinations where she interacts with Nina's ghost. It is also possible to argue that Claire's suicidal ideation is connected to Nina's death, because the film establishes Nina's suicide and how the support group responds to it from the very beginning.

10.3.2 Emotional pain

High psychological pain, which is defined as 'the introspective experience of negative emotions such as dread, despair, fear, grief, shame, guilt, frustrated love, loneliness and loss', has been identified as a risk factor for suicide (Olié et al., 2009, p.226). It is also important to note that physical pain is one of the causes of depression, which, in return, heightens the emotional pain of the sufferer (Vastag, 2003). Clients with emotional pain are considered to be in a high-risk position because the motivation to avoid emotional pain fuels their wish to die (Dunkley et al., 2018). Claire, therefore, is trapped in a vicious cycle of emotions. Her physical pain, which does not go away even with medication, feeds her depressed state. Her depression combined with her grief contributes to her emotional pain. Her only option to end this unending misery seems to be to kill herself because her existence is now only defined through suffering.

10.3.3 Mental pain

It is argued that suicidal ideation is strongly linked to an array of self-critical emotions such as guilt, shame, and despair (Verrocchio et al., 2016). The multiplicity of these emotions creates mental pain which feeds into an individuals' self-narrative of hopelessness, especially when they do not see any chance of a positive outcome in their future. As an unfortunate result of this constant anguish present in their thinking, these individuals might choose to end their suffering by taking their lives. This systematic review also shows how mental pain is strongly associated with suicidality and how its roots can be found in unfulfilled psychological needs such as love and approval.

The burden of mental pain can be so enormous for people that it creates a problem without a possible solution (Levi et al., 2008). This impossibility occurs especially when these individuals cannot articulate their stress, cannot deal with their negative emotions, and are unable or unwilling to get help. Claire is certainly depicted as a woman in the middle of this impossible situation which triggers her suicidal behaviour. From the beginning of the film until the end of the third suicide attempt, she is unable (and unwilling) to communicate her pain. She refuses to verbalise her feelings in front of Annette and the support group. Her grief remains unaddressed and (due to her combative behaviour) psychological help is not even an option. She deliberately lies to her doctor to get more opioids just to shut down her mind and sleep. Therefore, her suicidal behaviour continues all throughout the film.

Claire's inability (and unwillingness) to get psychological help is also mirrored by Roy's situation. During the scene at a bar where Roy and Claire are having drinks (45:17), he tells Claire what happened at his support group for suicide survivors. He describes a small exercise they did where the participants were paired with each other, and they pretended to be the one who died to each other. Roy, as a newly traumatised widower, describes how he expressed his intense feelings of fury and emotional damage.

His raw anger and grief about his wife's suicide appear to have been too scary for the group to handle so he quits attending. In Claire's case, however, she is asked to leave the group after she deliberately derails the session by revealing all the gory details of Nina's suicide, just to shock the people in the room and undermine the authority of the facilitator. Even though Roy finds the inner strength to carry on for his son Casey, Claire is further crippled by the loss of her son and her multi-dimensional pain gets translated into belligerent behaviour. Within this context, Claire cannot be expected to genuinely engage with a mental health professional. Because, as Schulte and Eifert (2002) argue, her basic patient conduct necessary for therapeutic interventions is lacking. Meaning, Claire is depicted as a woman who will be uncooperative, resistant to change, and will refuse to change her behaviour in a therapy setting. As she keeps on numbing herself with opioids, her grief and anger remain suppressed without any outlet. She appears despondent almost in every scene and her negative assessment of her own situation contributes to her inability to ask for help, and in return, makes the situation impossible to resolve.

What makes *Cake* quite unique in its layered narrative is not just the candid portrayal of Claire's pain and grief. It also manages to bring together all the themes and choices depicted in the six films I have investigated previously. Claire, just like Chris Kelvin in *Solaris* (2002), displays characteristics of prolonged grief disorder: she constantly avoids reminders of her loss and the accident; she is in extreme difficulty moving on with her life; and she is self-destructive. She is, just like Erica Bain in *The Brave One* (2007), suffering from PTSD, due to the traffic accident: she rejects sitting upright in a car and travels without looking at the road or traffic; she also unleashes her intense rage on Leonard and is physically violent when provoked. She can, just like Jim Doyle in *The Bank* (2001), act in a deeply vengeful manner due to her embitterment: after she gets kicked out of her support group, she does not hesitate to threaten Annette and L.A. County with a discrimination lawsuit as her trauma fuels her wrath.

On the positive side of things, Claire is also able to form a human connection with Roy, no matter how eccentric. Just like George Falconer in *A Single Man* (2009), she shows an effort to maintain this bond and finds an unconventional camaraderie energised by Roy's raw honesty as a widower. She, just like P.L. Travers in *Saving Mr. Banks* (2013), gradually learns to let go of her guilt, which certainly gives her relief from her mental and emotional pain. When it comes to forgiveness, Claire is definitely halfway there. Even though she does not forgive Leonard, even when he confesses how sorry he is, she is shown to finally understand the dynamic between confession and forgiveness. In the scene where she turns up at Annette's office, apologises for her behaviour and gives her a huge bottle of vodka as a conciliatory gift, she is forgiven by Annette. In other words, Claire actively mends a damaged relationship just like Becca Corbett and Jason do in *Rabbit Hole* (2010).

However, *Cake* also adds an indispensable ingredient to the bittersweet mix of pain and healing: self-compassion. Not seen or observed in the earlier film analyses, Claire's choice to acknowledge herself as a good mother becomes the key to unlocking her crypt. The way she sets herself free prompts me to ask a few important questions about the nature of grief. Can healing be a choice? Are bereaved people really that emotionally helpless? Can they actually become a participant in their own recovery if they want to? Or will they choose to continue to be locked in their crypts and mourn until the end of time?

While *Cake* does not aim to answer these questions directly, its metaphorical narrative opens up new discussions about grief, suicide, and healing. In the last section of this chapter, I will revisit the study about the people who jumped off the Golden Gate Bridge and survived with a focus on Claire's journey.

10.4 Choosing to live – life after death

As mentioned earlier, *Cake* starts with the support group scene. Annette, impersonating Nina for the session, is gently steering the participants towards a meaningful closure and separation with herself (as Nina). She invites them to vent their feelings, and after each participant she asks them the same simple question: will you forgive me? This group exercise starts to annoy Claire, and she gets more and more visibly irritated. When it is her turn, she flatly refuses to engage. But Annette does not take no for an answer, and she pushes Claire to talk. This little power game makes Claire turn brutally honest and she reveals all the grisly details of Nina's death, shocking everyone in the room with her sarcastic comments on suicide.

Throughout the film, Barnz never deviates from delivering this combination of honesty and dark humour, which makes *Cake* a special film in its handling of two difficult topics: suicide and grief. That is probably why the film starts and ends with two different scenes where Claire's defiant attitude is visible. As described above, Claire rebels against Annette's attempts to make Nina's suicide easier to process because of this simple fact: Nina killed herself due to her chronic pain, something Annette has never experienced. Therefore, she can never personally understand how that pain drove Nina to suicide. For Claire, who shares a similar chronic pain, it is almost like an insult to the memory of Nina, and she slaps Annette down with facts.

There is no doubt that Claire's attitude in this scene comes across as rude and aggressive. However, Claire actually benefits from this raw anger in her. Out of her pain, grief, hopelessness, and desperation, rises a woman who fights her battle against her own self-destructive urges and wins. It is important to remember her three suicide attempts here: even though she gets to the edge of death every time, she always chooses to live and stops. However, only on her last attempt does she understand the reason why she is choosing to live: she is not guilty for her son's death. By admitting this to herself, she conquers her inner demons with self-compassion.

Jung argues that depression is a harbinger of change, an angel to be wrestled with until it reveals its surprise benefit. In a letter to an anonymous woman, dated 9 March 1959, he described this battle and its outcome candidly (Jung et al., 1973). He wrote that in every excess, in every overindulgence or immoderation, there is a reversal of nature. Therefore, depression should be fought with courage, knowing that it will be over.

During the final attempt when Claire is in the full grip of her mental, physical, and emotional pain and ready to end her life, there are no alcohol or drugs in her system to cloud her judgement. When she willingly surrenders to her destructive impulses, she finally acknowledges what she has been so unwilling to understand. Her simple but powerful appreciation of her own past capability of being a good mother activates her self-healing process and paves the way to her resolution of grief. When she becomes aware of the very core of her crippling grief, namely her self-blame, her courage to face the past, present, and the future is renewed.

It is important to remember the reason behind the film script: coming to terms with and finding peace with pain. This is symbolically depicted in two separate scenes after the third suicide attempt: the first one is in her house, and she sees the photograph of her son back on the wall (as a gift from Jason). As a complete contrast to the scene where she could not stay in her son's room, she now faces his big photo smiling back at her, lets her tears run freely, and finally owns her grief. Her newfound courage to face her reality and pain does not stop there. In the very last scene of the film, she takes the simplest but ultimate step of looking forward. After hanging the wind chime over her son's grave, she chooses to sit upright in the car, directly looking ahead. As a powerful representation of her transformation, Claire is now ready to face her future. Her physical pain may not be over completely, but her battle against her 'dark angel' is now won. She can now start healing slowly, one step at a time.

This shift in Claire's psyche is similar to what Rosen describes as a sublime and ethereal regeneration (Rosen, 1975). In his study of people who survived jumping from the Golden Gate Bridge in San Francisco, Rosen explains how these individuals talk about an inner renewal which emerges after they yield to something stronger than themselves (Rosen, 2002). He explains this with the death of the negative, self-destructive ego, which leads to an experience akin to rebirth. As explored in the chapter for *Solaris* (2002) and in Jungian terms, this situation follows one's encounter with their *shadow* and their alchemical stage, *nigredo*. Claire, of course, does not miraculously survive after suicide; hers are only attempts. These attempts, however, appear potent enough, and produce similar results. She discovers a new way towards acceptance, self-compassion, and finding meaning after she destroys her former perspective of life based on guilt.

It is also important to remember the Jungian concept of 'compensation' discussed in relation to *The Brave One* (2007). Compensation refers to the balancing act of the psyche, namely homeostasis. Jung wrote that every activity in the psyche will trigger a compensation if it becomes too powerful to contain (CW 16, para.330). Claire's wish to die, unlike Chris Kelvin's in *Solaris*, is balanced by her wish to live. Her self-hatred and guilt are balanced with self-compassion. She is not saved by a sentient planet. She saves herself by facing her shadow, acknowledging its power, and consciously choosing to live. In other words, her way out of her crypt becomes an example of what Jung calls a transformation of a state of mind which leads to a self-achieved freedom (CW 11, para.784). This peaceful resolution in the psyche is a consequence of self-awareness and it can transpire after a period of reflection.

Claire's conscious choice to live, to get better, and to heal is both an announcement and an act in the film. Her second meeting with her physiotherapist Bonnie (60:50) and the dialogue between them proves her determination. Mirroring Claire's brutal honesty, Bonnie asks her if she really wants to get better without any shortcuts or cheating. Claire's reply is short and frank: she says she does.

Therefore, the hopeful ending of the film, the final shot of Claire now sitting up and conquering her amaxophobia, brings together all the symbols and story threads, interweaving the different meanings and ideas explored. Free from the painkillers poisoning her mind, she has allowed her physical and psychic wounds to change the relationship with herself and others on new terms. Coming to a crossroads in her life, she chooses to part with her old ways of life and finds a reconciliation with her own self, acknowledging her own shadow in the most constructive way. As she hangs the wind chimes over her son's grave, she lets in the flow of a new life that awaits her, not feeling trapped in a crypt anymore.

When Clare is first introduced in the film, she is depicted as a woman who is aggressive, rude, and unlovable. As more details are revealed about her, it becomes clear that she acts like that because she is unable to move on and change her situation. With her physical pain and the torment of her grief pushing her towards a point of no return, she is forced to change from inside. This change leads to a positive transformation in her relationship both with herself and with the external world. Her internal bitterness, which defines and dictates the whole film, slowly fades away at the end. When she brings a homemade cake to Casey's birthday (which is an indirect fulfilment of Nina's wish and where the film's title comes from), that cake becomes the epitome of alchemical change and sweetness which she now allows herself to accept and enjoy without any guilt.

10.5 Wounded healer

Germer and Neff (2013) define compassion as being mindful of pain with a desire to relieve it. Self-compassion, in this context, is the internal awareness and gentle care which tend to invisible wounds. It is a special type of kindness that people frequently forget when they discount themselves with self-criticism. Growing research on the positive aspects of self-compassion suggest that the more self-compassionate one is the less psychopathological they are (Barnard and Curry, 2011). The study of Breines and Chen (2012) also indicates that self-compassion helps individuals recover from past mistakes and makes them more enthusiastic to change for the better.

Entirely connected to my own experience of losing a loved one to suicide, I started exploring different tales of cryptic mourning with *Solaris*, with its rather gloomy look on this act. I specifically wanted to end my series of tales with *Cake* because in many ways it looks at the same topic with less melancholy and with more passion for life. As I said in Chapter 4, if Chris Kelvin had been able to think that Rheya's suffering ended with her suicide, he might not have chosen the same route to oblivion. Now after *Cake*, I would like to add one more thing to that statement: if Chris, just like Claire Bennett, had been able to show compassion to himself, things would have been very different for him. He would have been less psychopathological, less self-critical, and more enthusiastic to start again back on Earth.

This is why this chapter ends with emphasising the importance of self-compassion within the context of trauma and loss. As Claire's case study shows, inwardly directed compassion not only offers relief for cryptic mourning, but also paves the way to a rather holistic recovery from deep, multi-layered traumas. Hollis-Walker and Colosimo (2011), and Neff, Kirkpatrick, and Rude (2007) also suggest that self-compassion does not mean forgetting the trauma. It means living alongside the trauma, and acknowledging that there is a new life, a transformed life, a wiser life after death.

This reminds me of the Greek myth of Chiron. Chiron was a wise, immortal centaur who was wounded by a poisoned arrow. Because he could not die, he spent the rest of his life in pain. However, through this pain he gained further wisdom and taught many Greek heroes how to reach their full potential. Jung describes Chiron as the wounded healer (CW 15, para.159). I see a similar pattern in Claire's transformation in the film. By embracing her pain and her loss, she gains mastery and wisdom over her traumatic loss. In other words, through self-compassion she becomes a wounded healer, unlocks her potential to heal, and finds her path towards a happier life out of her inner darkness.

Filmography

The Bank (2001) Directed by R. Connolly [film]. Australia
The Brave One (2007) Directed by N. Jordan [film]. USA
Cake (2014) Directed by D. Barnz [film]. USA

Rabbit Hole (2010) Directed by J.C. Mitchell [film]. USA
Saving Mr. Banks (2013) Directed by J.L. Hancock [film]. USA
A Single Man (2009) Directed by T. Ford [film]. USA
Solaris (2002) Directed by S. Soderbergh [film]. USA

Notes

1 Nina's ghost seems to appear as 'the shadow self' of Claire because she is the recurring figure in all her dreams and visions. According to Louise-Marie von Franz (Jung and Von Franz, 1983) the shadow self makes one aware of their qualities –such as egotism, schemes, cowardice, etc. – which they see in others but deny in themselves.
2 It is a lie because, on the wall, there used to be a big, framed photo of herself and her son smiling together. This is revealed at the end of the film as the second cathartic moment.
3 I specifically read this vomiting act in the bathroom as hesitancy because a person determined to kill themselves would not necessarily care about the mess they might/ would leave behind. Their focus would be on suicide itself. The fact that she chooses to throw up in the bathroom is an indication of her reluctance.

Bibliography

Abraham, N. and Torok, M. (1994) *The Shell and the Kernel: Renewals of Psychoanalysis. Volume I.* Chicago: University of Chicago Press.

Barnard, L.K. and Curry, J.F. (2011) 'Self-compassion: Conceptualizations, correlates, and interventions', *Review of General Psychology*, 15, 289–303.

Breines, J.G. and Chen, S. (2012) 'Self-compassion increases self-improvement motivation', *Personality and Social Psychology Bulletin*, 38(9), pp.1133–1143.

Chevalier, J. and Gheerbrant, A. (1996) 'Bell' in *The Penguin Dictionary of Symbols*. London: Penguin.

Dunkley, C., Borthwick, A., Bartlett, R., Dunkley, L., Palmer, S., Gleeson, S., and Kingdon, D. (2018) 'Hearing the suicidal patient's emotional pain', *Crisis*, 39(4), pp.267–274.

Fareri, Y. and Stocker-McLane, E. (1999) 'Don't phooey feng shui', *SwissWORLD*, 3 (June–July), p.22.

Fishbain, D.A. (1999) 'The association of chronic pain and suicide', *Seminars in Clinical Neuropsychiatry*, 4(3), pp.221–227.

Frankl, V.E. (2004) *Man's Search for Meaning: The Classic Tribute to Hope from the Holocaust.* London: Rider.

Germer, C.K. and Neff, K.D. (2013) 'Self-compassion in clinical practice', *Journal of Clinical Psychology: In Session*, 69(8), pp.856–867.

Hitchcock, L.S., Ferrell, B.R., and McCaffery, M. (1994) 'The experience of chronic nonmalignant pain', *Journal of Pain and Symptom Management*, 9(5), pp.312–318.

Hollis-Walker, L. and Colosimo, K. (2011) 'Mindfulness, self-compassion, and happiness in non-meditators: A theoretical and empirical examination', *Personality and Individual Differences*, 50(2), pp.222–227.

Jung, C.G. (1966) *The Collected Works of C.G. Jung, Volume 15: Spirit in Man, Art, and Literature.* Princeton: Princeton University Press.

Jung, C.G. (1966) *The Collected Works of C.G. Jung, Volume 16: Practice of Psychotherapy.* Princeton: Princeton University Press.

Jung, C.G. (1967) *The Collected Works of C.G. Jung, Volume 5: Symbols of Transformation*. Princeton: Princeton University Press.

Jung, C.G. (1969) *The Collected Works of C.G. Jung, Volume 8: The Structure and Dynamics of the Psyche*. Princeton: Princeton University Press.

Jung, C.G. (1970) *The Collected Works of C.G. Jung, Volume 11: Psychology and Religion: West and East*. Princeton: Princeton University Press.

Jung, C.G. (1970) *The Collected Works of C.G. Jung, Volume 14: Mysterium Coniunctionis*. Princeton: Princeton University Press.

Jung, C.G. and Von Franz M-.L. (1983) *Man and His Symbols*. New York: Dell.

Jung, C.G., Adler, G., Jaffé, A., and Hull, R.F.C. (1973) *C.G. Jung Letters, Vol. 1: 1906–1950*. Princeton: Princeton University Press.

La Torre, M.A. (2006) 'Integrative perspectives', *Perspectives in Psychiatric Care*, 42(4), pp.262–264.

Levi, Y., Horesh, N., Fischel, T., Treves, I., Or, E., and Apter, A. (2008) 'Mental pain and its communication in medically serious suicide attempts: An "impossible situation"', *Journal of Affective Disorders*, 111(2–3), pp.244–250.

Neff, K.D., Kirkpatrick, K.L., and Rude, S.S. (2007) 'Self-compassion and adaptive psychological functioning', *Journal of Research in Personality*, 41(1), pp.139–154.

Olié, E., Guillaume, S., Jaussent, I., Courtet, P., and Jollant, F. (2009) 'Higher psychological pain during a major depressive episode may be a factor of vulnerability to suicidal ideation and act', *Journal of Affective Disorders*, 120(1), pp.226–230.

Parry, R. and Boon, J. (2015) 'The true story behind Jennifer Aniston's *Cake*', *Daily Mail*, 24 February. Available at: www.dailymail.co.uk/news/article-2962358

Racine, M. (2018) 'Chronic pain and suicide risk: A comprehensive review', *Progress in Neuro-Psychopharmacology and Biological Psychiatry*, 87, Part B, pp.269–280.

Ronnberg, A. and Martin, K. (eds) (2010a) 'Crossroads' in *The Book of Symbols: Reflections on Archetypal Images*. Cologne: Taschen.

Ronnberg, A. and Martin, K. (eds) (2010b) 'Wound' in *The Book of Symbols: Reflections on Archetypal Images*. Cologne: Taschen.

Rosen, D.H. (1975) 'Suicide survivors: A follow-up study of persons who survived jumping from the Golden Gate and San Francisco-Oakland Bay Bridges', *The Western Journal of Medicine*, 122(4), pp.289–294.

Rosen, D.H. (2002) *Transforming Depression: Healing the Soul Through Creativity*. York Beach: Nicolas-Hays.

Rossbach, S. and Lin Yun (1994) *Living Color: Master Lin Yun's Guide to Feng Shui and the Art of Color*. New York: Kodansha America.

Schulte, D. and Eifert, G.H. (2002) 'What to do when manuals fail? The dual model of psychotherapy', *Clinical Psychology: Science and Practice*, 9(3), pp.312–328.

Slattery, D.P. (2000) *The Wounded Body: Remembering the Markings of Flesh*. Albany: State University of New York Press.

Vastag, B. (2003) 'Scientists find connections in the brain between physical and emotional pain', *JAMA*, 290(18), pp.2389–2390.

Verrocchio, M.C., Carrozzino, D., Marchetti, D., Andreasson, K., Fulcheri, M., and Bech, P. (2016) 'Mental pain and suicide: A systematic review of the literature', *Front. Psychiatry*, 7, 108. doi: 10.3389/fpsyt.2016.00108

Further examples and concluding thoughts

Combining clinical theories with Jungian concepts is a new and creative way to think about grief. Looking into cinematic narratives, no matter how fictional, helps each story reveal its depth and breadth in depicting human suffering and recuperation. Expanding on the metaphorical journey of each protagonist provides an inspiring parallel tale. As I wrote in the Introduction, this new transdisciplinary perspective can be useful for artists, authors, and mental health professionals who prefer a deeply holistic view of loss and recovery. Before I write my closing words, I would like to give a few more examples to advance the discussion and illustrate the diversity of this approach.

C.1 Tales from the big screen

The Final Cut (2004) – Director Omar Naim wrote and directed this unique tale of traumatic loss and self-compassion. As a futuristic sci-fi, *The Final Cut* depicts the use of memory implants in people which record every living moment continuously, from birth to death. The information on these implants is then used to create curated films (hagiographies) to be shown at people's funerals as a celebration of their lives. At the beginning of the film, the protagonist Alan Hakman (Robin Williams), a famous curator/cutter, is living like a social recluse and also suffering from prolonged grief disorder. One day, he accidentally discovers in one of his clients' memories that his childhood friend, Louis Hunt (Peter Hall), whom Alan thought he had lost after a traumatic accident, is alive. This prompts Alan to hack into his own memory implant to discover what really happened and produces an example of enantiodromic change in his psyche. As Alan revisits his traumatic memory, he realises that he remembered the accident incorrectly, and he was not guilty. His choice to liberate himself out of his crypt is similar to Claire's situation in *Cake* (2014)

The Dark Knight Trilogy (2005–2012) – Director Christopher Nolan provided a new, dark, and edgy superhero depiction of Batman in his trilogy. Based on the childhood trauma of Bruce Wayne (Christian Bale), Nolan built up his tale of a hero trapped in a crypt. Witnessing the murder of his parents in *Batman Begins* (2005), Bruce becomes a masked vigilante of Gotham City, burdened by his traumatic loss. His story and fight for justice, blighted with PTSD, continues with

DOI: 10.4324/9781003292630-14

The Dark Knight (2008). However, with the third and final film, *The Dark Knight Rises* (2012), Bruce's cryptic mourning reaches its unique end. Introducing a way out for his protagonist, Nolan depicts Bruce making an unexpected choice: tired of grief and being trapped in his intrapsychic tomb, he chooses to leave Gotham City with his newfound love Selina Kyle (Anne Hathaway) and start a new life in Italy, away from the trauma and constant fighting. His choice to form new bonds helps him find his way out his crypt. This trilogy is a good example for Jung's teleological model of psyche, shadow archetype, and individuation, as Bruce Wayne fully realises his potential and achieves his destiny.

Inception (2010) – Another blockbuster from Christopher Nolan, *Inception* tells the tale of Dominick Cobb (Leonardo DiCaprio), a corporate spy who uses special technology to steal ideas from his targets' subconscious via a drug induced dream state. However, he is also suffering from complicated grief due to his wife Mal's (Marion Cotillard) suicide. The film's consciousness-bending tale portrays the actual crypt: a special place within Dominick's subconscious where Mal is still present and a constant source of guilt. When Mal starts to interfere with Dominick's last assignment, Dominick chooses to make peace with her death and let her go as she is killed by an associate of Dominick in a shared dream state. *Inception* is a film rich in Jungian dream symbolism and alchemical changes in the psyche.

I Origins (2014) – Written and directed by Mike Cahill, this film blends romance, drama, and science-fiction. In this touching story, a PhD student called Ian Gray (Michael Pitt) meets Sofi (Àstrid Bergès-Frisbey) through a series of mysterious events which bring the two together. Before Ian can complete his research on the evolution of the eye, Sofi dies in front of him due to a horrible elevator accident. Seven years later, now an established scholar in eye evolution but still grieving for Sofi intensely, Ian makes an eerie discovery: that reincarnation is real and iris scans can prove it. As he comes across a little girl's iris scan which matches Sofi's, he desperately flies to India to meet a (possibly) reincarnated Sofi. The film depicts a mix of PTSD and complicated grief where Ian is trapped in his crypt with his memories of loss. His healing and way out of his intrapsychic tomb resemble *Solaris* (2002). It only comes after a reunion. *I Origins* is full of symbols and events which demonstrate the Jungian concept of synchronicity in an engaging way.

Captain America: Civil War (2016) – Directed by Anthony Russo and Joe Russo, this thirteenth blockbuster of the Marvel Cinematic Universe shows what happens when superhero Tony Stark (Robert Downey Jr.) learns that the traumatic death of his parents (which he thought was caused by a traffic accident) was a murder. Apart from depicting Tony's complicated grief turning into revenge, the film also includes a unique scene where he uses a special technology (BARF) to transform his painful memory into an interactive three-dimensional hologram, clearly identifying his cryptic mourning and his desire to face it. As the story flows towards its inevitable and sombre conclusion, the PTSD of the main antagonist Helmut Zemo (Daniel Brühl) is also intertwined with all the destructive choices depicted in the film. *Captain America: Civil War*, while being another good example of the link between confession and forgiveness, can also be an interesting case study of the shadow archetype.

A Dark Song (2016) – Written and directed by Liam Gavin, this Irish–British film deals with the supernatural with chilling eccentricity. Sophia (Catherine Walker) is a bitter and grieving mother after the murder of her seven-year-old son. Unable to find the justice she needs, she resorts to ceremonial magic to summon her guardian angel in order to exact revenge. Locked in a house during the year-long invocation ritual, the film portrays a dual-layered crypt: Sophia's intrapsychic tomb and the house which her dead son visits but she cannot get out of. A complex case of PTSD and embitterment, Sophia finally succeeds in summoning her angel. Tortured by demons but dazzled by the angel's power and beauty, she chooses not to ask for revenge but for the power to forgive. Symbolically even richer than *I Origins* (2014), *A Dark Song* is a testament to forgiveness, and the Jungian concept of enantiodromia fits in with its narrative arc.

Arrival (2016) – Directed by Denis Villeneuve, this mind and time-bending science fiction film is truly exceptional in terms of cryptic mourning. With the sudden arrival of aliens, famous linguist Louise Banks (Amy Adams) is recruited by the United States army in order to decipher the aliens' language, which consists of symbols. As she slowly masters its semantics and syntax, she realises that the alien language is a tool to see through time and perceive the past and future simultaneously in any given present moment. Through the use of this new language, she sees into her own future: falling in love; having a daughter; losing her to an incurable illness; and grieving greatly afterwards. Even though the film does not portray Louise's trauma in detail, the circular narrative depicts her choice: she chooses to live that destiny and accepts her future loss knowing every detail of it beforehand. In other words, she gladly accepts her future intrapsychic tomb in order to enjoy every moment with her daughter. Her future grief finds its healing in her past knowledge in a truly Jungian ouroboric pattern which turns the teleological model of the psyche upside down.

The Rhythm Section (2020) – Directed by Reed Morano, this action film takes the ideas explored in *The Brave One* (2007) to a new level. Based on Mark Burnell's novel of the same name, the story focuses on Stephanie Patrick (Blake Lively) who survives a plane crash but loses her family. As a result of PTSD and complicated grief, she becomes a prostitute with a drug addiction just to numb her mind. Through one of her clients, she learns that the plane crash was not an accident. Fuelled with revenge, she meets a former MI6 agent Iain Boyd (Jude Law) and asks him to train her as a ruthless female assassin. The film then shows Stephanie, now with a new identity as Petra Reuter and funded by the Kaif family who supports her retribution, bringing violent closures to her losses. Similar to Erica in *The Brave One*, Stephanie is angry, helpless, trapped in her crypt, and the only imaginable way to achieve relief is to kill and destroy. Another good example of the shadow archetype, the story arc also provides an interesting look into the origins of criminal activity where people lose their fear of dying and become an agent of death and destruction just to deal with traumatic bereavement.

C.2 Tales from the small screen

With the Covid-19 pandemic and rolling lockdowns, especially the period between March 2020 and July 2021, the world saw the unexpected shutdown of most of the cinema industry globally. During this dark and tragic period, people had no choice but to stay at home. As a result, TV industry has enjoyed a new golden age which changed people's entertainment choices and priorities. Even though I have chosen to focus on cinematic narratives in this book, it would be unfair to disregard some of the exceptional grief narratives depicted in TV series that were released around this period.

Watchmen (2019) – Created by Damon Lindelof but directed by an ensemble, *Watchmen* picks up where the famous graphic novel of Alan Moore and Dave Gibbons finishes. Continuing the story arc of the book, this nine-part TV series deals with both the moral dilemmas and duties of masked vigilantes. The main storyline contributes to the political and social movement Black Lives Matter, and builds on the Tulsa massacre in 1921. As a child survivor of this massacre, Will Reeves (Louis Gossett Jr.) not only suffers from prolonged grief disorder and PTSD, but also becomes a vigilante to fight a racist organisation. Even though he was unable to succeed on his own the first time, he teams up with his granddaughter Angela Abar (Regina King) years later to finish what he started. As a tale which bends space and time, *Watchmen* includes many of the threads explored in *The Brave One* (2007) in terms of its depiction of vengeance, murder, and choosing to kill as a way of out a crypt. Jung's shadow archetype and his concept of alchemical changes in the psyche can unlock further layers in this outstanding narrative.

DEVS (2020) – Created, written, and directed by Alex Garland, *DEVS* is an eight-part science fiction miniseries about freewill and determinism, centred around a quantum computer system named DEVS which can see/compute both into the far past and future. In this context, *DEVS*'s main theme of knowing the future resembles *Arrival* (2016). However, it also depicts a relentless and grieving protagonist named Lily Chan (Sonoya Mizuno) who tries to discover why her boyfriend killed himself. As she slowly solves the mystery around his death in eight episodes, she also fights a mix of PTSD and complicated grief. Her way out of her intrapsychic tomb is a blend of *Solaris* (2002) and *Rabbit Hole* (2010): via the quantum computer, she learns that she is destined to kill Forest (Nick Offerman), the CEO of the company which created the computer. Knowing this upcoming murder, she chooses not to kill Forest, and therefore breaks the chain of events and the rules of a predetermined universe. *DEVS* finishes with an intriguing twist where the universe which Lily existed corrects this deviation with a nod to the symbolic meaning of the computer's name.[1] The finale is an interesting example of Jung's idea of numinosum in which irreconcilable opposites are dissolved in a new, mystical existence.

The End (2020) – This superb ten-part Australian TV series is written and created by Samantha Strauss. Directed by Jessica M. Thompson and Jonathan Brough, the story deals with three generations of a family confronting two age-old questions with dark humour: how to live and how to die. The narrative arc of the grandmother Edie Henley (Dame Harriet Walter) is similar to Claire Bennett in *Cake* (2014). Scarred by breast cancer and burdened by the mental and emotional pain of her past, she goes through several suicide attempts in order to get out of her intrapsychic tomb. With the help of her daughter and two Generation Z grandchildren, she learns self-compassion and rediscovers the unconventional joys of living, including getting high and providing euthanasia drugs to terminally ill people. *The End* includes particularly good examples of two Jungian concepts: mother archetype; and individuation.

WandaVision (2021) – Directed by Matt Shakman, *WandaVision* is the first miniseries of the Marvel Cinematic Universe, and debuted on Disney+ in January 2021. Continuing the story arcs depicted in the previous 24 Marvel films, *WandaVision* focuses on the traumatic loss and healing of a skilled witch and superhero called Wanda Maximoff (Elizabeth Olsen). After the horrible death of her lover Vision (Paul Bettany), Wanda's grief becomes uncontainable. As a result of PTSD and complicated grief, she unwittingly casts a powerful spell and traps a whole town with its residents in an alternate universe disguised as a TV show. Giving a new definition to cryptic mourning, she physically creates her intrapsychic tomb with a reanimated Vision in it as her husband. After a series of reality-bending events, she slowly faces her loss and chooses to let go of Vision in a way that is similar to how P.L. Travers comes out of her crypt in *Saving Mr. Banks* (2013). *WandaVision* provides new and interesting perspectives on the Jungian concepts of shadow and compensation.

Mare of Easttown (2021) – Directed by Craig Zobel, *Mare of Easttown* follows the story of Marianne Sheehan (Kate Winslet) who works as a police detective on a recent murder case. Through a series of seven episodes, the narrative slowly reveals why she is so aloof, unhappy, and rude to other people: she has prolonged grief disorder and is trapped in her crypt after her son's suicide. Similar to *A Single Man* (2009), and with the help of new human connections in her life, she gradually builds up the courage to revisit the memory of her son's suicide. The last scene of the final episode depicts Marianne ready to face the attic of her house where her son hanged himself, now prepared to forgive herself and let go of this haunting memory. *Mare of Easttown* depicts good examples of deep alchemical changes in the psyche which gradually bring about psychological growth and positive change.

C.3 Concluding thoughts

According to Abraham Lincoln, mercy creates better results than firm and exact justice. For those who need directions and assistance, compassion and understanding can be helpful tools. This perspective can be applied to several grief theories as well. People who suffer after a traumatic loss do not need to be labelled as 'ill'. They do not need strict, inflexible theories. They do not need tasks to complete or several stages to pass through on their way to recovery. They need another human being, hearing their pain and loneliness. They need to hear and be patiently reminded of the fact that there is life after loss. They need to be told that they have the agency to choose, to reconstruct their lives in a positive way.

The choice to write this book has helped me to review and reassess my own experience of traumatic loss. My recovery blossomed through combining intellectual thought and artistic expression. Even though I do not want to be prescriptive, I have to acknowledge the wisdom of Princess Leia. Every broken heart deserves to be turned into art.

Life is creation. Create.

Filmography

Arrival (2016) Directed by D.Villeneuve [film]. USA
Batman Begins (2005) Directed by C. Nolan [film]. USA
The Brave One (2007) Directed by N. Jordan [film]. USA
Cake (2014) Directed by D. Barnz [film]. USA
Captain America: Civil War (2016) Directed by A. Russo and J. Russo [film]. USA
The Dark Knight (2008) Directed by C. Nolan [film]. USA
The Dark Knight Rises (2012) Directed by C. Nolan [film]. USA
The Dark Knight Trilogy (2005; 2008; 2012) Directed by C. Nolan [film]. USA
A Dark Song (2016) Directed by L. Gavin [film]. Ireland, UK
The Final Cut (2004) Directed by O. Naim [film]. USA
Inception (2010) Directed by C. Nolan [film]. USA
I Origins (2014) Directed by M. Cahill [film]. USA
Rabbit Hole (2010) Directed by J.C. Mitchell [film]. USA
The Rhythm Section (2020) Directed by R. Morano [film]. USA
Saving Mr. Banks (2013) Directed by J.L. Hancock [film]. USA
A Single Man (2009) Directed by T. Ford [film]. USA
Solaris (2002) Directed by S. Soderbergh [film]. USA

TV series

DEVS (2020) Directed by A. Garland [TV show | HULU]. Available at: www.hulu.com/series/devs
The End (2020) Directed by J.M. Thompson and J. Brough [TV Show | Sky Atlantic]. Available at: www.sky.com/watch/the-end
Mare of Easttown (2021) Directed by C. Zobel [TV show | HBO]. Available at: www.hbo.com/mare-of-easttown
WandaVision (2021) Directed by M. Shakman [TV Show | Disney+]. Available at: www.disneyplus.com/en-gb/series/wp/4SrN28ZjDLwH
Watchmen (2019) Directed by N. Kassell, S. Williams, A. Parekh, S. Green, D. Semel, and F.E.O. Toye [TV Show | HBO]. Available at: www.hbo.com/watchmen

Note

1 The computer's name, DEVS, is revealed to be DEUS, written in Classical Latin.

Index

For Product Safety Concerns and Information please contact our EU
representative GPSR@taylorandfrancis.com
Taylor & Francis Verlag GmbH, Kaufingerstraße 24, 80331 München, Germany